Walter—

    For keeping me on my toes.

           Eric.

The Politics and Economics of Eric Kierans

The Politics and Economics of Eric Kierans

A Man for All Canadas

JOHN N. McDOUGALL

McGill-Queen's University Press
Montreal & Kingston • London • Buffalo

Legal deposit fourth quarter 1993
Bibliothèque nationale du Québec

Printed in Canada on acid-free paper

This book has been published with the help of grants
from the Social Science Federation of Canada, using
funds provided by the Social Sciences and Humanities
Research Council of Canada, and from the Canada
Council through its block grant program. The author
also acknowledges the assistance of the J.B. Smallman
Publication Fund, Faculty of Social Science,
University of Western Ontario.

Canadian Cataloguing in Publication Data

McDougall, John N.
    The politics and economics of Eric Kierans: a
    man for all Canadas
    Includes bibliographical references and index.
    ISBN 0-7735-1122-9
    1. Kierans, Eric W., 1914– . 2. Politicians –
Canada – Biography. 3. Canada – Economic policy –
1971–1991. I. Title.
FC626.K54M34 1993   971.064'092   C93-090334-X
F1034.K54M34 1993

Sections of chapters 10 and 11 are taken from J.N.
McDougall, "Nationalism, Liberalism and the
Political Economy of Eric Kierans," *Journal of
Canadian Studies* 25 no. 2 (summer 1990).

For

Ian and Nancy

Jennifer and Fiona

Contents

Preface

A play and a movie about Sir Thomas More bore the title *A Man for All Seasons*,[1] not because More became a different man from one season to the next but because, on the contrary, he held consistently – stubbornly, some felt – to the same approach to life throughout the tumultuous political changes of his country. Similarly – and partly for the same reason – Eric Kierans has held consistently to the same political and economic principles through all the "Canadas" he has witnessed and served in over thirty years of public life, and he does so still in the firm conviction that they will apply equally to all the "Canadas" that might possibly emerge in the future. Kierans, like More, entered the public life of his community with a set of profound beliefs – philosophical, political, economic, and spiritual – and has had the intelligence and courage to apply those beliefs to the concrete political choices that he and his community have faced.

Canada may be in greater need of such principles and beliefs now than ever before. For almost four years, Canadians have shown signs of almost universal discontent. They have also displayed increasingly widespread pessimism: a leading political commentator writes a remarkably dark and sour series of columns with the premise that the unity of Canada is a lost cause; a book itemizing the "trouble with Canada" sells out several times and, when it is available, ranks at or near the top of the best-seller lists for over thirty weeks; a comparable pace of sales is achieved by two other books celebrating Pierre Elliott Trudeau and his years in government, as though Canadians can now find solace – or renew their hopes – only by looking back on better times; a national task force on Canadian unity finds it difficult to move "ordinary Canadians" beyond condemnation of current office-holders to careful examination of national unity. In short, it has seemed recently as though Canadians had gone beyond mere dissatisfaction with the policies that their political representatives have been pursuing; they had given up on politicians altogether, as well as on those politicians' conventional approaches to making decisions.

Despite this general climate of discontent and growing rancour, however, no single statement of gloom carried the same force and profundity as George Grant's *Lament for a Nation* had done twenty-five years earlier. This thinker's cri de coeur was for the loss not of Canadian unity but of Canadian independence. However, Grant predicted that the defeat of nationalism in Canada, the central subject of the book, would precede its defeat in Quebec, by the same enemy and for the same reason: the overweening goal of economic prosperity in both Quebec and the rest of Canada foreclosed the survival of their respective national traditions. For Grant, "continentalism," or the absorption of Canada into the American economy and culture, was but a sub-case of the globalization of the United States's corporate power and liberal creed, the combination of which seemed destined to destroy the national identity and autonomy of all other peoples.

This book is about a Canadian who is both a Liberal and a capitalist, but who "nevertheless" (if Grant was right) has spent the past thirty years speaking, writing, and acting in the service of unity, independence, social justice, and – not least – responsible government in his country. He is also, it must be acknowledged, one of the Canadians whom George Grant placed in the continentalist camp, despite the affinity that existed between the political and philosophical outlooks of the two men. The key to this apparent contradiction is the fact that, as Kierans has believed deeply and argued tirelessly, by the mid-twentieth century there were two forms of capitalism – or, rather, there was capitalism proper and something else that he liked to call "corporatism" or "managerial capitalism," a recent, predominantly American perversion of capitalism.

Kierans has shared the core belief of capitalism that all members of a community benefit when a variety of its individual economic actors – business men and women – create economic enterprises that succeed and prosper within the implicit and explicit rules derived from the other goals and values that sustain the community. (This was his own experience as owner and president of a moderately successful Montreal manufacturing firm.) He also fought all his life against the core ideology of managerial capitalism, for mostly the same reasons that George Grant condemned

American liberalism. Kierans deplored the growing tendency of advanced capitalist societies to make the individual members of a community, and everything else in it and about it, secondary to the accumulation of capital, a process that defies limitations of any kind – least of all, national boundaries.

Moreover, Kierans has argued that achievement of capitalism proper within Canada would not only protect Canadian independence from the perverse forms of both capitalism and liberalism in the United States but also provide the solution to Canada's problems of unity, social justice, and political accountability. Indeed, one of the central points of this book is to show how Kierans's view of the major challenges facing Canada is particularly compelling, if not altogether unique, precisely because he starts from the understanding that the major problems facing Canada are interdependent. Both the origins of and the solutions to the challenges of national independence, national unity, social and economic justice, and political accountability are inseparable from one another; putative solutions to one or only some of these challenges in isolation from compatible solutions to the others are likely to fail and may even be counterproductive. In this vein, Kierans's diagnosis of the Canadian quandary has identified its origins in two fundamental errors – overconcentration of power and failure to recognize the primacy of politics over economics.

To that extent, this book both reports and endorses the "Kierans view" of these matters. However, I did not undertake this study of Eric Kierans because I felt that he had some vitally original ideas that Canadians needed to consider more intently. In fact, his thought as such, whether original or not, has never been the basis of my interest in him. What has impressed me since he first captured my attention in the late 1960s is the depth of his convictions and the manner in which he has brought his principles to bear on specific, concrete public choices. What should interest Canadians and students of politics about Kierans is less the principles of his political and economic thought than the way in which he gave practical expression to those principles in both his own public actions and his public judgment of the actions of others.

A lot has happened since Eric Kierans first made the front page of Montreal's newspapers in 1960. Internationally, we have witnessed such historic events as the election and later assassination of John F. Kennedy as president of the United States, the Cuban missile crisis, the war in Vietnam, the Soviet invasion of Czechoslovakia, the assassinations of Martin Luther King, Jr., and Robert F. Kennedy, the American victory in the race to the moon, detente with the Soviet Union during the early 1970s, the demise of the gold standard, the oil-price shocks of the 1970s, the emergence of Margaret Thatcher, Ronald Reagan and the "new conservatism," the Iranian revolution in 1979 and the subsequent rise of Islamic fundamentalism, the Soviet invasion of Afghanistan, the unification of Germany, the collapse of the Soviet Union, the emergence of Japan and the European Community as economic superpowers, Tiananmen Square, the Gulf War, and the global revolution in finance, telecommunications, and computing.

Meanwhile, closer to home, and against this background of world events, Canadians have witnessed the emergence of a new form of Quebec nationalism and its nemesis in the person of Pierre Elliott Trudeau, the increasing activism and power of provincial governments, bitter interprovincial and federal-provincial disputes over oil and natural gas pricing and exports, the election of the Parti québécois, the Mackenzie Valley pipeline inquiry, the challenge posed by multiculturalism to the "dualist" conception of Canada, repatriation of the Canadian constitution and the accompanying Charter of Rights and Freedoms, the national election and re-election of Progressive Conservative federal governments, the ballooning of the federal deficit, the Canada–United States Free Trade Agreement, and the failure of the Meech Lake and the Charlottetown accords.

Eric Kierans has had much to do with and much to say about almost every item on the Canadian list, and he has always done so with a keen sense of the global context within which Canadians have confronted such issues. The bulk of this study, therefore, is really about the fights that Kierans has waged against other public figures over the correct way to proceed on a variety of critical national questions. These have included provincial ownership of natural resources, provincial-government finances, foreign control of Canadian business, provincial development strategies, government procurement as an instrument of industrial policy, Canada's tax system, labour-management relations in the post office, political patronage, federal-provincial relations, the Mackenzie Valley pipeline and other aspects of energy policy, the Free Trade Agreement, and, last but not least, Quebec's place within Canada. Moreover, given that Kierans has been both outspoken and (as I believe) correct on most of these issues during the last three decades, and precisely because he approached them explicitly as questions of principle, the story of his public life is a useful vehicle for reviewing the substance and significance of Canadian public policy over the past thirty years.

The point of this study, then, is not to help Canadians learn more about who Eric Kierans is, and why (although I hope that happens, too), but rather to discover what someone with his background, abilities, and outlook faces when he or she tries to improve government policy in this country. The book acknowledges, quite bluntly, that Kierans was generally on the losing side, at the federal level, in government; however, it proceeds to argue that this may say more about the government of Canada than it says about him. I believe that what his public career says in this way about Canadian governance is not only of significance and interest to most students of Canada and its politics, but is of political importance to the country.

In sum, it is important to recognize throughout the discussion that follows that Eric Kierans, whatever else he may have been, has been a capitalist and, in that fundamental sense, a classic liberal. However, it is equally important to appreciate that the materialism and obsession with technique that George Grant condemned so vehemently and sorrowfully as the enemies of an independent Canada and autonomous communities everywhere were not part of the capitalism espoused by Kierans. The characteristics of American liberalism that Grant decried were the limitless pursuit of capital accumulation and economic concentration, the unending search for new technique, and the apparently insatiable need to draw less "advanced" societies within the capitalist system. Kierans simply did not believe that these characteristics were necessary to the economic well-being of any country. Rather, he believed that economic prosperity was simply one of the good things that a community could enjoy as a common benefit from the business success of enterprising individuals who were able to act free of intrusive government interference but still within the limits set by the community's laws, customs, and non-economic priorities. In this sense, the successful, publicly minded entrepreneur might well qualify as an example of the "human excellence" in which Grant expressed his faith when, in the introduction to the second edition of *Lament for a Nation*, he denied that he was a pessimist. At any rate, Kierans himself has said and done as much as any Canadian of his generation to promote the cause of an independent, capitalist Canada – not only as a good thing in itself, but also as the first line of defence against the imperial reach of managerial capitalism.

Acknowledgments

As I have discovered once before, by the time a book is completed, it represents an enormous accumulation of debts to people and institutions. I am pleased to acknowledge a burden of such debts even greater this time than last. The list must begin with the assistance of the Social Sciences and Humanities Research Council of Canada in providing both a generous research grant and the supportive efforts of, in particular, Leslie MacDonald. Denis Smith, as dean of Social Science at the University of Western Ontario, arranged seed money at an early stage in this project. Denise Kuzin provided able and reliable wordprocessing services until improvements in my own computing hardware and skills allowed me to take over. The capable staff of the Social Science Computing Laboratory at Western made a number of strategic contributions to the information storage and retrieval involved in this work. Pierre Coulombe and Leon Surette graciously prepared translations. Finally, Thomas Courchene, Robert Young, and Eric Kierans read early drafts of the manuscript, from which efforts the final product greatly benefited. To all of these, my profound thanks; I remain solely responsible for the book's contents.

A number of people have helped the book by assisting its author. Most important among these is also Thomas Courchene, whose keen personal and professional enthusiasm for this project dated back practically all the way to its inception. By a happy turn of events, I was able to complete the manuscript while I was a visiting professor at Queen's University's School of Policy Studies, where Tom was serving as director. Bob Young – as both friend and colleague – also "kept me honest" in his inimitable fashion, as different chapters took shape. In addition, the aid and comfort of several good people in Halifax helped to sustain my interest in this project – or, more important, my determination to see it through – especially Greig and Linda Macleod and Sean and Jody Wood. "The Smiths" offered similar encouragement in Ottawa. For a time in lieu of grants, and afterward in spite of them, help from friends was needed; these friends provided it.

Finally, of course, I want to acknowledge my debt to the subject of this biography. Most of this debt I believe I share will all Canadians, but I am pleased to give my unique form of it special recognition.

The Politics and Economics of Eric Kierans

CHAPTER ONE

The Many Canadas
of Eric Kierans

Throughout his public life, the Canadian policy questions that Kierans has addressed as a political actor and thinker have been fundamental and extraordinarily wide-ranging. He has been part of just about every major political issue that this country has faced during the past thirty years, making him a man for most, if not all the "Canadas" that have commanded attention during that period. The Canadas of which he has become part in this way can be briefly delineated.

There is the Canada challenged by an assertive, energetic, and increasingly confident Quebec society. Kierans was there at the beginning of the revitalization of Quebec and both contributed to and articulated the province's growing power and significance.

There is the Canada of small-to-medium, independent businesses attempting to survive and prosper in a competitive world. Kierans owned and ran two businesses and prospered doing it. There is the Canada plagued by federal-provincial conflict. Kierans was a member of both Quebec's and Canada's cabinets, was involved in some of the great struggles between the two levels of government after the Second World War, and ever since has passionately promoted decentralization as the only realistic and praticable response to Canada's regional differences.

There is the Canada marked by resource dependency and foreign ownership. As Quebec's minister of revenue, Kierans experienced directly the limitations that foreign-controlled resource companies have imposed on provincial governments. He later wrote a major study of Manitoba's resource policies, in which he set out a strategy of economic development based on the provincial government's capture of resource rents.

There is the Canada troubled by popular disillusionment with all levels of government and with politicians in general. Kierans has been unswerving in his dedication to the national interest, to high standards of conduct in all public offices, and to the ideal and practice of responsible, individual citizenship.

There is the Canada under siege from economic globalization. A consistent theme of Kierans's speeches and publications for years has been an attack on the "cosmocorp." His position on this crucial issue stems from his convictions concerning the evils of economic concentration and the assertion of political priorities over acquisitive behaviour, of community over market.

There is the Canada overshadowed by American economic and political might. Eric Kierans has long been wary of the United States' excessive power in the world, as witnessed recently in his passionate denunciation of the Persian Gulf War of 1991 and President Bush's "new world order."

There is the Canada in the grip of neo-conservatism and Brian Mulroney's Progressive Conservative government's apparent determination to dismantle the Canadian state. From Kierans have come repeated warnings that preoccupation with efficiency and the smooth functioning of markets cannot excuse the immoral failure to seek equity and just distribution of the social product.

There is the "new" Canada, about to be formed by the country's younger generations. Kierans has always appealed, in both senses of the word, to young Canadians, and he generally believes in the old giving way to the new, in political and economic power.

There is the "next" Canada that yet may emerge from future constitutional bargaining between Quebec and the rest of Canada. Kierans's contribution to constitutional discussions has been to offer not a blueprint for a "new and fully formed" Canada but rather a set of principles fundamental enough to be beneficially applied to whatever reconfiguration of political space Canadians may finally decide to institute.

In the remainder of this introductory chapter, the way in which Kierans's experiences and beliefs bear on each of these Canadas will be examined in more detail. This will also serve as a brief overview of Kierans's public career, which we look at in three parts. Part I (chapters 2–5) considers his activities in the public life of his native province – as president of the Montreal Stock Exchange (1960–63) and provincial politician – in government (1963–66) and in opposition (1966–67). Part II (chapters 6–8) examines his brief period (1968–71) in Ottawa as a member of Pierre Trudeau's first cabinet. Part III (chapters 9–11) analyses some of his many contributions as "public intellectual" since leaving Ottawa. Major philosophical and political-economic issues touching on these concerns will be high-lighted. The first section of this chapter, on Quebec nationalism, also provides a brief sketch of Kierans's formative years.

KIERANS AND QUEBEC SOCIETY

It is not surprising that, for all his public life, Eric Kierans not only has been sympathetic to the economic and political transformation of Quebec but has played an important part in it. Some of the domi-nant characteristics of Quebec's society – or, at least, Montreal's – are part of Kierans's very make-up, and there is an intriguing degree of interconnectedness between some of the outstanding qualities of the mature Kierans and those of an increasingly assertive Quebec. These interconnections were formed out of Kierans's early experi-ence of the deep rifts in Montreal society, his classical Jesuit education, and his life as a successful, independent businessman in a community whose prevailing language he did not speak.

Eric Kierans was born on 2 February 1914, and his early childhood therefore coincided with one of the most intense periods of French-English conflict that Canada has ever seen. Moreover, he grew up in the city where that conflict was most pronounced. Montreal from 1914 to 1918 was at the centre of what developed into a fierce political battle between Canada's two primary language groups, a social cleavage widened and embittered by the Great War between Europe's imperial powers.

There were, however, few indications of such tensions during the first weeks and months of Kierans's life. Indeed, on the day he was born, Montreal's English newspapers, the *Gazette* and the *Montreal Daily Star*, contained hardly a hint that Canada – along with most of the world – was heading towards the bloodiest war in its history. One small exception was a *Star* editorial criticizing the Liberal opposition in the Canadian Senate for its resistance to the acquisi-tion of the large naval vessels (Dreadnoughts) which many believed might be needed "to defend our common heritage."[1]

However, a contemporary review of the year 1914 indicates that even the first months of the war engendered antagonisms that were to develop into a terrible feud between French- and English-speaking Canadians over participation in the war.[2] Not only was the world in general riven by a huge struggle between great powers, but the corner of it into which Kierans was born was beginning to come apart over it. Nationalists in Quebec were linking French-Canadian involvement in the war to the language question in Canada. For instance, Henri Bourassa, editor of *Le Devoir*, had written, somewhat caustically, that "Frenchmen" were "better treated in language matters in Alsace-Lorraine than in Ontario." Similar sentiments accumulated in the francophone community during the course of the war, and before it ended Quebec society – and much of Canada – was convulsed by English-French hostility over conscription.[3]

Kierans's life in Montreal thus began during one of the darkest moments of animosity between its two major communities, which underscores the fact that the Kierans household did not comfortably belong in either one. Although Kierans was English-speaking, his heritage was not English; instead it was (of all things in 1914–18) Irish on his father's side and German on his mother's – two nationalities unlikely to be embraced with enthusiasm by the majority of English-speaking Montrealers either during or after the war. This was neither an incidental nor an inconsequential aspect of Kierans's early life. For one thing, his characteristic combativeness is probably a legacy of having to defend himself, literally and physically, as an Irish-German kid in frequent contact with the children of English-Canadian families who had participated, and probably suffered losses, in the war.[4] For another, it was the first instance of Kierans's "socio-economic marginalization."

Given the importance that the idea of community has held for Kierans throughout his life as a thinker and political actor, it is surprisingly difficult to identify precisely the community within which he has lived his life. Among North Americans, Kierans was a Canadian; among Canadians, a Quebecer; among Quebecers, an English-speaking Montrealer; among English-speaking Montrealers, a man of Irish and German descent. Even as members of the city's Irish community, his family lived not in the Irish quarter, but in a tiny Irish enclave within the working-class, French-speaking neighbourhood of St-Henri.[5] Like his neighbours, therefore, he grew up about six blocks away physically, and a world away economically, from the city's "English" (in fact, mostly Scots) establishment. In sum, Kierans has been a member "in, but not of" the communities in which he was located. He lived at the margins of whatever community one might wish to say he was a part.

Thus Jamie Swift titled his 1988 biography of Kierans *Odd Man Out*. However, all his life Kierans has been not so much "out" as "not all the way in." He was, more to the point, a straddler of social groupings and economic classes, a man in both camps, neither quite here nor there. This picture, of course, is entirely inconsistent with the clarity and decisiveness of his attitudes towards important issues, but it does describe the circumstances within which those views emerged and perhaps accounts for the depth and forcefulness of some of them. The real danger associated with his indeterminate location was, of course, that circumstance could force him to abandon one focus of identification in favour of the other. This danger gave Kierans a powerful incentive to soften the conflict between opposing elements of the world in which he lived, to make their reconciliation a personal priority, and to fight hard against those who, on the contrary, were likely to sharpen the conflict between them.

THE PEOPLE'S CAPITALIST

For most of his adult life, Kierans was an independent businessman, and quite a successful one. However, as we have just seen, he was from the beginning a different kind of businessman, although the label "socialist millionaire" that some (including Kierans himself) have used to describe him is a misleading oversimplification.[6] Kierans was not merely a businessman; he was and remains a thorough-going capitalist. Indeed, the critique of advanced industrial economies that Kierans drew from his capitalist inclinations and experience is far more fundamental than that of many socialists in recent and current Canadian discourse. Kierans has expressed the core proposition of this critique with the trenchant observation that "the growth of capital within a nation is not necessarily synonymous with growth in capitalism."[7]

Most of the evils that Kierans has associated with advanced capitalism he attributes to the distorting effects of accelerated depreciation and other forms of investment subsidy in Canada's post–Second World War tax policies, which expanded capital at the expense of capitalism. As he has argued many times, the general thrust of such subsidies was borrowed from the United Kingdom, whose central economic problem at the time was almost diametrically opposite to Canada's:

domestic prosperity in Great Britain was threatened by industrial obsolescence and, therefore, they took measures which admittedly favoured the employment of capital as a factor of production over labour. In Canada, our internal growth is threatened, not by a shortage of capital investment, but by a surplus of labour.

The unemployment problem hangs like a dead weight over our efforts to speed economic development with its burden of overhead costs, charge on government expenditures and clear testimony to the world that we seem powerless to react to this overriding challenge. This is not to say that we should not encourage a high rate of capital investment but we do say that, in a country in which labour is plentiful, we should not discourage the use of labour by granting special tax concessions and privileges which could have the effect of replacing labour by capital. Where the productivity of capital facilities is greater than that of labour, then we must obviously make the economic choice and employ additional capital even when this has to be imported. But when the relative productivities are equal, it would only be common sense in Canada to use labour which is in excess supply and to save on capital of which this country is very short.[8]

According to Kierans, a number of other economic problems stemmed from this fundamental mistake – most notably, a decline in corporate profits, encouragement of foreign control of business, proliferation of inefficiently sized firms, and a decline in price competition among major firms in many industries.

While Kierans had no doubts about the economic virtues of capitalism, he was also convinced that the final guarantor of those virtues is the individual investor, not the corporate manager. As their last and decisive defect, public incentives to corporate investment promoted "capitalism without capitalists" and defeated "people's capitalism." The latter, superior form of capitalism is attainable only in an economy that permits a major role for the small entrepreneur and the individual investor, who is constantly on the look-out for new and more promising ways to deploy capital to maximum benefit.

Moreover, when corporate managers take over this crucial role, they undermine the highest value of all for a society – citizenship in the community. As Kierans has put it,

Our 'people's capitalism' will not long survive if corporations persist in financing via internal funds or debt ... Profit is a reward for investing property at risk and our entire system is based on the acceptance of the principle that property ownership is essential to the development and independence of the individual and to his growth as a free and responsible citizen. Clearly, a corporate philosophy that reduces the role of the owner to that of a passive 'rentier' is to change private capitalism into a system of managed capitalism which is capitalism, and capital, without the capitalists. There is little difference between this and crown capitalism and all, who pursue this course, contribute to the weakening of our enterprise system.[9]

Kierans's condemnation of the concentration of economic power in the hands of corporate managers, as opposed to individual entrepreneurs and investors, derives ultimately from his concern for democracy. So, too, does his opposition to all types of concentration of power and over-centralization – political, cultural, intellectual, academic, and, perhaps most important, governmental.

"ALL POWER TO THE PROVINCES"

Among those who continue to support a united Canada, Eric Kierans may well be the most thorough-going decentralist (or "provincialist"). Indeed, "sovereignty-association," but for all provinces, is not an inaccurate formulation for his vision of the relationship among Canada's provinces (or regions) and between them and the federal government.

Some of this radical decentralism is broadly characteristic and, at root, philosophical: it is the application to federal-provincial relations of his more deep-seated distrust of concentrations of power of any kind. Some of it, too, is based on personal experience, going back to his days as a minister in the Quebec government during the Quiet Revolution. The rest is derived historically, from his reading of the record of swings in the pendulum of power from federal government, to the provinces, and back again, that seem to have marked the country's 125 years.

Kierans blames Canada's recent intergovernmental turbulence unequivocally on the excessive centralization that occurred during the Second World War. Or, to be more precise, he blames it on the dominion-provincial conferences of 1945–46, when Ottawa consolidated for peacetime purposes the powers that it had assumed, without significant opposition, to pursue the ultimate common purpose – the war effort. This conversion of wartime necessity into peacetime convention was, to Kierans, a mistake. Moreover, its final legacy could well be, with equal doses of irony and tragedy, the destruction of Canada by internal rather than external forces in a matter of a few more years. The reason for this possibility lies in the provincial sentiments, by no means confined to Quebec, that first arose in 1945–46 and have simmered and occasionally boiled over ever since.

Kierans is extraordinarily sensitive to these provincial sentiments. He recently invoked them during his testimony before the Special Joint Committee on the Meech Lake accord. Since the failure of that accord he has been given to quoting with approval the statements of several provincial premiers at the 1946 conference during his discussions of the appropriate English-Canadian response to renewed nationalism in Quebec.

One premier so quoted is Angus L. Macdonald of Nova Scotia:

Let me ask you, Mr. Chairman, and the delegates here, whether they represent the Dominion government or the provinces, let me ask anyone who is within sound of my voice, let me ask that great body to which we as public servants are all accountable, the citizens of our provinces or of Canada, let me ask any of these people whether they think that it is a fair or honourable or dignified position in which to place the provinces of this dominion. Provincial autonomy will be gone. Provincial governments will become mere annuitants of Ottawa. Provincial public life – and I do not think these words are too strong – will be debased and degraded. I cannot think that such a state of affairs is desired by the representatives of the government of Canada here today, my one-time colleagues.[10]

Another is Maurice Duplessis of Quebec: "The issues of this Conference are not racial issues, they are national issues; it is bureaucracy against democracy; parliamentary institutions and prerogatives against bureaucrats. In Quebec we believe in democracy; we believe in parliamentary institutions, and these cannot live if representatives of the people do not have the financial power to implement their legislative and administrative prerogatives. Confidence is the very basis of stability."[11]

Duplessis itemized the ways in which federal taxing and spending powers were invading provincial jurisdiction, repeating the phrase "confidence is shaken" and "again confidence is shaken" five times in four paragraphs. Duplessis summed up his remarks as follows: "the present federal proposals amount to the most definite attempt at centralization, to one of the most dangerous assaults on against our federative system. The uncompromising attitude taken by ... the federal government, is only compromising the very foundation of Confederation. The country needs stability and certainty. The federal proposals would be conducive to instability and uncertainty."

As Quebec's minister of revenue from 1963 to 1966, Eric Kierans learned how capricious, from the point of view of one responsible for provincial finances, federal initiatives could become; hence his recognition of Duplessis's concerns about confidence, stability, and certainty. It was a story of federal programs sprung on provincial governments, dangling the lure of 50-per-cent financing, which made them irresistible. But "half-priced" programs, while attractive, disrupted the provinces' own priorities and planning: central or nation-wide standards and priorities lead to stability and predictability only if they are established and administered in a predictable, responsive, and responsible manner. Eric Kierans would say that it has been a long time since these adjectives could be properly applied to the major initiatives emanating from the federal government.

More important, though, were Premier Macdonald's references to the potential of such federal programs to degrade provincial public life. Kierans's distrust of the overconcentration of political power had the same root cause as his distrust of the overconcentration of economic power. Both threaten to erode over time the responsibility of individuals, as investors or as citizens. In the case of federal-provincial relations, excessive concentration of power at the federal level threatened to reduce the role of the residents of the provinces and of the politicians accountable to them.

DEMOCRATIC CENTRALISM?

It is time now to turn to the deep malaise of a troubled nation that is the source of intense frustration, if polls are to be trusted, for increasing numbers of citizens. It may or may not be of some solace to these "cranky Canadians" to know that a man of Eric Kierans's stature came to hold the same view of the federal government – from the inside – as they do, twenty years later, from the outside. Here, the discussion departs from the premiss on which the title of this study is based, for there is at least one facet of Canada for which Eric Kierans proved not to be "the man" at all – Ottawa.

After the energetic excitement of the Lesage government in Quebec, Kierans moved to Ottawa in 1968 to become minister of communications and postmaster general in the first government of Pierre Trudeau. He found no excitement in being part of the government of Canada – only obstruction, frustration, bitterness, and, finally, ostracism. The story of this descent from the political highpoint of his years in the Lesage cabinet is a tale of the triumph of banality over the spirit of public service. Three events stand out as examples of the problems that Kierans faced in attempting (almost in isolation) to promote his idea of the public good through the exercise of national power: the government's refusal to implement in any significant way the recommendations of the Royal Commission on Taxation (the Carter Commission); the collapse of the government's authority over the Canadian postal service; and Kierans's almost-futile battle to prevent the government from succumbing to special interests over the acquisition of Canada's first communications satellite. These episodes will be recounted in some detail later in this book. However, it is worth pausing in this introduction to consider exactly what all three of them were fundamentally about.

The three issues that most divided Kierans from Prime Minister Trudeau and most of the cabinet concerned the "national interest" – that is, the general interest of Canadians, those interests that Canadians hold in common with other Canadians. This is, on the face of it, not a particularly original concern, but an appreciation of what is at stake can be enhanced by a brief review of Charles Taylor's analysis of Hegel. According to Taylor, Hegel believed that the "drive to dissolution" of civil society (or the bourgeois economy) must be contained by the state on behalf of the "more ultimate" community.[12] To perform this task, the state has to be more than the sum of its parts. Taylor writes, "Hegel argues strenuously against the type of constitution or constitutional provision which is based on this atomistic or composite view of the state. This is the view of men in society as simply 'a heap,' as against an articulated unity. If we start with men fractioned into individual atoms, no rational state or indeed common life will be possible."

For Hegel, France and England, unlike Prussia, exemplified two of the great disruptive forces endangering the unfolding of the modern state: "The first was the kind of mob action inspired and controlled by revolutionary elites of which the Jacobins provided the paradigm example. The second was the force of private interest, inherent in civil society, which always threatened to overflow its limits and dissolve the bonds of state. Both these were dangers implicit in the modern principle of free individuality, but corresponding to different philosophical stages. The first was in a sense Rousseau on the rampage, the second was utilitarianism run wild (Bentham gone berserk)."[13]

In these terms, Kierans's struggles can be understood according to Hegel's interpretation of the political struggle in Britain over the Reform Bill of 1832. Hegel felt that the English had confused freedom with particular rights. There was no real dominance of the universal, but only a chaos of negotiating private rights. And what is worse, according to Taylor's summation of Hegel, the matter was irremediable: "For the only force which could cure this would be a strong monarchy, like those of the late medieval kings which forced through the rights of the universal against their refractory barons. But the English have crucially weakened their monarchy; it is powerless before parliament which is the cockpit of private interests."

Kierans would never have sought "strong monarchy" to override the modern Canadian muddle of private interests. He was, however, hoping for a strong cabinet – unswervingly committed to good, efficient government and determined to promote the interests of "the ultimate community," that is, Canada as a whole. What he encountered instead, especially during the debates on the Carter Commission's recommendations and Telesat Canada, was a cabinet that had become a cockpit of special interests: mostly corporate in the case of Carter's report, and mostly departmental and local in the case of Telesat. As for the post office, Kierans's attempts to rationalize rural postal outlets, raise general rates, and increase second-class rates provoked a continuous flow of Benthamite agitation, while his attempt to introduce competitive bidding on contracts for postal trucking service in Montreal exposed him to a Jacobin phase of Quebec radicalism.

Kierans quit the federal government in 1971 out of frustration, which had to do almost entirely with what he saw as Trudeau's appalling and dangerous lack of attention to Canada's economic problems. Kierans was also irritated with Trudeau's "style of government," which stood in contrast with his earlier experience in Quebec. Was Kierans justified in this assessment? Was what he did about it the right thing?

Help in making this assessment is available in Tom Kent's reflections, which are grounded firmly in his experience as the principal policy adviser in the Prime Minister's office with L.B. Pearson and a deputy minister with the government of Pierre Trudeau. Here the very title of those reflections, *A Public Purpose* (1988), is a starting point, and a useful first step is to consider Kierans's admiring review of Kent's book in the magazine *Policy Options* (June 1988).[14] Almost everything that Kierans admired about Kent's study, as well as the accomplishments of Lester Pearson's government as described in it, was absent from Trudeau's government.

Kierans's review centred on the story that it tells of the growing subversion of democratic government by the power of business, especially big business. Ironically, Kierans dates the early signs of the expansion of that power at the point in 1963 when Walter Gordon was forced to withdraw his budget in the face of sustained attack by the business community, financial interests (which, of course, included Kierans himself, on behalf of the Montreal Stock Exchange), and financial press:

Where democracy had originally meant rule by and for the people, the corporate community now began to assert the great power invested in their control of the economy and its financial levers. Tax policy, corporations insisted, must favour investment, research and development, productivity, global competitiveness. Growth and accumulation of wealth in the hands of large corporations was the way to go, and so it has gone ... The most important institutions affecting political decision-making in Canada today are the large corporate associations such as the Business Council on National Issues (Canada's largest 150 corporations) and their affiliated research institutes. The common good that they insist upon will be a by-product of their own aggrandizement, not the first purpose of government.

Against this background, Kierans places a summary of his reasons for thinking so highly of Kent's efforts while in government: "The Pearson-Kent achievement is that they accomplished as much as they did under these circumstances and in little more than two and one-half years. The moot result of the 1965 election left the prime minister dispirited and Kent frustrated. They need not have been. It had been a glorious period with a great reduction in unemployment, strong economic growth and an enormous strengthening of the social contract."

Kierans concludes with a thought that owes an unmistakeable debt to his own battles in Ottawa, some of which are reviewed below: "Unless corporate leaders, who now possess the substance of power in the democratic nations of the West, accept political authority and the legitimacy of social goals, the people and their representatives will look for alternatives to corporate capitalism. For a brief period in our history, the common good was the overriding goal of our political leadership. As *A Public Purpose* shows, it wasn't easy."

As Kent's volume also reveals, Trudeau's government scarcely even tried to assert a conception of the public good against the vested interests of these powerful corporations. As a consequence of his disappointment, Kent quit his post as deputy minister (to Jean Marchand) of the Department of Regional Economic Expansion – about six weeks after Kierans left cabinet, for much the same reason.[15]

Two issues are tied together in the kind of frustration that these two public-spirited men experienced. One is the principle of accountability of government and the responsibility of leaders to those who elect them. The other is the substance of the policies – in this instance, primarily the economic ones – for which governments take or do not take responsibility. Kierans resigned because the government was a failure on both counts. It was guilty of economic mismanagement and failure to give economic issues adequate priority, and it was guilty of a related failure to defend firmly the national interest in the face of powerful groups with special, vested interests.

WHOSE RESOURCES ARE THEY,
ANYHOW?

During the decades following the Second World War, especially during the 1960s and 1970s, provincial governments were caught between heavy dependence on resource-based revenues and pressures from industry for high levels of after-tax revenue to support (as industry argued) further resource development. Eric Kierans is responsible for the definitive single study of the dimensions of this problem and its most desirable solution. His report on Manitoba's natural resources policy was a seminal work, whose legacy can be easily traced, if not precisely measured, in a substantial body of scholarly literature.[16] Numerous Canadian academics have singled out the report for attention in their own work on resource policy in general and on the public capture of economic rents in particular. The report also received substantial attention from many of the people involved in making changes to resource policies at both the federal and provincial levels following publication in 1973.

Kierans's report presented strong arguments along three lines. First, substantial economic rents were available from Manitoba's stock of mineral resources. Second, mining companies in the province were appropriating those rents and denying them to their rightful recipients, the people of Manitoba, who owned the stock of resources but who were not well served by past and current government policies in obtaining revenue from them. Third, the most effective method to rectify the situation was creation of publicly owned exploration and production firms.

These arguments drew a considerable amount of attention, and there is evidence that they were also highly influential. Certainly, the number of references to the report is substantial.[17] However, and more significant, several prominent students of Canadian resource policy have shown how it helped redefine debate and policy in this country. As one example, Richards and Pratt cite the study as "a significant intellectual stimulus to the central planners" in their move to form the Potash Corp. of Saskatchewan in 1975. They described his influence on provincial governments: "Kierans wrote as a nationalist who had recently resigned from the federal cabinet in disappointment at its refusal to place a high priority on policy to counter foreign ownership of Canadian industry. His report was in effect a political manifesto. It eschewed radical rhetoric but it provided strong succour to the entrepreneurial ambitions of the Fabian bureaucrats within the central planning agencies of the three contemporary NDP governments across western Canada."[18] Similarly, a more recent study of natural resources and economic welfare in western Canada, co-written by John Richards, adopts the report as its "point of departure" and clearly considers it a pivotal analysis.[19]

A line can also be traced from the Manitoba report through much of the resource-policy analysis conducted by academic economists during the 1970s. R.D. Cairns treats it favourably in "Ricardian Rent and Manitoba's Mining Royalty," which defends Kierans against the frequent, ad hominem dismissal of his conclusions and recommendations as "socialist."[20] (Cairns's own understanding of resource rents later formed half of what a recent textbook in resource economics has labelled the "Cairns-Grubel Debate."[21] Furthermore, Kierans's report appears to have inspired a recommendation to create a national crown corporation to bid on all projects for mineral resource development.[22]

A recent review of Canada's post-war mineral policies describes the impact of the report in more dispassionate terms: "The Kierans Report created much controversy and some bitter criticism. It was not implemented, but it left a lasting impression that it had voiced the previously unthinkable. In some ways it made the industry more placatory and prepared to envision changes, providing these were less radical than Kierans had suggested."[23] This assessment was published by the Centre for Resource Studies, itself a legacy of Kierans's report – or, more precisely, part of the industry's massive attempt to deflect its impact.

In any case, the decade that followed publication of the study saw numerous governments in Canada adopting new policies to capture the rents available from resources under their jurisdiction. Over the past twenty years, however, the record of such policies has been mixed, at best. Even so, the report's legacy has not been exhausted. A recent task force on Canadian energy policy, headed up by Kierans's son, Tom, endorsed the essence of the 1973 strategy in its own report, *Energy and Canadians into the 21st Century* (1988). Its recommendations implied public application of resource rents to the development of human capital as the only viable way, over the long term, of achieving balanced and self-sustaining growth on the foundation of a resource-intensive economy.

THE NEW AMERICAN WORLD ORDER

Eric Kierans rose to national prominence in January 1966 because of a speech that he made in Toronto before a meeting of the Society of Financial Analysts.[24] It attacked the US government for issuing guidelines to its multinational corporations that encouraged them to conduct their operations in ways that would help to alleviate a growing balance-of-payments problem. Kierans's many objections to this move related to two concerns. First, the US government expected multinational corporations to conduct operations in light of US national interests rather than either their own economic interests or the national interests of the countries in which they operated – including, of course, Canada, which hosted more American investment than any other country in the world. Second, as the United States increased its military presence in Vietnam, the government intended to draw on the nation's economic power to support its status as a global superpower. Twenty-five years later, almost to the day, Eric Kierans was condemning the Persian Gulf War on CBC radio for almost exactly the same reasons. Quite simply, the power that the United States displayed during events leading up to the Gulf War, not to mention the course of the war itself, is very close in Kierans's mind to absolute evil.[25]

It is crucial to understand that Kierans can hold this belief that US power in the world is evil without believing that Americans themselves are evil – or, at least, any more so than the rest of humanity. For him, the evil represented by US power does not stem in any way from the fact that it is American; it stems rather from its violation of both of Kierans's most fundamental moral convictions. First, the economic power of the United States and its multinational corporations is simply too massive and too concentrated. Second, American power in the world is the single most threatening example of the harm that can be done to humanity when politics is subordinate to economics, rather than the other way around.

In short, the evil of American power derives from a conjunction of two ultimate evils to which Canada, largely by virtue of its location, is exposed more immediately and more vulnerably than any other national community in the world – namely, economic globalization and American world hegemony.

Kierans composed his most recent pronouncements on the political and economic implications of "globalization" – the fact that an increasing number and variety of significant economic transactions are beyond the control of the governments of individual nation-states, acting alone – in a talk that he prepared on the fate of the Baltic republics of the Soviet Union in an era of glasnost and globalization.[26] He noted two similarities between the Soviet Union and Canada: both were having to deal with the claims of nationally distinct identities for increased power-sharing and greater independence, and both were seeking to satisfy the needs of their peoples in the context of the current thrust towards a global marketplace. Both challenges – not new for either country – were nevertheless being confronted in the new circumstances generally summed up as "globalism": "Globalism is the buzz word. Books are written about a Borderless World, the Competitive Advantage of Nations, Triad Power, and the race to be Number One. Is the nation-state just about through as an economic unit, as Charles Kindleberger suggested in 1969?"

Kierans's answer was, of course, no; but he began his argument with the concession that, rather, yes, "it would seem so": "Triad power means the assembling of hitherto independent nation-states into one of three major economic power centres – the United States, Germany and Japan. Economic goals, priorities and expectations will no longer be located in separate nation-states but will be subsumed in the overall objectives of the bloc leaders. The ability of a national community to meet the material needs of its citizens will be replaced by the drive, desire and will of each of the Triad to achieve power, accumulation and growth as a bloc."

This situation holds two severe dangers from Kierans's point of view. One is the spectre of a renewed imperialist economic struggle as emerging economic giants such as Germany and Japan attempt to throw off the bonds of American economic pre-eminence. This can lead only to a wasteful and dangerous economic war between these three expanding giants, with all the uncertainty about its final resolution and the enormous cost in resources and vitality that the struggle itself must consume in the mean time. The other is the fate of the smaller countries caught up in this struggle: "If they are constrained to follow the goals of any one of our triad, their goals can no longer be equity and redistribution but become, as satellites, the goals of the imperial state – growth, accumulation of wealth and power in the drive for control of the global economy. The care and feeding of the imperial power [take] precedence over the priorities of the nation, republic or province."

For Kierans, the evil of economic imperialism – the hallmark of the twentieth century – is simply the global manifestation of one of his ultimate evils, the triumph of economics over politics, which in the present context means the overwhelming of local priorities by the international – and, at the limit, global – accumulation of capital: "The cruellest hoax of all in this post–World War II environment has been the imposition of economic goals and wealth, accumulation and power over the political need for distribution and fairness. What is a borderless world? It is a world emptied of every value and principle save one, accumulation."

The evil represented by American power in the world can be re-stated in terms of the preceding discussion of globalization. American imperialism is simply a sub-case, in fact one of three extant sub-cases, of the struggle for unrivalled imperial power and global domination. All the implications for politics that flow from globalization thus flow from American economic power, except that in the case of American domination, they flow most directly for Canada.

For Kierans, the American economic challenge to Canada is simply a single instance of a world-wide challenge to the independence and viability of political communities everywhere. Among other things, it lends to the quest for Canadian independence a universal moral dimension. For Kierans, the ultimate justification of Canadian nationalism is grounded not in material well-being or any other specifically economic objectives but in concern for the political value of individual participation in the collective life of an autonomous community. He asks: "What is an economy anyway? Is it an end in itself or is it the means by which the members of a community, a given space, organize themselves and their resources to provide for their own standard of living and their material needs?"

The implication of this question – which brings the discussion back to Kierans's belief in decentralization within the Canadian federation as well – is that smaller countries must simply find a way, or strive to find a way, to fend off and stand outside the centralizing, imperial game: "Reconstruction must start from the bottom up, from the regions. Only the regions can be concerned with the unemployed, the poor, the small and medium-sized firms that survive outside the corporate umbrella. From this pool is coming the pressure for reform, the demands of smaller communities for the right to manage their own affairs and to refuse assimilation into larger entities. For a community, the good is that it should be able to maintain and reproduce itself, its people, and their environment."

Thus, for Kierans, one of the most vital, practical concerns of Canadian public life must be to avoid excessive entanglement with the United States itself and with the international, hemispheric, and continental institutions that it tends, inevitably, to dominate.

This, at any rate, was the central theme of Kierans's review of Robert Keohane's *After Hegemony* (1984), a study of the supposed decline of US power in the final quarter of the twentieth century.[27] As Kierans points out, the author was in little doubt that hegemonic leadership is unlikely to be revived in this century for the United States or any other country. The key political challenge for the United States then becomes organizing cooperation without hegemony – that is, "how international cooperation can be maintained among the advanced capitalist states in the absence of American hegemony." Kierans's review of this study finds two faults with its central argument: it has posed a false problem and proposed a bad solution.

Kierans argued that it is ludicrous to suggest that the United States is not the dominant and dominating nation in the Western bloc that it has been since 1945. The international monetary and energy crises of the early 1970s clearly caused some anxious moments, but the instigation of "summitry" – regular conferences among the heads of government of the seven largest industrial nations – soon smoothed over these and other emerging problems of the international economy. "These conferences have invariably ended with agreement on American positions, with little concern shown for the political and economic costs to other members," Kierans observed.

Moreover, Kierans anticipated by six years his subsequent reaction to the dramatic developments in the Soviet Union that were just getting under way in 1985. Kierans was gravitating toward the realization that the demise of the Soviet Union and its empire could well promote the expansion and consolidation of an American empire:

By seeking to regain what has not been lost, American hegemony over the Western alliance, what would Professor Keohane's plethora of international institutions accomplish? Each new institution, charged with finding common solutions to monetary, fiscal, commercial and defense policies, would in effect be limiting the sovereignty and responsibility of national governments, 'denationalizing' the nation-state. In this new book, he seeks to obtain for the United States, via the creation of numerous new international regimes, the same tight control over the policies and priorities of the allies that Moscow exercises over the members of the Eastern bloc.

Kierans, however, was not convinced that the American leader could be certain of followers: "Professor Keohane's warnings that substantial hidden costs face nations which insist on keeping their options open just might be counter-productive. Before agreeing to economic sacrifices and giving up political sovereignty, nations will want to know what American global purposes are. The book lacks any description of the United States view of its world historical mission. Until this is clearly defined, the entanglements proposed by Professor Keohane could well be more costly to nations than 'if they had never joined at all.'"

By March 1991, of course, the world had witnessed the unrelent-ing devastation of an army and a people that had the bad luck to be subordinate to a tyrant created and armed to the teeth by the same countries – most notably, of course, the United States – that brought that devastation. All this was done in the service of something that US President George Bush labelled "A New World Order," which, for one thing, did not preclude a new round of arms sales to most if not all countries in the region. It seemed entirely unlikely that big powers in their own right, such as Germany and Japan, would accept this vision voluntarily and would lend any more support to it than the United States could exact from them using its end of the levers of military and economic "interdependence." Kierans's advice would simply be that for smaller countries, like Canada, the costs of interdependence, American-style, were almost certain to prove terminal to anything resembling a respectable degree of national autonomy in its external affairs or political responsibility in its domestic ones.

EACH OTHER'S KEEPERS?

Several major policy debates in Canada's recent past have seen seeming opposition between a new nationalism and a domestic version of the "neo-conservatism" that held ascendancy in both the United States and Britain during the 1980s. As public policy, this neo-conservatism has appeared in the form of the Canada–United States Free Trade Agreement, cuts to Via Rail and to the CBC, erosion of national standards for health care, capping of transfer payments to the provinces in several areas of social policy, proposed reduction of the powers of the central government in the Meech Lake and Charlottetown accords and, for some, support for the United States in the Persian Gulf War. A common ingredient of the opposition to these and other initiatives has been strong resistance to the (perceived) weakening of the federal government in all of them. It is as though, in Canada, centralism were identified with nationalism or, to personalize the same point, as though Pierre Trudeau's vision of Canada – especially following the National Energy Program of 1980 – were the only patriotic one: anything else is a cover for the sell-out of the country to the Americans.

Against this background, Eric Kierans's agenda is a non-starter, almost a contradiction in terms. He claims to be an advocate of both national independence and social responsibility, yet he is also an impassioned decentralist. To escape this apparently contradictory position, one can hear his critics argue, he must abandon either his centralism or his social conscience. Kierans can square this circle (assuming that he needs to do so) with some faith in his fellow Canadians, combined with an assumption that provincial governments are – or would be, if they were given the chance – democratically responsive to the people who reside in them. In other words, he challenges the premiss that anything that the federal government stops doing would, for that reason, not get done at all. Kierans would argue that the real contradiction reposes in that premiss. It is a premiss that requires the belief that the same Canadians who demonstrate their commitment to such values as social justice and economic equality through their support for national programs would prove devoid of such sentiments as citizens of their respective provinces.

For Kierans, the base measure of interprovincial equality is not how much – on a per capita basis, say – is spent in each jurisdiction, but rather the success with which residents' priorities are being satisfied and their needs, as they define them, are being met. Clearly, vast quantities of "federal" money can be spent in provinces without meeting this test. It will be objected that this argument ignores the unequal resources available to different provinces. Here, for now, three short answers will have to suffice. First, nothing in Kierans's decentralized vision denies any role at all for the central government and forms of income equalization – especially among individuals, not governments – implemented by less intrusive policy instruments, such as the national income tax.

Second, Kierans believes that the exercise of federal power in this country since the Second World War has led to a net transfer of resources not from richer to poorer Canadians or parts of Canada, but from here to the United States. He posits a direct relationship between the centralization of power within this country and Canada's participation in a centralized process of international capital accumulation, which is clearly not centred here. His decentralized Canada would cease to be part of this wealth-absorbing system by, at the very least, ensuring that the surpluses generated locally are retained locally, which situation of course would logically precede any question of how they might be redistributed within the country as a whole.

Third, alleged signs of relative material deprivation in some parts of the country may, in fact, be manifestations – no doubt, seriously distorted by forty years of federal manipulation, but signs nevertheless – of regional preferences. Denied by circumstances "development" of exactly the kind that they wanted, some provinces may have forgone development altogether. Faced with a greater share of direct economic responsibility, provincial governments and populations might surprise us all, even perhaps themselves, with the kinds of self-sustaining economic activity that are adopted and adapted to local circumstances and preferences. Some of them might even prove to be exportable innovations in approaches to development.

But the key moral point in all this is that Kierans objects to Ottawa's essentially coercing Canadians in their local provincial circumstances into conformity with its own vision of social responsibility, economic equality, and caring. One of his favourite classical (in fact, biblical) references in recent years has been the story of Cain and Abel. When challenged by God to account for his treatment of Abel, Cain demands of God, "Am I my brother's keeper?"; as Kierans pointedly reminds us, God does not answer him. It is a question that is up to us humans to answer for ourselves. By implication, Kierans's further question to Canadians is, "If it's not up to God to answer this crucial moral question for us, why should a bunch of bureaucrats in Ottawa do so?"

In short, if Canadians generally, or in particular regions, are incapable of compassion, generosity, and mutual responsibility, the federal government's efforts to take them off the hook will ultimately prove futile. If, instead, they possess these qualities – and Kierans trusts that they do – such efforts will be superfluous. His answer to the neo-conservative agenda is, ultimately, to point to the Canadian citizen as a responsible moral agent. Since Kierans would include collective provision for the disadvantaged and unlucky as a hallmark of the public virtue of a community, this is not, as some would misuse this notion, to "privatize" welfare and social services into incidental acts of individual charity, but it is to localize them. The rhetoric and, to an increasing degree, the reality of Canadian neo-conservatism seem to turn on a grand strategy of leaving former national responsibilities to "impersonal market forces." This sloughing off of all public responsibility is not a vision that Kierans shares; but he would leave much to the immediate, personal forces that bind local societies.

CANADAS TO COME

Eric Kierans ran for the national leadership of the Liberal party in 1967. It was not a campaign trailed with glory, but among the groups that did support him in disproportionate numbers were student Liberals and young Liberals. This is not surprising, for a good part of Kierans's pitch was aimed at youth, but not expediently.

Kierans had for some time been framing his public appeal to audiences in both Quebec and the rest of Canada with particular attention to the present youth of the country and, beyond them, to succeeding generations. In fact, Kierans is a man for the "Canadas to come" in at least three senses.

First, Kierans accepts, as a principle of political economy, the obligations that every generation bears to the next, and following, generations. Sensitivity to this issue was palpable in his study of Manitoba's resources policy, for example, but it also informed his condemnation of Quebec separatism in the late 1960s: the current generation of Québécois might be willing to risk economic dislocation for the sake of political autonomy, but how certain was it that it was not placing in jeopardy the economic future of the province's youth?

More broadly conceived, Kierans's political and economic thought has always been framed by adherence to a notion of limit. One of the limits that human beings properly place on their current actions and aspirations derives from concern for the legacy that they will leave behind, in terms of both the example and the concrete results of their actions. As the moral political agents and civilized people that Kierans takes them to be, Canadians must see the conduct of their own lives as conditioned by time as well as by place, by their dual obligations to what they inherited and to what they pass on. To quote but one illustration, he has said recently, "Invisible hand economics has never worked in the long-term interests of mankind. Witness the pollution, poverty, unemployment and debt that we, the richest nations on earth, are passing on to our children."[28]

Second, Kierans is philosophically disposed to be surprised. Youth is the ontological source of the innovative, the unprecedented, the better way. Kierans has consistently disliked orthodoxy, consolidation, centralization, concentration of power, monopoly. A vital antidote to all these ills, if not evils, is creativity, and the existential ground of creativity is birth, or as Hannah Arendt labels it in *The Human Condition*, natality. Kierans likes to quote Thomas Jefferson, one of the chief architects of the American constitution, that each generation should rewrite its own. "How else," Kierans asks, "to respond to change?"

Third, and in keeping with the spirit of the last observation, Kierans's political and economic principles are, in fact, so fundamental that they are applicable equally to almost any eventual configuration of political space on the upper half of the North American continent. This is not to say that they would be of equal value anywhere in the world, although this might be true of some of them. No; Kierans's view of the political is Western, in the sense that it is Judaeo-Christian, and emphatically liberal and capitalist. But it is profoundly moral with respect to individuals, and local with respect to collectivities. Unless (until?) Canadians become Americans, they will be living some particular version of the "Kierans challenge" regardless of whether they constitute themselves into two or more sovereign states, associated or otherwise; a confederation of two, four, or five regions; a federation of nine, ten, or twelve provinces; a European-style "superstructure"; or a unitary state with a number of préfectures.

Any of these systems will still confront, as the present one does, the proximity and enormous cultural and economic pull of the United States. They will remain export-dependent economies heavily tied to natural resources, faced with globalization of industrial production, an enormous burden of public debt, unprecedented pressures for immigration, deep-seated regional differences and cultural diversity, comparatively high overhead costs for infrastructural services, and a long list of other socio-cultural and economic "givens." In the context of the Canada of his time, Kierans has had specific answers for all of these kinds of problems, but his answers were not specific to that context. His answers were derived from certain philosophical and political-economic fundamentals, all of them comprehensive enough to be the source of new solutions for the Canada to come. Of course we cannot know, though we are entitled to hope, that the Canada of the future will embody the fundamentals towards which Kierans has guided us; however, if it does not, then we will all not only be the poorer for it, but we may not be Canadians at all.

PART ONE

The Quiet Revolution

CHAPTER TWO

Professor and Polemicist

Eric Kierans's public life began with his involvement in the political and economic transformation of Quebec. Indeed, Kierans affected the politics of his home province more than that of his country. However, these early, Quebec years shaped his subsequent contributions to national political life.[1] This chapter and the next three chapters, therefore, are devoted to Kierans's commercial and political activities in Montreal and Quebec City between 1960 and 1967. In the former year, Kierans left McGill University's School of Commerce (of which he had been director since 1953) to become president of the Montreal Stock Exchange (MSE).[2] In 1967, he quit the presidency of the Quebec Liberal party and ran for the leadership of the Liberal party of Canada, and the following year he joined Pierre Trudeau's first cabinet. For three years – from August 1963 until the provincial Liberals' defeat in June 1966 – he played a central role in the government of Jean Lesage during Quebec's Quiet Revolution.

Kierans's involvement in the politics of Quebec's emergence through the early and mid-1960s includes activities of interest from a national perspective. Part I of this study highlights five of these: his campaign to restore the vitality of the MSE, including making it more relevant to the economic aspirations of the province's French-speaking majority (chapter 2); his partnership with René Lévesque during the second phase of the Lesage government's interventions in the province's economy (chapter 3); his frustrations, as a provincial minister, with Ottawa during pivotal federal-provincial negotiations (chapter 4); and his growing opposition to the conversion, within the Liberal party, of French Quebec's increasing activism and nationalism into separatism, which led ultimately to a break with Lévesque (also chapter 4). Throughout these years he displayed a penchant for making controversial declarations on national and international issues, starting with his attacks on the Créditistes and on Walter Gordon's 1963 budget, while he was still at the MSE (chapter 2) and culminating with the spectacular "Kierans Affair," in the winter of 1965–66 (chapter 5). To all of these the discussion now turns, in a more or less chronological story of how an Irish-German Montrealer fared in a province more and more consumed by French-Canadian nationalism.

A PROVINCE IN TRANSITION

Chapter 1 underscored the facts that Eric Kierans's infancy coincided with one of the most bitter conflicts between French and English Canada and that, consequently, he began his life in Montreal during one of the most intense flarings of Quebec nationalism that that city has seen. His life as a politician began with his joining the government in mid-1963, about a year after the Liberals had won re-election with the slogan "maîtres chez nous" ("masters in our own house"). (More ominously, it also coincided roughly with the earliest in a series of increasingly violent acts perpetrated by the Front de libération du Québec, the group that was eventually to murder one Quebec cabinet minister and kidnap a British consul in Montreal.)[3] Kierans did not simply join the government but became one of the strongest and most consistent allies within its ranks of the most prominent Quebec nationalist of them all, René Lévesque. What was there about Eric Kierans and about the Quebec nationalism of the early 1960s that drew from Kierans a degree of intellectual sympathy and active support that was rare, even unique, among Montreal's business elite?

First of all, the conflict between Canada's "founding" language groups was not the only element in Kierans's early circumstances that placed him between separate, or at least largely divergent, worlds. Another was his Jesuit education. His parents were working class, but cultured within their means, and held high ambitions for their oldest child. By a happy coincidence (enhanced by some strong pressure to succeed from his mother's "Protestant work ethic"), young Eric was an excellent student.[4] School grades consistently at or near the top of the class won him a successful nomination from the St Thomas Aquinas Parish school for a scholarship to attend Loyola College, also in Montreal. Kierans enrolled in the four-year high-school program at Loyola in the fall of 1927 and graduated with a four-year college degree in 1935.

While Kierans eventually chose a business career over more advanced studies, he never lost touch with the values represented in the brand of classical learning, most notably in philosophy, propounded by the Jesuit fathers, two of whom Kierans rates as among the most influential people in his life.[5] For Kierans, to contradict St Matthew by attempting to serve two masters, God and mammon, was almost beyond the realm of possibility; business opportunities can be pursued, but only in so far as they are part of the more encompassing business of the human spirit. This kind of tension between material and spiritual pursuits was much more profound and pervasive in Kierans than one suspects is the case with the vast majority of business people who consider themselves Christian. It underlies Kierans's unqualified conviction that politics must supersede economics and is grounded in the extra-economic ends of people in their respective communities. This insistence on the primacy of politics is not, on the evidence, a common prescript among even religious adherents in the modern corporate world, and it certainly goes further than the current fad in business circles of bringing "ethics" back into business.[6]

His Jesuit education, however, does not explain Kierans's entry into public life. His relationship with the best of his teachers added poignancy to one of the definitive experiences of his life – his refusal to enter the Jesuit order, complete his higher education, and become, like them, a teacher. Kierans gave this pivotal decision some long, hard thought.

The contending considerations were heavy: in favour were his respect for the Jesuits' learning, his admiration for some of them as men, and his own genuine intellectual interests and sense of academic accomplishment. In opposition were his sense of obligation to his family – next to his father, he was most responsible for the welfare of his mother and younger brother and sisters – and possibly a touch of foreboding that, as intellectually stimulating and challenging as the academic life promised to be, its horizons might turn out to be a little confined when compared to those of business.

Kierans, in the event, chose business, but the perplexity of the choice – made almost bitter by an unshakeable sense of letting his mentors down – left a lasting impression on him. This not only added weight to the "businessman with a conscience" strand in his own character but also made him very sensitive to the character of Quebec's French-speaking community. It is as if Kierans felt that his Jesuit mentors might (just) acquiesce in his choosing business over academe – and thereby letting him out of his obligations to the spiritual side of his nature – if, but only if, he promised to be "a capitalist with a difference."

On graduation from Loyola in 1935, Kierans became a regional salesman in the Maritimes for Ogilvie Mills. But after five successful years in this capacity, and having married and started a family, he began to look for something that would allow him to settle in Montreal. He spent most of the Second World War as a partner in a small sales-promotion business and as a member of the reserves with Montreal's Victoria Rifles. In 1946, he bought an insolvent Montreal adhesives firm, and he gradually brought it back to economic health.[7] He was aided in the purchase by a loan from the Royal Bank – a business connection that has remained with him the rest of his life. However, after a few years he began to feel bad about making a living in the province "without putting anything back." This feeling was amplified by the fact that the majority of its people were of a different language and culture. Worse, an increasing number of francophones harboured legitimate resentment against the minority community with which he was, in their eyes, identified – the anglophone business elite.

Two conclusions about Kierans's entry into public life stand on this evidence. First, it seems highly probable that he would not have undertaken a political career at all if he had succeeded in business in any other province. Second, he might not have entered politics even in Quebec without the extra impetus provided by his sense of owing something to the people who made up the majority of a society in which he did not fully belong.[8] (He first came to public attention as director of McGill University's School of Commerce for showing a unique concern for the development of the social conscience of the business student.) By bridging the gulf between the English-speaking business community and the French-speaking, Roman Catholic majority, Kierans played not only his most significant bridging role, but the one for which he was perhaps uniquely gifted. At any rate, it was a call that he answered with a high degree of conscience and commitment.

Thus, the image of marginalization and the accompanying ambition to reconcile existing differences fits more easily the significant facts about Kierans's life than Swift's implied image of the loner, outsider, gad-fly, and "odd-ball."[9] For instance, Kierans was neither peripheral nor an oddity during some of the government's major initiatives in the early 1960s, but he did provide a link between Quebec City and the anglophone business community. Kierans was an important, English-speaking, Catholic businessman who – a rare thing among the breed – supported the creative public entrepreneurship urged by Quebec's most inspired nationalist, René Lévesque. He was also strategically positioned, ideally suited to mediate between Québécois activism and English-speaking entrenchment. A businessman whose schooling had imbued him with a deep sense of morality and community-centred values, he stood on the line dividing Quebec's two major communities, committed to the idea that the success of both its parts could be made to serve the highest good of the whole.

Second, the Québécois nationalism of the Quiet Revolution was very different from that of the conscription crisis during the First World War. A comprehensive account of that crisis identifies three primary roots of the earlier nationalism: "The evolution of the spirit of French Canadian nationalism has been a gradual one, but by the outbreak of the World War the French Canadian's deep allegiance to his faith, his language and his institutions had become a sacred code to which the vast majority of the inhabitants of Quebec adhered."[10] By the 1960s, the Quebec state had replaced the Catholic church as "the guardian and almost the very expression of French Canadian civilization."[11] Indeed, it seems likely that what René Lévesque had once called the Quebec state – "un de nous, le meilleur d'entre nous" – was a sentiment that French-speaking Quebecers had once held towards their church.[12]

The intensifying conflict between Québécois nationalism and Montreal's anglophone establishment was essentially a product of a long process of modernization and secularization in Quebec. Industrialization had come long before. Following Britain's defeat of France's forces at Quebec City, British capitalists in Montreal had accumulated large fortunes through development of the timber trade, steamships, canals, and railways.[13] In the second half of the nineteenth century, they brought the industrial revolution to Montreal with profitable investments in clothing, textiles, tobacco, brewing, and leather-processing. Through most of this period, French-Canadian society was inward-looking, turning its talents and energy into the professions, the church, the trades, and farming.

During this period of urbanization, a great many French Canadians left their traditional rural homes, mainly because of the very high rural birth rate and the lack of good new agricultural land. A good portion of this redundant agricultural population migrated not just to Quebec's industrializing centres, but to the United States and elsewhere, thus changing the relationship between the Québécois and the church. Sancton observes that, "Despite their obvious preference for an agricultural economy, the leaders of Quebec's Roman Catholic church eventually realized that the church would be better off if French Canadians could find factory work in Quebec rather than in Massachusetts. Consequently, by the early twentieth century, church leaders became reconciled to the province's industrial development." This accommodation dampened the emergence of Québécois radicalism that might otherwise have accompanied such a profound transformation and the severe economic and social dislocation that followed in its course. To quote Sancton again:

When Quebec's displaced agricultural population flocked to the factories and the cities, the Roman Catholic church came with them. Catholic trade unions flourished, and externally controlled secular trade unions were kept out. The Catholic school system was perpetuated, despite its limited ability to prepare pupils for skilled work or management. Social services in the city remained strictly a matter for local priests and volunteer organizations. These distinct Catholic institutions perpetuated the separation and isolation of the two linguistic communities in Montreal and helped maintain the cultural barrier between French-speaking Quebec and North America as a whole.[14]

Kenneth McRoberts similarly argues that "the traditional nationalist ideology contained a strong suspicion of the state," so that for a long time it was still deemed "safer and more in keeping with French-Canadian traditions to rely on autonomous French-Canadian institutions, especially the Church, to deal with social problems." Moreover, it was in the increasingly critical areas of health, education, and welfare that "the lag in political modernization was especially acute." The breakdown of this church-centred social system, primarily through the eventual overloading of the church's capacity to meet these needs of urbanized francophones, contributed to the new politics of Quebec after 1960. However, especially after 1945, increasing numbers of well-educated lay people – many trained outside the province – gradually began to take over important positions within this system. Owing to its nontraditional educational and social background, Sancton tells us, this growing new section of the French-Canadian middle class found the existing roles of church and government restrictive and illegitimate: "While generally remaining loyal Catholics, they looked to the provincial government of Quebec as the most appropriate institution to implement new policies to control and modernize Quebec's education and social service systems and ultimately to gain control of its economy. Accordingly, they opposed the Union nationale government of Maurice Duplessis, seeing it as catering only to the patronage concerns of rural Quebec and to outdated emotions of traditional French-Canadian nationalism."[15]

Meanwhile, the Catholic church was undergoing something of a transformation itself, a fact that William Coleman insists we must not overlook:

Virtually all discussions of the change in ideology by intellectuals and political elites in Quebec in the early 1960s have ignored the impact of Pope John XXIII's encyclical of 1961, *Mater et Magistra*. This encyclical ... gave an added legitimacy to direct state intervention in society. It caused a stir in intellectual circles in the province, particularly among traditional thinkers who had viewed any state intervention as socialistic and hence atheistic. The idea of using the provincial government as a tool for promoting the francophone collectivity in Quebec could now be seen as quite consistent with Catholic thinking.[16]

The stage was finally set for a clash between this newly legitimate activism of the emerging French-speaking classes and of their reform government and the pillars of English Montreal. Kierans, who was English-speaking, but Irish and Catholic rather than English or Scots and Protestant, first witnessed and then joined this clash as an outsider to both camps.

Levine points to an important dimension to this clash. Not only was Montreal's anglophone business elite soon to be under siege from Quebec nationalism, but it was to face this assault in a severely weakened and deteriorating state. For at least thirty years Montreal had been losing to Toronto its position as Canada's primary commercial centre, because of such fundamental factors as the shift in Canada's export orientation from Britain and Continental Europe to the United States, the massive concentration of American branch-plant headquarters in Toronto, and Toronto's displacement of Montreal as a Canadian transportation, financial, and communication hub. Reflecting the adage that, historically, Montreal's business elite did not so much rule Montreal as it ruled Canada from Montreal, Levine concludes succinctly that "on the eve of the Quiet Revolution, Montreal was no longer the economic centre of English-speaking Canada."[17] It seems to have been inevitable that as the status of this elite shrank within Canada, it should be usurped within Quebec; but that fact was less perceptible at the time and, in any case, was hardly likely to diminish, and may have intensified, the determination with which it struggled to hang on.

THE PROFESSOR JOINS THE MSE

Eric Kierans became president of the Montreal and Canadian stock exchanges in January 1960. It was the turning point from a private business and academic career to a public one. The job itself lasted only three years, but by 1963 Kierans was launched on a lifetime of public commentary on the state of Canadian business that reached its apex in October 1988, with his comprehensive critique of Canadian capitalism, *Wrong End of the Rainbow* (written with Walter Stuart). On the face of it, this twenty-nine-year metamorphosis from scion to scourge of the Canadian business community looks like a major reversal, but, on closer examination, Kierans's career as an observer of Canadian capitalism represents a less than revolutionary path of development.

For one thing, three decades afford plenty of time for countries to change, too, and the subtitle of *Wrong End of the Rainbow*, "The Demise of Free Enterprise in Canada," suggests that Kierans's attitude towards Canadian business changed greatly as it began to take directions that he did not like. For another, there is a remarkable continuity between what Kierans had to say about the underlying problems of Canadian capitalism in his speeches on behalf of the MSE in 1960 and what he had to say about the same subject in his book in 1988. At the core of this continuity are the non-economic values to which he held, even as a businessman, along with a firm conviction that modern economies, including Canada's, were no longer truly capitalist.

In chapter 1 of this study, Kierans was described as "a businessman with a difference." This difference was already in evidence even before he made the transition to public life. Kierans had begun part-time work towards a PhD in economics at McGill in 1948; his presence in academic circles, combined with his ongoing business activity, had won him appointment as director of the university's School of Commerce in 1953. Comments by the editor of McGill's student newspaper provide a measure of Kierans's impact:

Professor E.W. Kierans is leaving McGill to become President of the Montreal and Canadian Stock Exchanges ... Since coming to the School, Professor Kierans has done much to improve the curriculum, calibre and reputation of the School of Commerce. He has done this by imposing the compulsory humanities continuation, broadening the curriculum, and by eliminating the haphazard choice of courses. In other words, Professor Kierans has incorporated the essential values of the liberal tradition in the program of the Commerce student ... Professor Kierans has a challenging task ahead of him. He will accept his responsibilities with the same zest as he showed so very well in his administration of the School of Commerce. He brings to the Exchanges a breadth of interest, as exemplified in both his business and professional activities, and a fine appreciation of national and international developments on the political and economic scene.[18]

Montreal's anglophone businessmen were about to witness, generally with less enthusiasm than his former students, similar signs of Kierans's distinctive approach. Over the next three years, the president of the MSE seized almost every possible opportunity to expose the threats that he saw to the survival of capitalism in Canada; worse, they were to be condemned by him for helping to undermine it. Worse yet, they were about to be told that the revival of capitalism in Quebec would require that the English-speaking corporate establishment make way for greater participation by Québécois entrepreneurs and individual investors.

Capitalism without Capitalists

Eric Kierans made five notable speeches during his first year (1960) at the MSE. They were in part aimed to revive the fortunes of a declining stock exchange. One of his main themes was thus the economic virtue of widely dispersed ownership of shares and the distribution of profits through dividends to shareholders instead of reinvestment, as retained earnings, by corporate managers. A second, less predictable common theme related to the inequities and inefficiency induced by the government's generosity to business, especially big business, in the form of accelerated depreciation and sectorally selective capital cost allowances. A third theme, not predictable at all, was concern over foreign control of the Canadian economy, chronic unemployment, and Canada's increasingly exclusive trade relationship with the United States. Departing from the business-community and governmental norm, Kierans quite candidly placed these developments at the door of misguided public policies and improper corporate practices, rather than of the external constraints that most government and business leaders liked to claim were beyond Canada's control.

However, the most striking feature of Kierans's speeches was the way in which he drew out the interconnections among his themes and lay bare a central core to the several ills of the Canadian economy.

It might be useful to point out that, to encourage a temporary investment boom by selective depreciation allowances, will not help in the solution of the problem of foreign control of our industries but will serve only to magnify those difficulties. Such measures reduce the reliance of all firms on the capital markets for their sources of funds. At a time when Canadians would welcome the opportunity to buy into the Canadian operations of foreign corporations, we are postponing this possibility indefinitely by introducing measures that make corporations increasingly independent of the shareholder or potential capitalist. It is pertinent to remark that the growth of capital within a nation is not necessarily synonymous with growth in capitalism.[19]

Kierans here expresses his concern over the fate of the small, individual investor in the climate created by accelerated depreciation, which was in turn connected to rising foreign control of the economy and the reluctance of foreign-controlled firms to sell shares to Canadians.

However, the harmful effects of accelerated depreciation went beyond the expansion of foreign control. In Kierans's view, all firms, wherever owned, were vulnerable to the complacency and ill-considered decisions of managers who worked in increasing isolation from the realistic and potentially harsh judgment of the marketplace: "I maintain that a good deal of the tremendous investment in Canada is the result of reinvestment of internal funds which do not and cannot meet the test of an impersonal capital market," he said to a group of fellow manufacturing executives.[20] Kierans also drew these themes together in an analysis of the Canadian natural gas industry, combining many of his general concerns into some fairly blunt advice on the securing of the funds needed to expand the industry. The key, he told the Canadian Gas Association, was to rely less on internally generated funds and to try alternative approaches, for example, by drawing more heavily on capital markets and engaging in more intense price competition. The solution to many of the problems facing both the industry and the country lay in increasing personal savings, which would meet simultaneously "the need for additional financing and the opportunity for Canadians to participate to a greater extent on an equity basis."[21]

On the key question of funds for future growth, Kierans saw the industry facing a choice between opposite directions: "Basically, you can adopt a policy of financing from internal sources, as have so many other industries, or you can decide to make full and effective use of external sources of funds through the institutions of a strong Canadian capital market."[22] Textbooks on corporation finance, Kierans pointed out, have shown that internal funds are the dominant source of new capital, in the form of retained profits and depreciation and depletion costs; however, he added, "to finance the growth of this industry from internal sources alone is to court many dangers."[23] In sum, while expanding capital investment may increase the efficiency of production, this is not necessarily associated with the increased efficiency of the firm as a whole or, indeed, of the national economy.

Quebec Capitalism and
Québécois Capitalists

Kierans's business speeches leave little room for doubt that he was a capitalist. However, even his addresses to his business audiences reveal a strong concern for public issues. The confrontational tone and controversial content of many of his arguments make it clear that he was performing a political function within Montreal's business community – he was promoting a shift in the status quo. Not the least of his causes was that of promoting the role of Québécois. The values that Kierans espoused as president of the MSE were increasingly compatible with, and conducive to, the transition of the Québécois from a passive and subordinate status to active dominance within their province's economy.

For example, Kierans outlined several steps to be taken at the exchange itself to spread stock ownership, such as advertising for wider participation, pressing business managers for more frequent information, encouraging more American subsidiaries to make equity available to Canadians, and urging more firms to offer stocks at initial prices of between $5 and $10 per share.[24] More important, some of his economic principles led him to identify with the dawning assertiveness of francophone Quebec, economically and politically.

First, with his suspicion of existing economic power, Kierans sought the company of Québécois activists who wanted to use the provincial state to "cut down to size" Montreal's domineering English-speaking economic community. Second, with his exaltation of the virtues of small over large business and of entrepreneurship over entrenched management, he sympathized with the small francophone business person over the continentally oriented corporate executive. Third, with his deep-seated belief in the idea that local business enterprises, and for that matter local stock exchanges, owe a responsibility to the society and political community in which they are embedded, he was not opposed to the economic agenda of the rejuvenated Quebec state that emerged after the death of Maurice Duplessis. Fourth, with his personal and professional interest in the revitalization of the MSE, he stepped towards rather than recoiled from the expanded participation of francophone investors.

Kierans served these ends in part through the cumulative effect of modest changes, such as publishing the exchange's monthly newsletter in French as well as English and easing its rules governing the awarding of new seats to brokerage firms.[25] However, Kierans's primary achievement may simply have been to help the exchange first survive a long period of decline and then begin to prosper again, for this meant that there would at least be a thriving, local capital market in Quebec to serve its indigenous business class once francophone firms began to grow in number and power. Kierans must be credited with relocating the offices and trading floor of the exchange to a new, fully modern facility at Place Victoria. Many of the old blue-ribbon brokerage firms resisted this change as unnecessarily disruptive; several others with a growing share of their business centred in Toronto were largely indifferent.[26] The Montreal press, however, mobilized around the civic and provincial pride that could be served by a revitalized, local financial institution, and so did French-speaking members of the exchange. It was not an easy battle, but by the fall of 1961, a majority of members of the exchange had accepted Kierans's plans. It was as if, by physically shifting the exchange – lock, stock, and barrel – Kierans also got it to turn its face to the future.

Thus, when Kierans warned of the danger that continental and international economic forces might bring on an era of "capitalism without capitalists" and smother the economic energy released by a purer form of "people's capitalism," he was philosophically and institutionally positioned to foster Quebec's embryonic version of "market nationalism."[27] The private-entrepreneurial element of Québécois nationalism was originally overshadowed by the provincial statism of the 1960s and the political nationalism of the 1970s. However, if people's capitalism was first pre-empted, and later promoted, by the Quebec state after 1960, Kierans consistently championed the former, even as he came to serve the latter. It is time, therefore, to trace the path that led from the presidency of the MSE to the cabinet of Jean Lesage.

THE AUDIENCE WIDENS:
CAOUETTE AND GORDON

Eric Kierans, capitalist and entrepreneurial evangelist, was about to become increasingly vocal about the fate of the Quebec and Canadian communities. The political character of Kierans's tenure at the MSE intensified between 1960 and 1963. With the help of growing media attention in Montreal, notice of him began to spread across and beyond Quebec, until it reached the upper echelons of the Quebec and national Liberal parties. Premier Lesage invited Kierans to contest a seat in the provincial legislature in a September 1963 by-election. Two public controversies, in particular, led up to this event – harbingers of a larger and more direct political role for Kierans.

The first stemmed from Kierans's public denunciation of the economic philosophy of the Social Credit party. This speech drew a wider range of favourable political notice to Kierans than he had attracted with his more strictly economic dissertations as president of the MSE. The second developed out of a letter that he wrote in June 1963 to federal finance minister Walter Gordon in response to Ottawa's new budget. This action contributed significantly to the defeat of that pivotal budget. Both actions, in different ways, opened an avenue to the provincial cabinet.

Taking on Caouette

It is generally agreed among journalists and contemporary political observers that a single, slightly bizarre episode first elevated Kierans to widespread public attention.[28] Kierans levelled his economist's guns on the already listing vessel of Créditiste (Social Credit) monetary doctrine, in a speech before a February 1963 meeting of the Saguenay and Lac St-Jean-area chapter of the Richelieu Club. Most observers feel (and Kierans seems to agree) that the speech itself had less to do with the political currency that Kierans won from the episode than did the enormous fuss raised in reply by Réal Caouette, leader of the Social Credit party in Quebec, who labelled him a "shark of high finance" and a "bloodsucker."

Neither speech nor riposte need detain us long. With the exception of its scattered references to Proudhon and Marx, the economic analysis was scarcely beyond the reach of a second-year economics major – a little above the level that the subject matter demanded. It made the point that the famous "social dividend," by which Social Credit promised to make up the gap between the value of goods produced by workers and the aggregate income (and, hence, purchasing power) of the workers who produced them, was inherently inflationary.[29] "It will," warned Kierans, "rob property, yours and mine, of all meaning and value." Apart from that, the basic ill that Social Credit's "free credit" was meant to cure – the shortfall between the value of production and aggregate demand in the economy – simply did not exist: "The basic error in Social Credit thinking is simply that the individual consumer should buy up the whole output of the country: In fact he will buy only about 2/3 of Canadian output on average but the balance will be consumed by business and government."

Nevertheless, Caouette was determined to take this set of simple and straightforward objections to his party's tenets as a red flag. At a major rally in the federal election campaign of that spring, he made Kierans's speech the primary target of a populist tirade against the national Liberals, Quebec's labour unions, René Lévesque, and the provincial government. Thus Caouette's retaliation against Kierans inflated the returns from his original speech. It won him both media attention and notice in the upper ranks of the Liberal party. Jamie Swift summed up the ramifications of Kierans's attack on Social Credit this way:

its importance lay not in its substance but in the fact that Caouette took the bait, deflecting his considerable oratorical energies away from the positive aspects of his economic appeal to the chronically disadvantaged and unrepresented people of Quebec's hinterland. He focused instead a negative-sounding attack on his opponents. Kierans was but a catalyst in this electoral reaction as Caouette proceeded to attack not only his federal Liberal opponents but the popular Quebec Liberals of Jean Lesage and René Lévesque ... Lesage was forced to respond by entering the ring and aiming a few jabs at Caouette, something he had not planned to do at the outset of the federal campaign. So Kierans had an indirect hand in bringing about the support of the Lesage government for the Pearson Liberals.[30]

Swift also suggests that Kierans may have prompted a few Quebec businessmen to increase their support for the Liberals, because his speech raised their apprehension over the instability that could follow Social Credit electoral successes.

Swift feels that Kierans's attack on Caouette can also be seen as a setback at Kierans's hands of some of those who were being left in the dust as Quebec accelerated towards its new economic and political status: "Caouette's support came from the poor and the working class in northern and eastern Quebec, people victimized by unemployment, shunted off their land by growing concentration in agriculture; people who felt their world turned upside down as the provincial government of the Liberal Jean Lesage attempted to integrate Quebec more completely into an industrial capitalism which had long since been embraced by the rest of the continent."

The anxieties and dislocations attendant upon social mobilization, in other words, were generating grass-roots political movements on both the left and the right in Quebec. However, Kierans's part in all of this deserves to be seen in broader perspective. He could answer Swift's concerns in part by saying that no one helps the dispossessed and deprived by adopting measures that spell economic disaster for the entire community. That, in essence, was his message in opposition to Caouette, the plebeian champion of the poor and disadvantaged on the shores of the St Lawrence, in the northern woods, and in the east end of Montreal. It was, however, also the essence of his opposition to Walter Gordon, the patrician delegate from Toronto's Bay Street to the government of Canada. Kierans was at least as hard on the economics of Canada's minister of finance as he was on that of the leader of the Créditistes.

Taking on Gordon

Kierans's attack on Walter Gordon's "nationalist" budget was controversial enough at the time, and ever since it has raised questions in the minds of some about the consistency and the depth of his own nationalist convictions. However, it is not as obvious as some have assumed that all the nationalist angels are on Gordon's side in this matter or that Kierans's criticisms were so thoroughly at odds with the more nationalist stance that, as we shall see, he was to take less than three years later.

The budget incident is summarized by Denis Smith in his biography of Walter Gordon.[31] Gordon had promised Canadians to confront increasing foreign control of the economy and in his June 1963 budget introduced two measures aimed in that direction. A 15-per-cent federal withholding tax on dividends paid to non-residents would now include a rate differential of 10 per cent applied to dividends of companies with 25-per-cent or more Canadian ownership and 20 per cent to those of other companies, including, of course, those wholly owned outside Canada. This differential, Gordon hoped, would promote a broader policy of "growing partnership between Canadian investors and investors abroad."

More controversial was a tax on certain types of sales of shares in Canadian companies. It was based on a distinction between new direct foreign investment, preferably in partnership with Canadian residents, and the non-resident takeover of existing Canadian companies. The former type of investment was deemed to be "of great value to Canada," while the latter rarely conferred "any benefit to the Canadian economy":

We shall therefore propose a measure of taxation of certain sales which might contribute to such takeovers. We shall propose that effective tonight a thirty percent tax be levied on certain sales by Canadians to non-residents and non-resident controlled companies, of shares in Canadian companies listed on Canadian stock exchanges. There is to be no liability for the tax when such sales are made on the floor of a Canadian exchange in the normal trading manner and do not form part of sales exceeding $50,000 per day by any single seller. Effective tonight also, we are proposing a similar thirty percent sales tax on the sale by a listed Canadian corporation of the whole or substantially the whole of its property to a non-resident or a non-resident controlled company.[32]

Predictably, neither the executives of Canada's major stock exchanges nor the Investor Dealers' Association were enthusiastic about these measures, and representatives of the Toronto and Montreal exchanges met Gordon on 17 and 18 June. The president of the Toronto exchange was reluctantly reconciled to the measures during his meeting with Gordon. The same could not be said of his Montreal counterpart, who met the finance minister accompanied by several prominent members of MSE houses (one of whom was apparently a Liberal senator and fundraiser) and handed him a letter "couched in highly intemperate language," which he had already given to the press. "He then proceeded," recalled Gordon, "to harangue me in my own office and practically incited the stock brokers present to sell the market short when it opened in the morning."[33]

Smith agrees with Gordon's assessment of the tone of Kierans's letter, noting that it "began in hyperbole." Indeed, the opening paragraph was laced with purple prose, probably intentionally, and set the tone for the entire letter:

The financial capitals of the world have had just about enough from Canada ... the initial reaction to the budget was one of bewilderment and dismay. Yesterday, it was anger and scorn. ... our friends in the western world fully realize that we don't want them or their money ... their reaction? If that is what Canadians want, let them have it ... This is complete and utter nonsense. ... *All this is elementary.* ... A not very proud role is assigned to the Canadian shareholder. His contribution will be to badger, to harass and to torment management and the 75% controlling interest. How futile and how unrealistic. ... if Canadian shareholders do not respond, are we going to solve the unhappy dilemma *by forced payroll deductions*? ... This new tax simply expropriates 30% of the asset at moment of transfer. ... if the government here is not concerned with revenue (and the unbelievable rate is evidence of this), the purpose of the budget must be to destroy (prevent) certain activities engaged in by its citizens. ... the government is in effect describing 'good' and 'bad' subsidiaries. This raises certain questions in the applied art of discrimination. Are Dupont and C.I.L. 'bad companies'? Less than 20% of their stock is in the hands of the public.[34]

Any objective observer would see this as unnecessarily strong language, but what about the letter's accuracy and economic validity?
Smith distils the letter's message:

Kierans objected to the foreign ownership measures on every conceivable ground. He denied that non resident takeovers offered no benefit to the Canadian economy; he argued that a twenty-five percent equity shareholding by Canadians would not result in the degree of control the Minister considered adequate, that Canadians were disinclined to invest in Canadian subsidiaries, that the takeover tax was an unjust capital levy which would seriously depress the securities market, that it was an invasion of property and civil rights and therefore within provincial rather than federal jurisdiction, that the tax would create two markets and two prices for Canadian securities – 'one in Canada where the tax is applicable and liquidity reduced and the other in New York where transactions can take place among non-residents free of tax' – and that the tax would encourage Canadians as well as foreigners to avoid the Canadian securities market. Kierans had not gone to Ottawa seeking compromise. His object was to force the government's surrender on the application of the takeover tax through the use of all the influence his position commanded.[35]

Most of these observations would strike many people informed on the issue as well taken, or at the very least as defensible on economic and business grounds.

One should recall, however, the concerns about excessive foreign control that Kierans himself had addressed, before business audiences. Kierans expressly acknowledged at the close of his letter to Gordon that "foreign ownership is a problem in Canada. You are quite right in this, but this investment is not financed by foreign governments or inspired by desires to impair our political sovereignty." The issue for Kierans was how best to counter foreign control. Takeover taxes, indeed any attempt by governments to control the operation of capital markets, was simply the wrong answer, according to him. Two other letters written by Kierans in this period provide some significant clues as to his views on foreign investment and the proper Canadian policies towards it.

Kierans v. Gordon

The first of the other two letters was also written to Walter Gordon, less than five weeks after the budget fiasco in June 1963.[36] It concerned a US tax on the sale to Americans of equity in Canadian firms, not to mention a US tax on the trading of American securities between Canadians and Americans, commonly referred to as the "interest equalization tax."

The Liberal government was here experiencing an early version of a form of political discomfort that would become more and more familiar over the next twenty-five years. It was engaging in intense negotiations with the US government over some way to exempt Canada from forms of American protectionist intervention that were bound to harm the Canadian economy. But it sought to plead for such an exemption in a manner that played down for the Canadian people the country's almost total dependence on the United States in economic matters and the full magnitude of the stakes involved. Thus Kierans's second letter to Gordon challenged the finance minister's public statement that the type of transactions affected by the American measures "have not been a major factor" over the past year. Kierans pointed out that sales to the United States of outstanding Canadian common preferred stocks, combined with Canadian purchases of Canadian equities from Americans, totalled $1,087.8 million in 1962 – "*not* insignificant amounts."

Kierans maintained that 'the new 15% excise tax will have a severe impact on the Canadian balance of payments and on the value of Canadian securities" and that Canadian officials were far from justified in claiming that the tax "did not unduly trouble" them and that it was something "that we can live with."[37] With some prescience, Kierans concluded his analysis with some "general comments," including the prediction that "the increasing deficit on capital account forecast above will make it difficult for Canada to continue its existing level of imports and might require the imposition by Canada of exchange controls or import restrictions." Finally, "Canada should not have been included in these measures in the first place since we are not accumulating gold at the expense of the U.S. The exemptions, therefore, should be complete, and I urge you to make the strongest representations to that effect."

As it turned out, Canada did win its exemption (albeit one that left Canada severely dependent on the discretion of the US administration), but at the price of a version of domestic exchange controls that Kierans could not have anticipated precisely. Canada promised to place a limit on the size of its foreign exchange reserves, a "voluntary limit" that came to be "interpreted strictly by the American administration" and that therefore amounted to "a significant inhibition on Canada's freedom to conduct an independent monetary policy."[38] Of course, several observers have speculated on the link between the tough stance taken by the

American negotiators over their interest equalization tax and the Canadian takeover tax proposed the month before.[39] Was Canada the object of American retaliation?

Smith's account certainly suggests that US impressions of Canada formed over the Gordon budget reduced the administration's willingness to grant Canada an exemption to its own interest equalization tax, something that it had already done for smaller countries such as Israel and Mexico. According to Smith, A.E. Safarian surmised that the US position emerged more out of thoughtlessness or incompetence than outright vengeance but that in any case it was done in the context of Canada's having first interfered with the flow of capital between the two countries. As Smith quotes him, "The Americans may have felt this freed them to experiment with controls on the flow of capital too."[40] Smith also records the interesting and subtle link between the two countries' provisions posited by Gerald Wright: Gordon's budget was part of several moves by Ottawa indicating growing disenchantment with the special relationship with the United States, precisely because special dispensations towards Canada carried their own price in national self-esteem. However, of these two perspectives, Safarian's is the most helpful in the present context, because the issue of government interference with capital flows informs all three of Kierans's major interventions on these matters in the mid-1960s.

Precise details of Kierans's third letter await discussion of his days in the Lesage cabinet, for that is when he wrote it. However, Kierans remained consistent in his view that, once the increasingly visible hand of government began to displace the myriad, uncoordinated decisions of private investors and corporate executives over the appropriate timing and location of their investments, international economic relations would begin to take on wholly new political implications. With prescience, perhaps, André Laurendeau wrote in reaction to the assault on Gordon's 1963 budget that Kierans "should have been more conscious of the dangers Mr. Gordon wanted to combat and less confident in the effectiveness of individual action. The state (provincial as well as central) must help in tilting the balance – if Canadians really want that balance to be tilted. But that is an open question."[41] It would be only a short time before Kierans began to take up his share of political responsibility, at least within Quebec.

THE AMES AFFAIR

Kierans's actions as president of the MSE opened the way to his eventual appointment as provincial minister of revenue. One of his most widely noted acts as minister – helping to free the province from its almost exclusive reliance on a single consortium of firms to float its bonds – was initially undertaken while he was still at the MSE.

According to Dale Thomson's account, on 28 January 1963, Jean Lesage met with representatives of A.E. Ames and First Boston Corp., firms that had been used frequently to float bond issues of the Duplessis government.[42] They proposed to raise $300 million on the New York market. Douglas Fullerton, "drawing on advice from Eric Kierans," urged that some of the money should be raised in Canada, a position that accorded with René Lévesque's preference for dropping the usual financial syndicate centred on A.E. Ames and the Bank of Montreal. Kierans, then, was drawn into this fight while still at the MSE. However, the "culminating round" took place in the fall of 1963, just as he was taking on the responsibilities of his new cabinet post, where he was to prove to be an "invaluable ally" in Fullerton's campaign to broaden the base of Quebec's finances.[43]

By early December 1963, according to Fullerton, "we decided to test things with an issue through a new group" of bond dealers, made up mostly of members of the Ames group who had little to lose, but possibly much to gain if an alternative group were formed, because of their relatively small share in the Ames syndicate. Kierans had helped to bring this new group together. It included the Royal Bank, Banque canadienne nationale, Greenshields Inc., and René T. Leclerc. On getting wind of this, Fullerton reports, Ames sent out a letter to all members of its group inviting their participation in a syndicate being formed to deal with all borrowing by Quebec, Hydro-Québec, and Québec Autoroute in the coming year. The usual provision was made that no member of the syndicate would participate in any other syndicate on Quebec issues with a term exceeding one year. As Fullerton recounts: "Kierans blew his stack at this letter, issuing a public statement after Christmas saying 'group managers would be well advised to withdraw their letters' arguing that no mandate to an underwriting syndicate had yet been given by Quebec for the year 1964. He added that syndicate members might find themselves involved in 'restraint of trade' proceedings."

During the following two weeks a battle was joined in both private meetings and the press between the old syndicate, attempting to make the government back away from its new procedures, and the government, becoming ever more determined not to be seen as yielding to pressure from anglophone financial interests.

While the reforms clearly had the backing of the press, inside government the original syndicate seemed to carry more weight. Kierans and Fullerton had arrived at what they saw as a reasonable compromise, but it was pre-empted in further direct meetings between the Ames group and Jean Lesage. According to Fullerton, "What Kierans and I had been shooting for was two separate syndicates, with individual shares appreciably different ... It was only through this kind of wholesale revision of the syndicate structures that the share of francophone dealers could be appreciably increased." Their proposal, therefore, included the recommendation that the different syndicates could alternate on all Quebec issues or divide the government's borrowing between Hydro-Québec and the rest, moving eventually toward competitive bidding on all Quebec bond issues. The question was settled, however, before the Fullerton-Kierans formula reached Lesage, who announced instead the setting up of two management groups to alternate on all Quebec issues, one headed by the older group – Bank of Montreal, Ames, and Lévesque Beaubien – and the other by a new group – Royal Bank, Wood Gundy, and René T. Leclerc – with practically no new room for more junior members.

This outcome was not in practical terms a major change in the province's method of financing, but according to Fullerton it was the best that one could expect, given the entrenched position of the old group. However, in announcing his compromise, Lesage had spoken of his intention to expand Quebec's sources of financing and to have further recourse to the US market. He also intended to broaden the list of financial advisers on whom the province could draw. This, of course, is not a particularly revolutionary change: one Québécois observer, Pierre Fournier, saw neither the changes, nor Kierans's role in them, as very significant:

since the nineteen thirties, a financial group headed by the Bank of Montreal and the Toronto-based brokerage house A.E. Ames had the exclusive responsibility for distributing Quebec government bond issues on the Canadian market. Each broker had to agree in writing at the beginning of each year that he would go through the 'syndicate' or cartel exclusively to distribute new bond issues.

As a result of the cartel's attempts to block the nationalization of electricity, and as a result of various other pressures from the cartel, Eric Kierans, then minister of revenue in the Quebec government, decided to break the cartel in two. Thus, in 1963, Kierans created another group centred around the Royal Bank of Canada. However, the two managing groups, each made up of four institutions, decided to take turns managing Quebec's issues rather than compete with each other. They formed a steering committee with another six institutions; and each of the 14 institutions was given one vote on decisions affecting an underwriting.[44]

Fournier's rendition, then, implies that the episode did not transform Quebec's relations with the financial community in Montreal. However, according to other people in the Quebec government at the time, it spurred on the Quiet Revolution. Perhaps most important, it cemented relations between Kierans and René Lévesque, who lauded Kierans over twenty years later for his role in denting Ames so soon after joining the government in 1963: "In short order and almost single-handedly this remarkable buccaneer succeeded in at last breaking the monopoly the dynasty of A.E. Ames & Sons had held on provincial loans. Besides getting rich at our expense, this company had the misfortune to be essentially WASP from way back, which made it a choice target for this self-made man who was Irish into the bargain."[45]

Lévesque waxed even more rhapsodic in an interview with Jamie Swift. He agreed with the general view in Quebec that Kierans was "the first highly placed Anglophone to associate with the mood of 60–63."[46] So, when English-speakers began to get their backs up over the gradual transition from Lesage's "good-government" orientation to Lévesque's more assertive economic nationalism, Kierans "zeroed in" on Ames, which, according to Lévesque, "had a monopoly on practically everything Quebec did financially." Kierans "knew about the street more than we did and he started organizing in that little gang" so as to break the hold of the English-speaking financial elite on the government. Prior to this, Lévesque recalled, this group's main link to the Lesage government had been provided by the establishment figures George Marler, minister without portfolio, and Paul Earl, minister of revenue; but all that was to change. "Eric was the one-man monopoly breaker. A very intelligent son-of-a-gun, and has diversified experience; Ames was the major big accomplishment in the field that he knew better than anyone else." As a result, Marler was broken, which Lévesque saw as central to the remaining years of Lesage's government. During the Hydro-Québec takeover, Lévesque recalled, he himself lessened Marler's hold on Lesage, "but the real stranglehold was broken when Kierans god rid of Ames."

The Ames affair thus marked the emergence of the alliance within the cabinet that launched such major moves as creation of SIDBEC, the provincial steel company, and SOQUEM, the provincial mining venture. Kierans's role there also receives high praise from contemporaries who credit him with being among the first English-speaking businessmen to recognize and support the bid by the Québécois for political and economic control of the province. Thus, for example, Gérard Pelletier has said, with a hint of irony or chagrin, that "Kierans was the first whose field was economics and took a distinct interest in the majority [he laughs] in this province. Let's face it." Generally in those days, Pelletier further remembered, "if you wanted to speak to anglophones of any importance in Montreal you had to take the initiative. So he was the first one to come in our direction. He was interested."[47]

The emerging partnership between Kierans and Lévesque, dubbed "Jean Lesage's terrible twins" by journalist Stanley McDowell, also seemed natural to many who witnessed it.[48] Even before Kierans entered the cabinet, the press had labelled him "the English René Lévesque," and the two men shared a strong appeal to the media, which they earned with a similarly candid, no-nonsense, and usually fresh approach to public issues. Kierans, of course, captured extra attention as the English Canadian who stood on the "wrong side" of many issues in Quebec. It counted highly with Lévesque that Kierans was on the side of rapid development by means of an expanded provincial government and a reduced role for the English-speaking elite. As Michel Bélanger, who had played a part in the Ames affair, described it, "Lévesque was at ease with Kierans. He felt that at heart he was a kind of a social democrat. I think they were both good at tilting at windmills – but not necessarily the same ones. They had a lot in common."[49]

This common ground adds poignancy to Kierans's forcing of Lévesque's hand on his increasingly separatist nationalism. It was following Kierans's speech to the party's 1967 convention that Lévesque left the hall with a tiny band of recalcitrant Liberals, determined to quit the party to pursue his objective of "sovereignty-association." However, before that point of departure was reached, the new partners had more provincial business to do.

CHAPTER THREE

Lévesque and Kierans, Ltée

The Caouette and Gordon episodes had brought public attention to the outspoken, candid, and energetic president of the Montreal Stock Exchange. In fact, Kierans's public visibility and reputation had grown rapidly from early 1960. In the aftermath of the Caouette exchange in February 1963 and the Gordon letter in June, his public profile transcended local and provincial bounds and began to expand nationally.

Less substantial incidents also showed Kierans to be shy of neither publicity nor controversy. For instance, in May, he declared before an audience of about 150 businessmen, in the posh dining-room of Montreal's Mount Stephen Club: "Neither the Liberals or the Tories have any coherent economic policy at all. The only people who have a coherent economic policy are the NDP."[1] A month earlier, he had told the annual meeting of the Canadian Citizenship Council (held in the Queen Elizabeth Hotel) that English Canadians had been "reserved, complacent and indifferent" to the challenges facing Confederation. He switched into French and told those who understood the language (or had managed to grab their earpieces) that "there is no intelligent English opinion" to compare with the new, dynamic force represented by Quebec's intellectual elite. Moreover, he warned, the separatists were moving forward dangerously.[2] While this sort of exposure added to the uneasiness about Kierans among Montreal's anglophone business people, it could only make him nearly perfect "copy" in the francophone media. After a while, and in turn, this fact caught the notice of English Canada. In *Maclean's*, for example, a strongly supportive article on 18 May 1963 saw Kierans as future leadership material for his party.

Kierans's political career can usefully be seen as a media creation. In the recollection of Gérard Pelletier, then editor of *La Presse*, "You know, you sometimes hear about 'trial by media.' Well, this was 'election by the press.'"[3] In May 1963, when a seat in the national assembly became open owing to the death of Paul Earl, the anglophone minister of revenue, Premier Lesage put out a feeler to Kierans. A meeting was arranged at the premier's office in Quebec City on a Saturday morning, the day after Kierans was to deliver a paper to the Canadian Economics Association during the annual Learned Societies Conference held that year at Laval University. It was agreed at this meeting that Kierans should contest the by-election in Notre Dame de Grâce, and he would be guaranteed a cabinet position if successful, which was assumed to be a formality. Kierans won with a huge majority on 25 September 1963; he had been sworn in as minister of revenue in August.

Ahead lay several roles and experiences that were among the most definitive in his life. From the start, Lesage had in mind for him to mediate relations between the government and the English-Canadian financial community. Kierans did this, but he also brought greater weight and legitimacy to the cabinet's reform faction. The government, and indeed Lesage himself, were generally quite conservative in political orientation, and Kierans's determination to get things done helped to tip the scales towards the kind of sustained activism favoured by René Lévesque and other reformers.

These circumstances exposed Kierans to a distinctive and rewarding sense of collective action and public responsibility during an extraordinary period. The government undertook unusually intense involvement in society and the economy and arrived at its decisions in a dynamic, collegial manner. Kierans was Quebec's minister of revenue, and later of health, while national economic and social policies were being redefined, and he developed strong and enduring concerns about the overcentralization of authority in Canada, which later surfaced in emphatic criticisms of Ottawa's encroachments on provincial powers.

During this and succeeding periods, Kierans was almost perfectly positioned – by experience, as well as personal background – to bridge the gap that otherwise might have opened more rapidly and convulsively between the province's growing activism and the mounting caution, if not outright hostility, of the English-speaking elite.

THE CONTRACTION OF ENGLISH-SPEAKING POWER IN QUEBEC

Kierans's move from the MSE to the revenue ministry brings into focus two questions about the Quiet Revolution. What was the attitude of English-speaking Quebecers, particularly business people, towards it? What part did the "French bourgeoisie" play in it? On the first question, the Quiet Revolution represented at the very least a break in the traditional accommodation between the province's anglophone business elite and its francophone political elite – what Kenneth McRoberts has termed "an acknowledged specialization of responsibilities."[4] Francophones would run the political system, and anglophones the economy. More to the point, as Levine puts it, "Francophone leaders would not deploy the powers of the Quebec state to challenge these linguistic hierarchies and would support 'probusiness' policies favoured by the English-speaking economic elite of Montreal."[5] To the extent, then, that the Quiet Revolution threatened to overturn this tradition, one might have expected the English-speaking community and business elite to have feared it and opposed it.

Nevertheless, the academic literature is not unanimous in the view that English Quebecers typically opposed Lesage's reforms. In fact, according to Andrew Sancton, English-speaking Montrealers strongly endorsed them: "English-speaking Montrealers were among the most fervent proponents of the new Lesage government. They supported its attempts to eliminate patronage and transform the provincial civil service into a more efficient and capable bureaucracy. In short, the Lesage government seemed to be transforming Quebec's political system so that it would actually be better suited to traditional Anglo-Saxon values and sensibilities."

This assessment, however, does not apply without qualification to the political side of those reforms: "Paradoxically, this very tendency toward convergence in the two groups' values eventually posed the greatest threat to English-speaking economic dominance. French-speaking Quebeckers were now eager to participate in all aspects of Quebec society and no longer saw any legitimacy in their virtually systematic exclusion from top positions in the private sector. The stage was set for overt social conflict based on language differences."[6] In other words, despite the convergence of political values, the awakening French community still threatened English-speaking economic dominance.

In fact, as Sancton suggests, the only English-speakers who had previously complained about the Duplessis regime were those "with an unusually highly developed sense of political morality." Consequently, as opposition to the Union nationale built during the 1950s, "most of it came from French-Canadian intellectuals rather than English-Canadian businessmen."[7] It could be predicted, then, that when opposition to the Union nationale finally triumphed, this outcome would be embraced much less warmly by the latter than by the former group. To this extent, Kierans would appear to have been an atypical, if not unique, member of the English-speaking business community.

This interpretation squares with two other examinations of Quebec nationalism. William Coleman notes a potential clash between the new trends in Quebec and anglophone business people by stressing the role of their francophone counterparts. Québécois business people, while not part of the separatist extreme of nationalism, were sufficiently at odds with the status quo to support attempts to turn the new assertiveness against entrenched economic interests.[8] Francophone business interests were therefore well served when the Quiet Revolution turned into "a massive effort on the part of French-speaking political leaders to gain some measure of control over Quebec's burgeoning economy."[9]

In the process of assuming these new powers, French-speaking leaders of course expanded the constituency for even further change. As Coleman puts it, "the existence, at a structural level, of a new middle class at the dawn of the Quiet Revolution, is not as obvious as has been assumed. In some sense, it is more sensibly argued that the new middle class was a product of the reforms of the 1960s than their instigator. The provincial state, in rationalizing the education and social service systems and in founding a series of public corporations during the 1960s, may have created this class in its wake."[10]

The election in 1960 generated further economic and social transformations that increasingly opposed the economic interests of anglophone "ins" to those of francophone "outs." Coleman observes:

The overall aim of the economic policy that emerged after the *Parti libéral* victory in June 1960 was to create viable and competitive capitalist enterprises controlled by members of the francophone community. These enterprises would be sufficiently strong to allow the francophone community to become a full participant in the advanced industrial economy of North America. The means envisaged was the establishment of institutions that would compete with the dominant enterprises controlled by non-francophones and that would eventually wrest some markets from them ... [T]he period saw a stronger push to integrate the francophone community into an advanced industrial capitalist economy.[11]

In sum, as Levine puts it, "Although Francophone businessmen did not control the agenda of Quiet Revolution *étatisme*, policymakers were nevertheless committed to using state power to expand the Francophone presence in the private sector."[12]

Another account of the Quiet Revolution tends to see the French-English economic antagonism in Montreal as more fundamental and thoroughgoing. According to Arnopolous and Clift, Anglophone business leaders moved from early suspicion of Lesage's government to real misgivings, to outright hostility.[13] One possible exception was reluctant readiness to promote more French-speaking people to managerial and executive positions in order to maintain effective contacts with the increasingly powerful and active government in Quebec City. Even these changes, however, were "largely cosmetic and did not reflect any attempt to revise the basis on which power was shared between English and French elements of the country." More generally, in these authors' view, Montreal's English-speaking business leaders constituted the only major group that failed to join the chorus of praise for the reforms of the Quiet Revolution: "At a time when public spending everywhere was rising giddily, the attitude of the Quebec government could only signal an attempt to obtain the political decentralization of Canada, with its inevitable consequences for the national economy. The business community feared the balkanization of an economy that already had enormous difficulties meeting foreign competition." The government's more aggressive moves – most notably, nationalization of private power companies – sharpened these anxieties and prompted warnings from financial institutions.

When some of these institutions began dumping Quebec bonds on the market, Lesage felt that he had to take the issue to the electorate in 1962 to protect the government's credibility.[14] The effect of those financial reactionaries on the perceptions of Quebec's French-speaking activists brings our discussion full circle to the A.E. Ames affair, in which Kierans had stood not with these reactionaries, but militantly against them. Kierans had thus not just chosen sides, but joined camps. The new alignment is well expressed by Arnopolous and Clift: "It was driven home to the French middle class that the Canadian financial community would vigorously resist any attempt to alter the direction in which the Quebec economy was developing or to modify its fundamental subordination to the more powerful one in Ontario. In this way, the negative attitudes of the financial community, particularly those of the Bank of Montreal and of A.E. Ames and Co. of Toronto who were handling the province's public borrowing at the time, sowed the seeds of the current confrontation."[15]

Theoretically, there were two ways in which the business sector could become predominantly French: conversion of English-speaking into French-speaking companies or displacement of the former by the latter. The hostility of the vast majority of anglophone owner-managers to Québécois ambitions ensured the latter course, and the retarded development of a francophone capitalist class meant that the early steps in that direction would be made by the Quebec state.

LÉVESQUE ET KIERANS, INC., PROVINCE BUILDERS

Kierans and Lévesque teamed up to promote "state capitalism" in two primary forms – creation of SIDBEC, a provincially owned steel company, and SOQUEM, a less fruitful move in the direction of a state mining company. The SIDBEC story illustrates several points made already about Kierans's role in the cabinet, not the least of which was counter-balancing the conservative inclinations of George Marler.

SIDBEC

Nationalist ministers felt strongly that Quebec should produce steel for its own use and export its rich sources of iron ore in the fabricated form of steel products rather than as unprocessed raw materials. However, the idea of a government-owned corporation was less keenly held by Lesage and his more conservative colleagues, who were more concerned about the impact on the province's finances if the project proved uneconomic. The issue of whether Quebec's steel mill was to be a public or private enterprise, or something in between, was to plague, and divide, the government throughout its six years in office. Kierans stepped into this issue in midstream and made several decisive interventions aimed generally at preventing adoption of a mixed-enterprise formula that amounted to private control with public risk, a formula that surfaced and resurfaced throughout the policy-making process.

In July 1961, Quebec's Economic Council had endorsed a proposal to build an integrated steel complex with a capacity of 500,000 tons a year on the south shore of the St Lawrence River at a cost of $109 million, to be provided in whole or in part by the government.[16] This recommendation won cabinet approval in September 1961, and the council struck a Steel Plant Committee to oversee the necessary preliminaries. By January 1963 the project had received favourable feasibility and profitability studies, and an option had been taken out on an eleven-square-mile site at Bécancour, across the St Lawrence from Trois-Rivières.[17]

In the mean time, however, an alternative, private project was emerging. The Dominion Coal and Steel Corp. (DOSCO), of Sydney, Nova Scotia, was contemplating an investment in a steel mill in Quebec, provided that it could obtain adequate support from the provincial government. The president of DOSCO, A.L. Fairly, Jr., in an apparent attempt to set back the growing momentum towards a public company, told members of the Steel Plant Committee that the premier had said that his government had no intention of competing with established Canadian producers. This news, according to Thomson, prompted quick action:

Alarmed, the committee urged Lesage to issue a formal repudiation of any such commitment. Claude Morin supported the committee; not only would the publicly funded scheme likely be profitable, he advised the premier, but a truly Quebec steel plant was essential if the government was to honour its pledge to reconquer the economy and institute comprehensive planning. Jacques Parizeau, too, argued in favour of a 'national' project, financed either through the Societé Generale de Financement [SGF] or directly by the government ... Jean Lesage continued to insist that whether sponsored by the public or private sector, the scheme should be self-financing and profitable.

On 31 October 1963, the Committee recommended construction of a plant at Bécancour at an estimated cost of $248 million and productive capacity of 600,000 tons of steel per year. A new corporation was to be created to carry out the project. However, the method of financing remained a major point of contention within the cabinet. The premier continued to resist pressures for a state enterprise, fearful of being saddled with an unprofitable venture and haunted by the reputation of publicly owned companies for going broke.

According to Thomson, Lesage was finally persuaded to accept the public-enterprise formula for SIDBEC by the combined arguments of Lévesque and Kierans: "The federal crown corporation, Polymer [Lévesque argued], was making handsome profits. Personally, he would not object if the government supplied all the funds, although he recognized that it was useful to associate the private sector with the project. Eric Kierans, at the time still a recent but prestigious recruit to the cabinet, played a critical role in the debate, offsetting the influence of Marler and Pigeon and supporting the Steel Committee. Still uneasy, Jean Lesage finally yielded." This did not end the controversy, however. By April 1965, the cabinet was still deadlocked over whether SIDBEC should be essentially a private or a public corporation, and ministers were inclined to air their differences in public, despite Lesage's warnings. Among opinion leaders in the press, Claude Ryan and Gérard Pelletier argued for government control and public financing.

In the assembly, the Union nationale demanded full information on the subject, and Daniel Johnson indicated his sympathy with René Lévesque's viewpoint. On 9 April, Quebec's Economic Council debated a proposal from the proponents of government control, which recommended that representatives of the public hold half of the seats on SIDBEC's board of directors. When this proposal went before the cabinet's committee on planning, Lévesque and Kierans took the position that it did not go far enough; a crown corporation was required: "In addition to its being a more efficient instrument of government economic policy, they argued, a Crown corporation would have a healthier financial structure and would not have to pay federal taxes; the role of the private sector would be simply to buy the bonds and debentures guaranteed by the province."

The public-enterprise formula, which came to be known as the "Kierans Alternative," was strongly resisted by Gérard Filion, president of SIDBEC (and former head of the SGF). Filion also had allies in cabinet, and a consensus on a precise delineation of the eventual financial structure of Quebec's steel company eluded the cabinet right up until the election of 1966. To Kierans, Lévesque, Parizeau, and others favouring provincial ownership, all versions short of full crown ownership amounted to private-sector control with public-sector risk. In Fullerton's words, "How could the province justify publicly its role as banker, and in effect silent partner, to someone in the private sector?"[18] Thus, throughout the process from which SIDBEC finally emerged, Kierans went to great lengths to ensure that the province, as by far the predominant investor, would hold and exercise the preponderance of decision-making power. This proved difficult, given that the premier (and the president of SIDBEC) seemed determined to retain both the image and the reality of a publicly owned steel company that was not in competition with the privately owned firms. Facing this recalcitrance at the core of provincial authority, Kierans moved against the premier's flank with a campaign for a crown corporation, waged both within and beyond government circles.

This campaign began almost inconspicuously during a television program on 25 January 1965, during which Kierans mentioned that he favoured the crown corporation formula for SIDBEC. According to a subsequent review of the steel company debate by Gordon Pape, this comment "passed almost unnoticed."[19] Kierans included a similar comment in a speech before the Drummondville Chamber of Commerce two weeks later. Kierans circulated the text to the Quebec press gallery prior to delivery and included a reference to "the ownership of the means of production" while endorsing crown corporations as a route to sustained economic growth.[20] The press began a chorus of speculation over disunity in the cabinet, which in turn prompted Lesage to haul Kierans onto the carpet for a breach of cabinet solidarity.

When the leader of the opposition probed him on this point in the assembly, Kierans quoted Sir Wilfrid Laurier to the effect that a difference of views between a minister and his colleagues need not lead to his resignation provided that he was prepared to "give way to the views of others." While the premier held his head in his hands in the midst of a rather bemused chamber, Kierans added that since the steel mill did not relate directly to his responsibility as minister of revenue, "my views have a weight that is neither greater nor less than that of any other individual in the Cabinet. In this instance of course, I accept the consensus, and that is government policy."[21]

Kierans also worked inside the government, communicating bluntly and insistently with Lesage, Filion, and others in the cabinet. For example, in a letter to the premier in June 1965, Kierans barely concealed his frustration over Lesage's tendency to bend over backwards to maintain an impression of an important private-sector role in SIDBEC: "Are you trying to do the impossible?" his letter opened. It went on:

Several years ago, you ordered feasibility studies looking to the possible erection of a Quebec steel mill; you commanded market and product studies; you took out options on land around Bécancour; you took up these options; you formed SIDBEC; you appointed the directors and named the first President; you undertook to guarantee and supply most, if not all, the financing.

How can you come along now, plaster a label on all this and say that this was done by private enterprise?

It seems to me that we are frantically trying to put our own baby out for adoption and begging others to give the child their name.[22]

Kierans felt that any offering of shares to the public was premature, and he listed six conditions that had yet to be fulfilled before SIDBEC could claim to have an "investment proposition." It would be simply unfair, and potentially "murderous" politically, to induce the public to invest "on the basis of nationalism and emotionalism." Instead, Kierans recommended that the government remain open and flexible as to the ultimate ownership of SIDBEC and, in the mean time, subscribe for $20 million worth of shares, along with $3–5 million from the SGF, with further financing to come via government-guaranteed debentures. After four or five years, when potential investors had more information, the government could consider selling shares to the public. Or, "if attractive partnership offers come from major steel interests, the government will give them full consideration."

Kierans's primary concern was that specific corporate interests be denied the opportunity of controlling SIDBEC without carrying a proportionate share of the financial risk. Kierans had to pursue this concern against the premier's anxieties over the risks of public ownership and Gérard Filion's apparent desire to head a corporation with only the slightest possible ties to government. Thus, Kierans wrote Filion following a cabinet meeting on SIDBEC financing and stressed again the advantages of a non-taxable, fully public enterprise: "What bothers me is that we are giving up so much in the way of tax advantages in order to gain so little ... There has been no enthusiasm in the private sector for SIDBEC and there will be even less when the full implications of the C.O.E.Q. [Conseil d'orientation économique du Québec] recommendations sink in." He went on, "We are paying lip-service to a form of business organization, the private corporation, which is not suited to this particular project and which can endanger the primary aims of the government and the people in creating SIDBEC. For a passive, if not sullen, collaboration we are giving up all the tax advantages that would influence your pricing policies and measurably reduce your break-even point."[23]

Filion must have turned a blind eye to this advice, however, for Kierans wrote to Lesage in August, with copies to members of "Le comité ministériel de planification économique," spelling out his criticisms of what he took to be a planned campaign by Filion to more than double the prospective capacity of the Quebec steel mill. According to Kierans, Filion also planned to draw in European financiers and make a share offering to the Canadian public. This planned campaign, he argued to the premier, was designed "to put the government in a situation where it must choose between private control and the *vision* of a 1,500,000 ton steel mill or public ownership and a paltry 600,000 ton plant. The government is forced into a position that is untenable financially and dangerous politically. *In either case, the people will invest directly or guarantee 90%–95% of the funds and the risks are public.*" After some more detailed criticisms of recent public announcements by Filion, Kierans made a blunt call upon the premier to put him in his place: "Perhaps the management of SIDBEC would prefer to operate as a private enterprise but as long as the government is taking the risks, this is not possible. Under these conditions, I hope they will stop trying to outmanoeuvre the government and get down to the business of producing and marketing steel. Ideologists may or may not have a place in Cabinets but they surely do not belong in the steel industry."[24]

Especially given SIDBEC's poor track record – after 1966 it became a sump-hole for government subsidies and never did make the intended strategic contribution to economic diversification – it may seem odd that the hard-headed businessman in Kierans was apparently unable to restrain his enthusiasm for such a high-risk public investment. The answer lies in the activist public entrepreneur who also resided within him. The cause that he had championed while president of the MSE against the forces of the establishment, it is true, had been that of the small investor, not the state. In this instance, however, it is important to keep in mind not what Kierans was chiefly determined to prevent, but, instead, what circumstances prompted him to favour.

His fundamental principle was that the Quebec government should not fund and underwrite a project that remained under private control and worked to private benefit. He felt that there should be no public support without government control and a public purpose. Once into the fight to improve the chances of the fully public option, he gave it his characteristically energetic and hyperbolic best. Thus, despite the doubt perhaps cast by his use of the Marxist phrase "the ownership of the means of production," his role here should not be taken as a token of absolute support for public over private enterprise. To the contrary, it speaks to his particular understanding of the proper relationship between government and business.

Kierans advocated recourse to public entrepreneurship only when private entrepreneurs were failing society – indeed, were absent; here lies the link between the president of the MSE and the activist minister. At the MSE, Kierans had advocated frequent distribution of corporate earnings to individual shareholders because he thought them in closer touch than corporate managers with the emerging needs and capacities of the society. As a minister, he felt that in the face of similar failures of corporate management – as measured by its recourse to public subsidy – the state also might make up for entrepreneurial deficiencies, especially if individuals lacked the means or the will to take the risk.

Kierans spoke of Quebec's new economic opportunities before a

Canadian Club audience in Calgary just before he broke ranks with his cabinet colleagues over SIDBEC:

The difficulty common to all developing nations today is to find the locus of entrepreneurship. If we are to increase the rate of economic growth and reduce unemployment, we must move massively, i.e., through large industrial units ... Private enterprise must be encouraged, but, to the extent that a gap exists in the employment of our human and material resources, state enterprise will have to be created ...

If entrepreneurship is a scarce commodity in Canada, then it is time, as we in Quebec realize, to produce a measure of government ingenuity and dedication ...

The stimulus of our own investment will *supplement and support private enterprise, not replace the efforts of our business men and industrialists. We need more effort and initiative from everyone, not less* ...

Heightened activity is a necessity in Quebec today and this calls for government investment that will support and boost output and employment. In my own mind, our program will be a success when the need for a high level of provincial expenditures abates.[25]

One of the advantages of a crown-owned steel corporation most frequently cited by Kierans was its exemption from federal income taxes: the extra cash flow would give the "public entrepreneurs" some money to work with. Kierans figured out for his cabinet colleagues the difference in cash flow that SIDBEC would generate as a privately and a publicly owned corporation. The difference was $19.8 million on sales of $200 million, or 40 per cent more for the crown version, primarily because of the absence of $14 million in federal taxes. This higher rate of cash flow would help finance expansion of plant capacity, research in new steel technology, technical assistance to customers, development of new uses for steel, and several more corporate benefits.[26] One almost gets the impression that Kierans would have loved, as a provincial minister, to get his hands on a steel company; failing that, he shows early signs here of his later attitude to mining and other sectors – namely, that provincial governments can and, when circumstances dictate, should act as creative economic agents.

SOQUEM

At any rate, one can clearly see this theme working itself out in two other key initiatives of the province's public entrepreneurs –

SOQUEM and the Caisse de dépôt et placement. Kierans was more active in the former than in the latter, although his role in the creation of Quebec's mineral exploration company adds little to the picture already drawn of his part in the Quiet Revolution. Once again, Kierans contributed moral support and some clout within cabinet to another of René Lévesque's grand but divisive schemes for the expansion of provincial powers, this time over the mining industry.[27] This fight was less protracted and less volatile, however, primarily because Lévesque was able to win Lesage's support by doing him a good turn in another, unrelated direction. It does, though, include one interesting twist: Kierans favoured an even more ambitious move against the mining industry but deferred to Lévesque's judgment that a bird in the hand – a provincially owned exploration and development company – was worth two in the bush – namely, the major reforms in mineral taxation that Kierans wanted Lévesque to achieve.

Kierans vividly recalls how shocked he was when he noticed that provincial revenues from taxes on mining firms were extremely small – less than the province's expenditures on infrastructural support to those same industries. Closing down Quebec's mining industry would provide a net benefit to the public treasury![28] Kierans was therefore convinced that the time was long overdue for substantial restructuring of taxes and royalties applied against mining companies – a message that he later carried to Manitoba.

Lévesque's priority, however, appears to have been an active public presence in exploration and development which he felt that private firms could not be counted on to develop to the optimum benefit of the public. Putting the case to cabinet in January 1965 Lévesque acknowledged that since the province needed foreign capital and access to foreign markets, it was not possible to change the basic framework within which the industry operated. Thomson records Lévesque's position as follows:

Yet, as owner of the resources and with a certain experience in exploration, the government was in a position to 'insert itself into the process' and influence the pattern of activity. Without interfering with the operations of others, a government-owned company could intensify the development of Quebec's mineral resources, encourage local processing and consumption, open up new markets, and increase the province's share of the profits.

Specifically, René Lévesque proposed the creation of an autonomous body similar to the Autoroute Authority, with $15 million in initial funding to be paid to it over ten years. ... Enjoying the same freedom of action as a private firm, it would carry out its own exploration, participate in the development of proven sites, maintain a portfolio of shares in other companies, and eventually even offer its own shares on the financial market.[29]

This proposal was met with general lack of enthusiasm, and Lesage himself had already gone out of his way to assure the mining industry that it need not fear the fate of the province's power companies with the creation of Hydro-Québec.

As usual, however, Eric Kierans lent his full support to the idea, and Lesage agreed at the end of February 1965 to accept the plan in principle and to strike a committee to prepare the legislation. A draft bill was completed by the committee in March, and Lévesque and his close media observers were already gearing up for another cabinet fight. Ironically, Lévesque was able to overcome this latent opposition with scarcely a shot fired in anger: he won Lesage's, and hence the whole cabinet's, acquiescence in creation of SOQUEM by agreeing to a peculiar deal with the premier.

The University of Montreal was to hold a public debate on patriation of the Canadian constitution. Lesage pressured Lévesque to represent the government in this debate and argue in favour of the Fulton-Favreau amending formula, which the premier was committed to run through the provincial legislature despite widespread denunciation by Quebec's nationalists. Lévesque lost this debate rather decisively, possibly because of his discernible lack of conviction, but he did get approval for SOQUEM. Despite this success, or perhaps because of the rather peculiar method of attaining it, Lévesque was simply not up to further battles in the cabinet over resource policy. The substantial increases that Kierans wanted in taxation and royalties simply fell by the wayside.

The fights within the cabinet over SIDBEC and SOQUEM illustrate the hard practicalities involved in implementation of the Quiet Revolution. As with most practical matters, these battles, while not exactly routine, did not carry the symbolism of the earlier fight over Quebec's finances. Indeed, a typical meeting would have included Lesage; George Marler, who was de facto finance minister, the government's primary contact with St James Street, and a staunch defender of A.E. Ames and the Bank of Montreal; René Lévesque, minister of resources and mastermind of Quebec's new plan of economic emancipation through provincial-government intervention; and Eric Kierans, representing the business community but not the Montreal establishment. Kierans would have stood between Lévesque and the other two men but leaned closer to Lévesque, and those two together would have widened the distance between Marler and Lesage.

Kierans and Lévesque, though, parted company as soon as Lévesque and his supporters were no longer content to be simply "maîtres chez nous" and set out to dismantle Canada. However, before this rupture occurred, the two nationalists had a few more years of productive collaboration, as the government of Quebec became caught up in other developments in the rest of the country and across the continent. Kierans was accordingly drawn into – or projected himself into – the politics of Quebec's relations with Ottawa and the other provinces, as well as Canada's relations with the United States. The rest of Kierans's part in the Lesage government thus allowed him to engage in and reflect on federal-provincial relations, national unity, and national independence, subjects that were to preoccupy him for the rest of his life.

CHAPTER FOUR

"Cooperative" Federalism and the Break with Lévesque

Two of Eric Kierans's major experiences with the government of Quebec and the Liberal party – both in power and in opposition – reflected and shaped his attitude towards federal-provincial relations.

The first experience involves Kierans's presence at meetings between Ottawa and Quebec City in 1965 and 1966 on a range of matters: fiscal arrangements, pension plans, and early moves towards a national health scheme. Kierans was simply appalled by federal politicians and bureaucrats, who struck him as insensitive to the needs of individual provinces, ignorant of the constraints with which provincial governments had to cope, and arrogant in their treatment of those, like himself, representing "junior governments." The intensity of Kierans's decentralist stance, while quite consistent with his general distrust of concentrations of power of any kind, seems to be a direct outcome of this series of contacts. Kierans felt considerable and growing frustration as he tried to do his best on behalf of the people of Quebec, while coping with the consequences for Quebec of federal policies.

The second experience, after the Quebec Liberals lost power in June 1966, presents an interesting, almost paradoxical, contrast with the implications of the first. In opposing the early separatism of René Lévesque, Kierans was to show that his strong advocacy of decentralization was yet predicated upon preservation of a united Canada.

The two episodes also led to Kierans's gradual realization that he might be able to contribute to national political life. He began trying to figure out how to build bridges between English- and French-speakers, between central and peripheral regions, and, not least, between Canadian and Quebec nationalism.

THREE FEDERAL INITIATIVES

Part of Kierans's preference for a looser federation was born out of Ottawa's failure to respect, or even comprehend, the economic realities faced by provincial governments. It was further strengthened by Ottawa's assumption that federal economic and social programs were certain to provide better solutions to provincial problems than the provinces themselves could achieve with comparable resources. Kierans was also frustrated on several occasions by the federal government's determination to proceed with such programs, whether or not the provinces wanted them, or wanted them in Ottawa's preferred form. As minister of revenue (and, for a short time, of health), Kierans thus saw at first hand the difficulties for provincial governments that accompanied two major federal initiatives – the Canada Pension Plan and the early phases of Medicare.

Tom Kent's superb memoir of his years with the Pearson and Trudeau governments illuminates Kierans's part in the initiation of these two pillars of Canadian social policy.[1] There are two significant connections between Kent's memoir and Kierans's outlook on Canadian federalism.

First, even during the era of Lester Pearson's "cooperative federalism," the clash between national social programs and expanding provincial responsibilities was evident. Kent's book presents flesh-and-blood examples in the form of the struggles between federal and provincial officials over how to realize major social programs such as the pension plan and Medicare. Kent, although he occupied a key federal position during these struggles, was sensitive to the provincial predicaments created by Ottawa's exercise of its fiscal clout, which adds poignancy to Kierans's growing disaffection resulting from Ottawa's arrogance and indifference. What Kierans would have us condemn the federal government for doing, Kent tells us it could not keep itself from doing. A starkly partisan impulse pushed the Pearson government headlong into a rough-and-ready version of Medicare; Kierans was stunned by the manner in which it was "proposed" to provincial governments.

Second, Tom Kent clearly approached federalism (and government in general) from assumptions very close to Kierans's. For example, Kent lays out as eloquently as Kierans himself the fact that the centralization from which the provinces began to recoil in the early 1960s was a hangover from wartime mobilization. It was an aberration rather than the "natural order of things" that those bound to Ottawa have tended, not disinterestedly, to claim that it was. Quebec's "opting out" of several centralizing initiatives was only an extreme case of a widely shared provincial concern. As another example, Kent expresses disappointment similar to Kierans's over the Liberal party's complete failure, beginning with Pearson's government and amplified enormously by Trudeau's, to strike an appropriate long-term economic strategy for the country, a complaint often repeated by Quebec nationalists and separatists down to the present day.

Kent's memoir deals with three federal initiatives that involved Kierans: the Canada Pension Plan (CPP), the early phases of Medicare, and the fiscal arrangements of "cooperative federalism."

To begin with the CPP, Tom Kent's formulation of the federal-provincial impasse over this widely endorsed social program starts with some elementary statistics of the sort that Kierans also likes to draw quickly into any discussion of federalism:

Before the war, tax revenues had been divided fairly evenly between the federal government, on the one hand, and the provinces and their municipalities, on the other. On average over the years 1926–39, the federal government levied 46 per cent of total Canadian taxation, the provinces 54 per cent. The priority ceded to Ottawa in wartime was only slowly eroded afterwards. For the last five years before the Pearson government, 1957–62, against 37 per cent for the provinces and the municipalities combined.[2]

Pearson's "cooperative federalism," according to Kent, sought to redress this disparity. Existing shares of total tax revenues were out of keeping with the new and expanding demands placed on provincial governments after 1945, especially in areas of provincial jurisdiction such as education and health services. Kent states the principle simply: "the federal government ought to have less money to spend, in favour of the provincial governments having more." One of the major points at issue between Quebec and Ottawa on the matter of pensions put Pearson and the federal Liberals to the test on this precise point, and Pearson's government soon discovered that this objective, so easily stated, was rather more difficult to achieve.

Quebec wanted its own arrangements, specifically a funded pension plan, to enable it to accumulate, through the steady stream of individual and corporate contributions, a pool of capital that could be invested in an expanded provincial economic and social infrastructure – roads, schools, hospitals, universities, and all the other provincial assets necessary to promote self-sustained economic growth. A fully funded pension plan for Quebec meant that contributions would significantly exceed pensions paid for the foreseeable future, and this would expand enormously the resources available to the government. Ottawa, for its part, preferred an unfunded national plan, requiring contributions only at the (initially) modest rate required to meet its obligations to an (initially) small number of retired recipients. It was also more willing to provide benefits after a short period of eligibility. In sum, Ottawa's plan showed signs of the relative abundance of resources available to it through its current tax revenues, while Quebec's showed opposite signs of its need for additional revenues.

Probably for this fundamental reason, the politics of the CPP became tangled up with the more general issue of tax-sharing, "opting-out" formulas, and almost the entire intergovernmental agenda. Not only did this add complexity to the issues themselves, but it complicated the national politics of the pension issue. Within national party politics, given its naturally centralist assumptions – federal governments, regardless of party, are supposed to promote national, not provincial interests – willingness to cede the provinces more room to tax was easily attacked as "caving in," "giving away the store," and all other manner of characterizations of weakness and lack of resolve. The Pearson government had already invited such accusations in spades over the failure of Walter Gordon's 1963 budget. For this reason, the most sensible trade-off to ensure Quebec's compliance with the federal pension scheme – to offer all the provinces more tax room so that they would have more funds to invest in provincial development – simply would not wash in the cabinet, let alone in the Liberal caucus or the House of Commons. This raised the fiscal-policy stakes in the contest over the pension plan.

That the issue of funding was at the centre of the scrap over the CPP is clear. There is evidence to this effect in Kent's recent account and in such secondary sources as Claude Morin's review of the issue and Richard Simeon's discussion of the role of the pension plan in "federal-provincial diplomacy."[3] It is further reflected in the very motives behind the two different concepts, with Ottawa seeing such a plan as a central component of what we call today the "social safety net" and Quebec City seeing it as a major thrust towards what was soon to be known as "province building."

Provincial use of government power for acceleration of development was the area in which Kierans made his major contribution to Quebec's version of the pension plan. Kierans's part in creation of the Quebec Pension Plan, and especially vis-à-vis use of the Caisse de dépôt as a major source of capital expenditures for the province, was not unlike his role in earlier confrontations with the A.E. Ames syndicate over Quebec's bond financing. He helped to convince Jean Lesage that the main object of the plan was feasible and worthwhile – as usual, against the grain of the premier's more cautious and economically conservative instincts – and he undertook to reassure the more reactionary elements of the Quebec establishment that the whole enterprise was a legitimate use of the government's powers.[4]

As Jamie Swift relates, and as many secondary accounts have suggested with their paucity of references to Kierans, Kierans's major contribution was assuring the general legitimacy of the Quebec scheme both inside and outside the government. (Lesage was his own finance minister and minister of federal-provincial relations and worked most closely on these matters with his deputy minister of federal-provincial relations, Claude Morin.) However, Kierans was reviewing Quebec cabinet material pertaining to the negotiations over fiscal sharing arrangements, and several times he accompanied Lesage to meetings of the Tax Structure Committee.[5]

One of Kierans's favourite stories from this period deals with the way in which the provinces were given notice of the federal government's hastily conceived program for Medicare. Kierans has told it many times, and it appears in Swift's biography, so the details can be kept brief here. According to Kierans, Prime Minister Pearson brought up what became the National Medical Care Insurance Act (1966) almost as an afterthought at a July 1965 federal-provincial conference. Little was said about the nature of the proposed plan, but Pearson did estimate the cost of the plan loosely at about $1 billion per annum, of which the provinces could be responsible for half. Kierans quickly calculated Quebec's portion of the provinces' share at about $125 million. Hence his frequent complaint about the politics of shared-cost programs: Ottawa can, without consultation if it so sees fit, practically commit provincial governments to spending huge sums of money out of their own treasuries, even when the federal plan might carry very low priority for them. What really seemed to bother Kierans on this occasion, however, was the sheer gall of his federal counterparts. "This was Ottawa," Swift quotes Kierans. "They were just so absolutely blind to this thing [about distorting provincial priorities]. They thought they were doing us a favour."[6]

Kierans makes the same complaint about a similar episode surrounding introduction of a federal plan on youth unemployment. The setting, again, was a federal-provincial conference.[7] According to Kierans, Tom Kent had noticed that the only item on the agenda was the pension plan and that the whole meeting could be over by 11 o'clock in the morning. "So Kent threw in his plan for youth employment. And here we were in [the province of] Quebec trying to take care of youth on farms, knowing that labour was an essential factor on many of our marginal farming operations. It just wasn't going to fit together with Kent's idea."[8] Kierans also recalls that other provincial representatives had equal difficulties with Kent's proposal. He quotes Premier Duff Roblin of Manitoba as asking, "Where the hell did this come from? Nobody in my government knows anything about this!" Nova Scotia Premier Robert Stanfield quipped, "Maybe the mails are faster to Manitoba than to Nova Scotia. I didn't get my copy of this until I boarded my plane ... " According to Kierans, Stanfield went on more seriously to sum up another difficulty that Kierans has always had with such federal initiatives. He remembers Stanfield saying to the conference, "There is no demand for this kind of plan in Nova Scotia, but at the same time there are demands there I can't possibly meet. Even worse, I can now predict that there *will be* a demand for this program – the minute [Premier] Robichaud picks it up next door in New Brunswick."

Kent's account of the introduction of Medicare, while different in tone from Kierans's recounting of such episodes, substantiates the lack of meaningful consultation with the provinces preceding Pearson's announcement of the plan at a federal-provincial conference in July 1965.[9] A special committee of officials from the Privy Council Office, the Prime Minister's Office, and the Department of Finance had been working up the four main principles that it felt should define a national health scheme. Kent had expected these principles to form the basis for consultation with the provinces, after which a firm federal position would be determined. This way of proceeding was consistent not only with earlier precedents but with the spirit of "cooperative federalism."

As Kent recalls the cabinet's deliberation of these principles, he was "taken aback" when Pearson acted almost immediately. According to Kent, the prime minister

submitted the committee's recommendation to Cabinet as the definite federal plan to be proposed to the provinces at the federal-provincial conference arranged for 19–23 July 1965. This meant that it would be made public as soon as the provinces heard it. Cabinet agreed. ... My first draft of the Prime Minister's main statement to the conference had to be written only five days before it was delivered. It was a long document dealing with subjects as varied as the 'poverty and opportunity' program as a whole, regional development, training, the Canada Assistance Plan, the state of the economy, the principles of federalism, the tax structure committee, off-shore mineral rights, and cooperation against organized crime, as well as the main item – medicare. The advance notice to the provincial delegations was therefore minimal. The most we could do was to invite a few of the principal officials to a meeting in my office when they arrived, the evening before the conference began, and give them a quick briefing on the federal medicare policy.

The provinces justifiably resented this peremptory federal con-duct, but politically Ottawa had the initiative. Kierans clearly had good reason to feel that provincial priorities had not been given a chance to register on Ottawa before the federal government publicly announced a medical plan that was certain to stir up expectations in all provinces. Provincial governments thereafter were unlikely to walk away from the health care program; electorates would know that they could provide such care using "fifty-cent dollars." The provinces nevertheless had to come up with this half-dollar and, moreover, to dig it out of budgets already under severe pressure. For Quebec in particular, prospective expenditures on medicare were about to conflict with ambitious programs of economic expansion.

Thus Kierans's reaction to the style of the federal plan seems vindicated by Tom Kent's admission of Ottawa's failure to provide proper notice to provincial governments. Similarly, Kierans's assessment of the plan's substance finds support in Malcolm Taylor's definitive study of the history of medicare: "The political costs to Ontario and Alberta of their 'cooperation' were large, and they and some others considered the arrangement less 'cooperation' than coercive 'political blackmail.'"[10] Regardless of these costs, ten provincial programs would eventually come into being: "Such is the power of the federal purse even in areas outside its constitutional jurisdiction." To an activist provincial minister such as Kierans, this power would be an extra-sensitive issue.

Kierans's personal reaction to the introduction of Medicare left him with an indelible impression of the potential abuse of federal power, which ultimately rests on the fiscal imbalance between Ottawa and the provinces. His response was far from unique, and it would find echoes among his contemporaries. Nothing that Kierans has said on the subject has ever matched John Robarts's anger: "Medicare is a glowing example of a Machiavellian scheme that is in my humble opinion one of the greatest political frauds that has been perpetrated on the people of this country. The proposition is this: you are taxing our people in Ontario to the tune of $222 million a year to pay for a plan for which we get nothing because it has a low priority in our plans for Ontario."[11] Such sentiments, of course, underlay the rationale for a separate Quebec pension plan as well as Quebec's determination to opt out of Medicare and any number of other nationally defined programs impinging on provincial jurisdiction.

As Quebec insisted when Medicare was announced:

When our plan is introduced, it will operate outside any joint Federal-Provincial program in line with our general policy of opting out in all areas within our competence. Quebec's decision on this matter rests on the acceptance of our obligations to our citizens and on the necessity to exercise our rights; it is not guided by any desire for isolation; it is still less connected with any strategy aimed at inducing each province to establish a program completely different from that of the others, which would make it relatively easy for private interests apprehensive about Medicare to play one province against another in order to postpone, or even prevent, its introduction in Canada ... in fact, Medicare may be one subject on which there is most agreement among Canadians generally, regardless of their ethnic origin. The Federal government can make it easier for provinces to exercise their constitutional powers, for example, by rectifying the present system of sharing revenue sources in Canada.[12]

The issue of opting out raises yet another one of Kierans's favourite anecdotes, concerning a visit to Laval University from Cambridge economist Barbara Ward in 1965. (Ward and Kierans had met in 1955 when she gave the Chancellor Beatty Lecture at McGill University.) During Ward's stay in Quebec City, the two spent an afternoon at Kierans's Department of Revenue office discussing Quebec's place in Confederation and the importance to the province of preserving and enhancing its powers by opting out of federal programs, despite the resulting national controversies and inter-governmental antagonisms.[13] Ward made what still impresses Kierans as a very astute observation for a foreigner so little versed in the ins and outs of Canadian federalism: Quebec, she hypothesized, might have avoided all this trouble if it could have induced just one other province to opt out of just one other shared-cost program.

In a similar vein, Kierans himself has always felt that "the worst thing that ever happened to the country" was that Quebec's strong opposition to Ottawa did not coincide with equally strong protest from some other province against federal interference.[14] Kierans, much later, expressed this point in his testimony before the parliamentary committee's hearings on the Meech Lake Accord:

when I first started to attend federal-provincial conferences in the 1960s - and I attended a great many of them - the federal government had done a wonderful job of isolating Quebec. The nine English provinces never opened their mouths about anything - just as in the late 1950s they had similarly done a marvellous job of isolating Tommy Douglas ...

... Now, with all your Peckfords and all the others that are around at these federal-provincial conferences, it is no longer just Quebec trying to argue for a position. Now there are half a dozen of them, and you have a much more federal system than when you have nine people nodding their heads up and down all the time while Quebec presents something.[15]

At this last point, an invariably anonymous "Hon. member" blurted out, "I love it!," no doubt spurring Kierans on to launch the diatribe against Pierre Trudeau's "one man centralism" that we consider in a later chapter.

Kierans is probably among the most "decentralist" of those Canadian public figures who see any role for the federal government at all, and this strong decentralism was "cemented" by his frustration with Ottawa while a member of an activist provincial government.[16] This frustration became as powerful as it did despite Lester Pearson's commitment to cooperative federalism and well before the enormous centralist thrust of Pierre Trudeau's second period in office (1980–84). It is also a clear indication of how difficult it has always been, regardless of anyone's intentions, to promote nation-wide solutions to Canadian economic and social problems. These almost inevitably appear to some province or region as an intrusion on its interests – as seen locally – and, on local priorities. Kierans simply concedes this as a fact of Canada's political and geographical landscape that must be respected and recognized in the design of national programs and political processes. It is for these reasons that he gives a blanket endorsement to the 1979 Pepin-Roberts Task Force's report on Canadian unity as the best public inquiry into such issues that he has yet seen and praises Thomas Heuglin for his profound theoretical understanding of why Canada can operate successfully only as a "heavily decentralized" federation.[17]

BREAKING WITH LÉVESQUE

Given Kierans's extreme decentralist outlook, his highly visible role in the split between René Lévesque and the Quebec Liberal Federation (QLF) is rather ironic. Several others have told this story in detail, and only an outline is offered here.[18] This episode leads one to wonder though, why Eric Kierans was not a Quebec separatist.

The short answer has two parts. First, Kierans has always felt that English-Canadian nationalism and Quebec nationalism, properly conceived and promoted, were mutually reinforcing rather than mutually defeating causes. The survival of each required the survival, indeed the self-confidence and assertiveness, of the other. Second, he has always been, and remains, sceptical that separation from Canada is in the economic interest of individual Québécois. The economic relationship between Quebec and the rest of Canada may hold its problems, but they are nothing compared to the stark vulnerability of a tiny, sovereign Quebec in a vast, anglophone North America and an increasingly competitive global economy. The latter reason is more central to the falling out between Kierans and René Lévesque.

The contest for the hearts and minds of Quebecers between economic rationality, as espoused and defended by Kierans, and political independence, as promoted by separatists such as Lévesque, spans almost the entire period between Kierans's taking office in the Quebec government in 1963 and the referendum on sovereignty-association in 1980. From the time of the 1967 convention of the QLF, this contest was personified in several intense battles between Kierans and Lévesque. In 1967, both men had recently suffered through the defeat of the Liberals by Daniel Johnson's Union nationale the previous year. Kierans had been elected president of the QLF with the support of Lévesque and his supporters as a compromise candidate between reformers and the status quo.

Lingering traces of these battles could be found right up to the end of Lévesque's life. In the mid-1980s, the two men had different views of the status of their friendship, especially in the aftermath of the 1980 referendum. Their divergent views had to do with Kierans's deliberately publicized resignation as a director of the Caisse de dépôt approximately one week prior to the 1980 referendum. The resignation itself was perhaps less consequential than Kierans's charge that the Parti québécois government had ordered the caisse to lend money to the province at less than market rates, contrary to the interests of Quebec's pensioners.[19]

It is hard to know how the publicity surrounding this episode affected those Quebecers who had not already made up their minds on the referendum issue. At the very least it would have drawn their attention to the fact that a prominent anglophone, who had once fought hard to promote the economic interests of Quebec, and had also promoted the Caisse in the first place, was clearly out of sympathy with the PQ government and stood firmly on the "no" side of the referendum debate. Lévesque was caught on this point, because he had pushed to have Kierans appointed to the Caisse's board of directors, precisely because he knew that Kierans would put the economic interests of the province first.[20] The episode represents the concluding instance of a long-standing campaign that may be one of Kierans's most significant contributions to Canadian public life: making the economic case against the separation of Quebec from Canada.

Some of Lévesque's bitterness and enduring anger over Kierans's resignation from the Caisse de dépôt et placement must surely have been fed by his growing sense that the referendum was going down to defeat. Worse yet, more and more Québécois were beginning to accept the same kind of arguments about the economic vulnerability of an independent Quebec that Kierans had marshalled against Lévesque and his separatist colleagues in 1967. Lévesque may have recalled, even repeated, some of the stinging denunciations of Kierans's economic arguments that he had uttered after being forced to leave the QLF's 1967 convention.

Peter Desbarats captures the mood of this reaction well. Lévesque made an anti-climactic speech to the 1967 convention shortly after it overwhelmingly rejected what was soon to become his sovereignty-association formula. He then made a dignified exit, accompanied by a couple of dozen supporters:

The bitterness erupted later that evening. An hour before midnight, as the delegates closed their convention [in Quebec's Château Frontenac] by singing 'O Canada' beneath the Canadian flags that had been hurriedly unfurled that morning beside the original display of Quebec flags, Lévesque held a press conference surrounded by about 200 supporters in the smaller Clarendon Hotel a few blocks away. He accused Kierans of having employed 'economic terrorism' against his thesis. 'It isn't the man in the street who is sowing the seeds of panic,' he said, 'but the newspapers and the dominant English-speaking element in our province - three or four dozen people of the same race that managed to put up very well with Duplessis as they finagled behind the scenes with the economy of Quebec.'

Kierans replied that the Liberal party had refused to permit 'an elitist minority to drag the Quebec population into a separatist adventure'.[21]

Then and later, Lévesque attacked his friend for "flagrantly distorting the facts," "psychological terrorism," "a funny kind of brutality," and "an intellectual billy-clubbing of the party and the whole population."[22]

The 1967 convention was thus a confrontation between Lévesque and Kierans, who was the front-man for a Liberal establishment determined to force Lévesque either to tone down his independence-oriented program or to leave the party.[23] Ironically, Kierans was the Quebec anglophone perhaps least deserving of Lévesque's bitter characterization of his community's political role. Furthermore, Kierans was able to force the issue only because Lévesque and his colleagues had helped him become party president the year before. Kierans had been a regular member of the St-Denis Club along with a few other reformers from the cabinet and several other Liberals from outside the assembly, such as Robert Bourassa.

There had been early signs that this group was not going to be able to maintain a common stance on Quebec's place in Confederation. Differences had appeared even in victory:

The election of Kierans as president of the Federation was an important victory for the reform element of the party, but it did nothing to advance the constitutional debate. Kierans made his own position clear at the [1966] convention: 'As an economist, I think the time isn't ripe for Quebec to go it alone without suffering a serious drop in its standard of living.'

'And when that time comes,' he added, 'I hope that Quebec won't make that choice. The solution lies in a Canada in which the rights of French-Canadians, as equal partners in Confederation as far as language and culture are concerned, are everywhere recognized and respected.'[24]

As a confirmed federalist, Kierans had no interest in furthering constitutional debate within the party. But for others, particularly Lévesque, this had been the main thrust of the club's discussions. After the 1966 convention, he continued to develop the issue with other members of the original group. It was the start of a process that quickly transformed relations between Kierans and Lévesque.

Kierans, of course, was not about to attack Lévesque as a person, or even as a politician; he was about to intensify his attacks against separatism. As Lévesque moved to the fore of separatist politics, and especially as he attempted to turn the QLF into a vehicle for the realization of independence, or something akin to it, he was bound to become a target for Kierans's strident, economics-centred dismissal of the whole separatist philosophy.

But Kierans's anti-separatist stance had been making headlines and receiving space in the press for at least three years. For example, in a prominently featured interview in the *Montreal Star* published two days before his by-election victory in September 1963, he was asked what he would do if separatists fielded a party in the next provincial election. "I'd make an all-out effort to expose the economic consequences of separatism" he replied, "in the same manner as I went after Social Credit in the last election." If Quebec did secede from Confederation, there would be a decline in economic activity and growth for years to come: "There would be such a lack of real challenge and opportunity that many of the best trained and educated young French Canadians would move to Ontario and the United States. How does a country build itself if its best young people find in it only frustration and lack of opportunity?" The fact that Canada is comprised of two peoples "should not be viewed as a cause of enmity but is in fact a Godsend," and he attributed the tolerance and peace-loving character of Canadians "at least in part to the fact that our two peoples see much to admire and respect in each other."[25]

By the late summer and fall of 1967, Kierans had begun to amplify his expression of these sentiments, especially on the economic costs of independence. His speeches attracted more and more attention from both the English and French media as the 13 October opening of the QLF convention loomed closer. On 1 October, he dropped a bombshell before a meeting of 600 Liberals in Sherbrooke, a platform that he shared with Jean Lesage.[26] Kierans was greeted by front-page headlines the next morning in Le Devoir: "Kierans: l'independence plongerait le Québec dans la pauvreté et le chômage" ("Independence will plunge Quebec into poverty and unemployment") and the Montreal Star: "Big Business Will Move out If We Separate – Kierans." Le Devoir also reprinted large portions of the text of the speech.

In the lead story, Le Devoir highlighted Kierans's prediction that, should Quebec separate from the rest of Canada, it would cost the population at least $2.3 billion in the first five years of independence. The paper also picked up on his use of federal accounts for the previous year to show that, while Quebec received 35 per cent of the federal government's spending, it contributed only 25 per cent of federal tax revenues. The paper also reported Kierans's prediction that, on separation, Quebec would become a foreign country to many large corporations currently with headquarters in Montreal. These companies would prefer to continue their trans-Canadian and global operations from places such as Ottawa and Toronto, reducing provincial revenues by as much as 10 per cent, or about $1.1 billion in five years. This loss of tax revenues, together with loss of net income from federal fiscal policies, would produce a large deficit, forcing either reduced social expenditures or greatly increased taxes. The former would set back recent gains in the quality of social services and education; the latter would lead to the departure of the best and the brightest of Quebec's youth and the most promising of its own businesses.

Le Devoir and the *Montreal Star* both saw these economic warnings as a major step in Kierans's campaign to confront the separatist faction within his own party, as well as to embarrass Premier Daniel Johnson and the Union nationale government into clarifying its own stance on independence. On the latter point, Kierans claimed that capital was already leaving or avoiding the province because of anxiety over separatist leanings within the Union nationale, about which Kierans had been attacking Johnson for several months.[27] His concern to tackle the government on the issue of separatism was related to his confrontation with Lévesque, for as long as separatists were able to claim a comfortable home in the ranks of the Liberal opposition, it was easy for Johnson to deflect any criticism of his own brand of provincial nationalism and his challenges to Canadian federalism.

That the battle had thus been joined with René Lévesque's version of Quebec nationalism was becoming evident in the days leading up to the Liberal convention. Lévesque himself received a lot of attention for a rebuttal of Kierans's economic arguments on 5 October, before a meeting of 250 members of Montreal's Gouin constituency.[28] Although the ultimate collision took place on the platform and in the back rooms of the convention itself, its most dramatic and widely observed version was probably a televised debate between Lévesque and Kierans on national television about three weeks earlier. Again Peter Desbarats has captured the mood and substance of this extraordinary, hour-long event:

Neither Kierans nor Lévesque had many illusions about the outcome when they met in Montreal for an hour-long television debate that was organized by the CBC and broadcast on September 26. As soon as Lévesque entered the studio, he went to Kierans, extended his hand and said, 'I'm sorry.'

'I'm sorry, too,' replied Kierans.

Kierans then said to Lévesque that one or the other was going to be out of the party by the end of the October convention. It was clear, he said, that whoever was identified as the man who had led the drive to oust Lévesque would himself have little future in the party and perhaps in Quebec politics, regardless of the outcome ...

'René and I are two predictable people,' said Kierans on the air that night. 'I knew he was heading for this. He knew I would fight him.'

'Basically, I'm a Quebecker first,' commented Lévesque, 'and Eric is a Canadian first.'[29]

The most striking differences between the two men to emerge during their debate had to do with the economic implications of Lévesque's "independence with association" and with the related issue of the increasing vigour and intensity of nationalism within Quebec, especially among young French Canadians. Kierans made the point that no class or group in Quebec could benefit from independence and that he saw it as a "tragedy" that "a people who have just begun to emerge from their isolation and make contact with the world, would enclose themselves in a ghetto of separation."[30] He also predicted that Quebec's standard of living would drop by 30 per cent, a claim that Lévesque rejected as "an inaccurately tragic portrait of the economic repercussions of independence." Lévesque gave greater emphasis, however, to "the growing feeling, among the younger generation especially, that Quebec must do what it does alone." In this case, independence might await the maturing of this generation. To this Kierans replied, "it would be a lost generation." He then added, "René is saying it's all right to make a thousand mistakes so long as they're our mistakes."

Commenting a day later in an editorial, Montreal's *Gazette* observed that the exchange revealed two characteristics of the separatism issue.[31] First, the debate, as it reached its climax, was turning from emotions to economics. "One can imagine that in the end, many Quebeckers will decide the issue on prospects for prosperity or poverty," although complete and objective studies of the economic consequences of separation were still lacking. Second, the debate was notable for its increasing "absolutism." "The issue as now defined with compelling clarity will soon force all the province's political activists into new alignments for or against separation."

The clearest indication, though, of the core issues lies in the language of Kierans's impressive speech the first evening of the convention. The speech was officially titled "Rapport du Président Monsieur Eric Kierans." However, on the title page of the archival copy, Kierans has written, "Defi a René."[32] And so it was.

In his speech, the president reviewed recent activities of the QLF's standing committees, of Jean Lesage, and of himself as president. He managed to touch directly on several of the questions dividing Lévesque from himself and, he clearly hoped, all the rest of the party. One of these was the issue of Quebec's young people:

nous avons pu constater que le parti libéral du Québec constituait vraiment le seul groupement politique valable pour la jeune génération québécoise grâce à son audace et à son habitude de relever les défis.

Les jeunes gens de cette province considèrent leur gouvernement comme le moyen de réaliser leurs objectifs nationaux. Ainsi, ils conçoivent un parti politique comme un moyen d'accroître les possibilités économiques, le progrès culturel et leur statut social. Je suis particulièrement fier du grand nombre de jeunes qui militent dans nos rangs.[33]

Another issue concerned the priorities of Québécois in general, as both he and Lesage had encountered them, in more than fifty counties, during tours in the aftermath of their recent electoral defeat: "En juin, M. Lesage et moi avons comparé les résultats de nos tournées respectives à travers la province. Indépendamment, nos conclusions se sont avérées les mêmes. La population québécoise n'a qu'un intérêt minime touchant les problèmes constitutionnels et le séparatisme, tandis que le fardeau des taxes municipales et scolaires, l'augmentation du chômage, le développement économique et régional, le logement, la protection du consommateur, etc. sont des problèmes d'intérêt primordial."[34]

A third issue underlined in his text concerned the need to make a clear and definite choice in the constitutional realm:

L'image du parti libéral à la suite de ce congrès doit être plus claire et plus précise que jamais. Nous voulons pour la nation canadienne française un statut d'égalité entière et nous avons l'intention de lutter pour obtenir les changements constitutionnels nécessaires à l'obtention de cette égalité. La route vers l'égalité ne se trace pas dans le séparatisme. Si telle est la décision de ce congrès, ceux qui proposent cette solution doivent en toute honnêteté envers eux-mêmes et leur parti prendre les décisions appropriées. Quant à moi, croyant fermement que l'option séparatiste sous toutes ses formes n'est pas dans l'intérêt de la population du Québec, je suis prêt à démissionner immédiatement, si tel est votre choix.

Certes, le défi est de taille, mais les libéraux du Québec, voulant d'une part un Québec fort dans un Canada vigoureux tout en refusant donner dans une querelle de mots sans fin et sans lendemain, prendront position définitivement et clairement en faveur de la seule option valable pour le peuple du Quebec.[35]

The response of the convention was uproarious and almost unanimous approval.

Kierans's confrontation with Lévesque, and indeed his opening speech, anticipated the terms in which the Quebec referendum would be fought thirteen years later. Those opposed to negotiation of sovereignty-association with the rest of Canada were inclined to propose the same alternative that Kierans offered the Quebec

Liberals: not separation from Confederation but the achievement of new status, new powers, and new opportunities through Confederation. Could Pierre Trudeau's promise to Quebec of "renewed federalism" have meant anything other than Kierans's implied invitation in 1967 to "Stay within Canada and we promise to work out better terms for Quebec and better conditions in Quebec"? For that matter, did not Lévesque's referendum proposition really offer the same future that he had offered the Liberals in Quebec in 1967 – namely, declare the objective of independence but promise to seek negotiations towards a new relationship with the rest of Canada?

Eric Kierans contended that Canadian federalism, and more specifically the Quebec Liberal party, could be the instrument with which a new generation of French Canadians would achieve their highest social, economic, and cultural aspirations. This was really the articulation of the toughest of all challenges to separatism. It was clearly intended to force separatists to confront the question "separation for what?" and then challenge them to show why the ends specified in the answer to that question could be obtained only by splitting from the rest of the country. Implicit was the simple message to Québécois that their interests were advanced best through improved federal relations with the rest of Canada, rather than Quebec independence. Kierans may not have been the first to adopt this response to Quebec nationalism, but he seems to have been one of the earliest to do so in a highly public way, and within Quebec itself. It has certainly been done since, though perhaps with no greater clarity and force.

CHAPTER FIVE

The Kierans Affair and After

Before his confrontation with René Lévesque at the QLF convention in the fall of 1967 – one of his last significant acts in the politics of Quebec – the "Kierans Affair" had attracted national attention. During the winter of 1965–66, while Quebec's Liberal government was still in power and Kierans a member of the cabinet, Kierans had been the key figure in another major event with national implications – a confrontation over foreign control of the Canadian economy.

THE KIERANS AFFAIR

The "Kierans Affair" was an enormous ruckus generated by a letter of 4 January 1966 from Kierans to Washington protesting guidelines issued to American multinationals in an attempt to improve the US balance of payments. It drew more press coverage and prompted more mail than Kierans has received on any other issue. (There is one full file of "Guidelines" correspondence in the Kierans Papers, and press clippings on the issue number in the hundreds in both French and English.) It also gained Kierans Canada-wide recognition as an economic nationalist. Less important, perhaps, this episode also provides clues as to Kierans's attitudes towards Lester Pearson's government, his notion of ministerial responsibility, and his extraordinary ability to exploit his popularity with journalists.

However, Kierans's action, whatever good it may have accomplished, was a major embarrassment to his premier and his colleagues in Quebec City and an affront to the Pearson government and its mandarins. The Kierans Affair was thus in fact a two-edged sword. It drew attention to the issue of Canadian economic independence and its new, outspoken, and vigorous advocate, but it also raised suspicion and hostility in the very institutions that Kierans would one day wish to convert to his ideas.

Dale Thomson's account picks up the story where it began, in December 1965:

At year's end, the United States government issued guidelines to American multinational firms asking them, in view of the country's balance-of-payments problems, to curtail their foreign investments and the reinvestment of profits earned abroad. Kierans was outraged at such a directive's being issued without apparent consideration of the consequences for countries like Canada and decided to protest in a manner designed to make the greatest possible impact. Without consulting Lesage, who was in Florida, he wrote to both the United States' Secretary of Commerce and the Secretary of the Treasury in his capacity as acting minister of revenue, sharply criticizing the policy as false in its basic premises, and also a violation of the accepted principle that firms operating in other countries should 'adapt to the political environment of the host nation and act as loyal citizens of that nation.' If such norms of behaviour were abandoned, he warned, others would have to 'adjust,' and that could well mean the establishment of further state enterprises (on the lines of Hydro-Quebec) that would not be subject to foreign intervention. In his letter to the Secretary of Commerce, he asked for a list of the nine hundred parent companies to which the guidelines were to apply, so that the implications could be discussed with their Canadian subsidiaries. Then having unburdened himself of his sentiments, he made the letters public.[1]

Having "achieved his purpose of making headlines," Kierans was surprised by the intensity of the reactions that he provoked. The governor of the Bank of Canada, Louis Rasminsky, telephoned Lesage on his return from Florida and asked indignantly what right his minister had to intervene in the matter and, even worse, to purport to speak for all of Canada. Prime Minister Pearson also criticized the initiative. As for the press, Thomson reports that *Le Devoir* described it as "a blunder," while the *Montreal Star* called it "silly." More significant, Jean Lesage was "furious." On the premier's return to Quebec, the two men had a sharp conversation and Kierans agreed to write a further letter to Washington, explaining that he had not acted in an official capacity. Lesage, further, "dissociated the government publicly from the whole matter."

Thomson's account, while a corrective to overly enthusiastic assessments of Kierans's role in the matter, is a little misleading on two points. It exaggerates the reaction of the press and fails to convey the substance of Kierans's protest. Kierans's letter to the US secretary of the treasury, Henry Fowler, documents a transformation in Kierans's political life and political-economic outlook. This incident moved Kierans from a generally favourable to a highly critical stance on foreign direct investment. He acknowledged this transition in the letter: "Speaking personally," he wrote, "I have long been identified in Canada as being completely favourable to foreign investment, and I am not sure that I can maintain the same unqualified stand ..."[2]

The letter also spelled out the exact reason for this change in attitude. The reason was not so much economic as political – the new American policy would convert multinational corporations from economic to political agents. Referring to a recent address in which Fowler had explained the guidelines, Kierans argued that they represented a major departure in US economic and commercial policy, such that multinationals would "have not only a commercial importance but a highly significant role in U.S. foreign policy." To Kierans, the new policy seemed inspired by Washington's belief that the national interests of "base and host countries" will rarely be identical and its insistence that, in the event of their conflicting, American multinationals must serve US national interests.

Kierans expressly acknowledged the "right" of the United States to take this stance but insisted that to do so broke with the traditional American view that investors and corporations going abroad should conform to the policies of the host nation. "If the rules are to be changed," he darkly suggested, "we must all adjust." Even more critical for host countries such as Canada were the consequences of this change. If the myriad of firms operating in foreign markets are to come under the direction of the US government, he argued, "We are no longer dealing with the large numbers [of firms] of economic theory but with a single directing voice, not with the disparate and independent decisions of thousands of businessmen but with hard government policy."

Kierans did not hold back from providing Fowler with some unsolicited advice as to the real source of the American balance-of-payments problem, along with some solutions. First, according to Kierans, American preoccupation with the rate and direction of capital flows, in the form of direct investment, was too narrow and missed the positive effects for the United States of other transactions associated with the operations of its multinationals, including imports and exports, charges for technology transfers, and managerial fees. The net effect of all these transactions could not possibly account for the nation's general balance-of-payments problems. Instead, "they are caused by the heavy obligations and responsibilities of world leadership, by Vietnam, etc."

Second, the United States was persisting with other policies that promoted excessive foreign investment in countries such as Canada. Alluding to the fact that US tax breaks for American firms with foreign subsidiaries gave them a competitive edge over local firms in other countries' markets, Kierans pointed out to Fowler, "If you withdrew the privilege of charging subsidiary or branch losses back to the parent company after 3 or 5 years, a great deal of over-investment will be avoided, the structure of Canadian industry would benefit, and hostility toward American investment would diminish."

In concluding his objections, Kierans underscored his insistence that the economic and the political implications of capital flows were separate matters and that he was protesting only the political turn that American policy had given them. "In sum," he wrote, "I believe, like you, in the international corporation but I do not believe it can be used as an agent of government." However, apparently fearing that this perfectly clear point could somehow be missed because of the reasonable language in which it was couched, Kierans chose to make the same point a little more vividly: "We hope that international companies, unlike armies of occupation, will always have a role to play. To accomplish this, they must conduct themselves as true citizens of the host country." The allusion to "armies of occupation" parallels a formulation by economist John Dales: "We did suppose that American subsidiaries were business enterprises, run by businessmen intent on making a profit. If they really are Trojan horses under the control of Washington, economists have nothing to say about them. We know nothing whatever about the behaviour of Trojan horses."[3] Dales captures Kierans's point precisely.

Reaction in Canada

Despite the strident tone and the clear breaches of protocol – not the least of which was the releasing of copies of the letters to the Canadian press on the same day the originals were sent to Washington – the most vehement reaction occurred in Canada, not the United States. Indeed, Washington's response was modest, and the American press's almost undetectable. In Canada, though, governments and press were vociferous. For neither the first nor the last time, an issue ignited in Canada primarily because of disputed claims about real or potential American reactions to Canadian actions towards Washington. As usual, there was considerably more "political heat" generated in Canada over the harm supposedly done to Canadian-US relations by such actions than there was south of the border.

Jamie Swift has described Canadian press coverage of this affair, but the atmosphere is also reflected in the Kierans Papers.[4] What level of exasperation prompted Lesage to send this telegram to Kierans within days of his letters of 4 January: "REUNION URGENTE ET IMPORTANTE CONSEIL DES MINISTRES MARDI SOIR 11 JANVIER A 8 HEURES VOUS DEVEZ ANNULER TOUT AUTRE ENGAGEMENT AUCUNE EXCUSE NE SERA ACCEPTE JEAN LESAGE"?[5] Clearly Lesage was feeling the heat from both political circles and the press.

In contrast, however, the broad Canadian public responded in a manner that Swift describes as "overwhelmingly positive." Press coverage of Kierans's letters, as well as a speech on them delivered three weeks later in Toronto, produced a deluge of favourable mail from an extremely diverse body of Canadians. Indeed, if this were a study of the political culture of Canadian nationalism, a systematic and comprehensive review of the support offered by such a wide variety of people to Kierans's protest would have been worthwhile. For instance, the number of favourable responses from executives of Canadian companies might seem surprising to people now grown accustomed to the complacency with which Canadian business has accommodated the largest concentration of foreign direct investment in any industrialized country.

Kierans took a great deal of satisfaction and encouragement from this support, especially when it came from other prominent Canadians. He could not resist, for example, passing on to Lesage "a few samples of my recent mail" that had poured in immediately following press coverage of his Toronto speech, often accompanied by a request for a copy of it.[6] Michael Oliver, then director of research for the Royal Commission on Bilingualism and Biculturalism, spoke of "the clearest and most compelling statement on the problems of the American influence on the Canadian economy I have ever read." Maurice Strong, president of Power Corp. of Canada, wrote: "Never have I heard a more lucid or better documented case for the kind of positive, realistic, forward-looking nationalism which Canada so badly needs ... If we do not wake up soon even those opportunities which are still available to us may well be lost by default." H. Scott Gordon, Department of Economics, Carleton University, offered "Congratulations! ... A landmark discussion of Canadian economic problems and policy"; Kierans replied in part, "How about raising a little 'hell' yourself?" Duff Roblin, premier of Manitoba, called the speech "a most stimulating piece of work. You have pulled together all the half-fledged ideas that were floating around in my own head and established them on a sound basis."

The Toronto Speech

The address that attracted all these compliments – "The Economic Effects of the Guidelines," delivered to the Toronto Society of Financial Analysts on 1 February 1966 – corresponded in most points to the letters to Washington. It stressed the distinction between the economic role of foreign investment and multinational corporations, which Kierans accepted, and their political direction by the US government, which he emphatically rejected.[7] The speech began on a note that several of Kierans's critics have insisted is one of his most glaring inconsistencies – namely, his attack three years earlier on the Gordon budget and its provisions for a foreign takeover tax and a dividend withholding tax. The opening sentence reminded Canadians that no country in the world should work harder for the removal of restrictions to the free flow of goods, services, and capital than Canada. "Trade on a per capita basis is three times more important to us than to the Germans, Italians, French or British." Moreover, "As Dr. H.E. English has pointed out, we are the only highly industrialised nation in the world which does not have a sufficiently large domestic market or free access to large markets. We must bargain and trade for such markets if we hope to raise our national income and to prosper as individuals. *We should not ourselves recommend or introduce measures which impede the flow of capital and goods and should resist, even if we cannot prevent, the introduction of such policies by other nations.*"[8]

This is an obvious allusion to Walter Gordon's earlier approach to the problems of foreign investment, and it underscores the differences between Liberal governments' "single issue" or "ad hoc" nationalism and Kierans's own, more broadly conceived approach. The speech continued:

Unfortunately, many Canadians believe that the only way to preserve their national identity and culture is by reverting to protectionism and various forms of restriction on trade, capital inflows, foreign ownership and the like. Nothing could be further from the truth because all such measures inevitably lead to a reduction in income and hence a loss of economic strength and independence. ...

... The net economic and social advantages of foreign investment such as increased employment, wages, salaries, taxes, reinvestment of earnings, etc., outweigh the ill-defined and vague dangers to political independence that some have seen. *The assumption is, of course, that economic and management decisions, if not made in Canada, are made in New York or Detroit by businessmen seeking profits and investment opportunities. On* this basis, the host country can reasonably predict the pattern and effects of such investment and frame its policies accordingly. Further, the decisions are made by thousands of business leaders acting independently and in their own special interests, so that only the most emotional and chauvinistic could imagine a *concerted* effort by businessmen to undermine political authority. *Actually, there need never be any fear on this score if the political authority is itself decisive, sets out clearly its economic objectives and defines the rules under which domestic and international corporations shall carry out their operations.*[9]

The main thrust of Kierans's speech is thus visible in the first two paragraphs.

The remaining nineteen pages insisted on three related propositions concerning foreign investment. First, as a matter of economics and business practice, there is nothing inherently damaging to the Canadian economy in the simple fact of foreign control of Canadian subsidiaries. By attacking or undermining international capital flows in the Canadian economy, Canada would be cutting itself off from valuable economic exchanges on which its prosperity depends.

Second, the positive net effects of foreign investment can be reduced or reversed if business decisions are driven not by the economic interests of a vast array of enterprises but by the economic, political, and even strategic interests of their home government. This, for Kierans, was precisely the problem represented by the new US guidelines, which used the parent-subsidiary relationship within the international corporation to direct capital flows in the form of factor payments, fees, and dividends from the Canadian subsidiaries to their American parents. Such superimposition of political goals on international businesses hurts a country such as Canada, reversing its own economic calculations with respect to the benefits of foreign investment. Moreover, it ultimately harms even the US economy because it severely complicates and obscures the proper business management of American multinational firms: "Canada could have performed a lasting service for our neighbours to the South if we had been able to convince them that this use of the international corporation was not in their long-run best interests."

Third, and most important, even in the extreme case of foreign governments interference with foreign-controlled firms, but certainly in the case of their conventional business activity, the net costs or benefits to a country of foreign investment are determined by the public policy set down by domestic authorities. "Responsibility for our present condition of over-investment and slow growth in manufacturing does not rest with foreign investors but, as Roger

Dehem has noted, 'in the lack of a proper framework devised by government to orient private initiative toward growth and welfare objectives.'"

Why Kierans Responded

This last point reveals Kierans's thinking at the time on foreign investment and clarifies some elements of the guidelines incident. Kierans's visceral reaction was in part the product of his frustration with Ottawa's economic failings. Kierans recalls, with some flourish of exaggeration, that in late December 1965 "Canada had no government whatsoever."[10] Lester Pearson was off in Barbados. Walter Gordon had resigned over the failure of the Liberals to achieve a majority government in November's general election (which he had pressed Pearson to call). Mitchell Sharp was acting minister of finance. In Kierans's mind, this left effective control to "the Rasminskys, the Reismans, the Bryces," with whom he associated the kind of debilitating tax policies and "corporatist" outlook that he had often attacked while at the MSE.

In fact, Kierans had written to Washington on his own initiative in an impulsive reaction to an argument with Louis Rasminsky. A newspaper had reported Kierans's initial outburst on the guidelines, which Kierans had thought was "off the record." Rasminsky had called Lesage and demanded that he "tell Kierans to shut up." Lesage asked Kierans to call Rasminsky and added: "Rasminsky is one of the few friends in Ottawa we have."[11] After a blunt exchange with Rasminsky over the telephone, Kierans got his dander up and wrote his letter. He was simply angry because nobody else in the country was going to "do a damn thing" about the guidelines, even though the United States was already running a balance-of-payments surplus on its Canadian accounts.

The incident, then, does not reveal a "flip-flop" by Kierans on the key issue of nationalism. He has always felt that Ottawa's mismanagement of the economy was more responsible for Canada's failure to harness effectively its abundant resources than were foreign investment and other American influences. It is also ironic that Liberals should seek to discredit Kierans's nationalism because of his attack on the Gordon budget of 1963 and the so-called reversal of his position in 1966. His Liberal critics have a few inconsistencies of their own. Not the least of these, Walter Gordon and Mitchell Sharp, as ministers of finance, traded away control of the money supply for exemption from the American interest equalization tax.

As we have seen, Washington had introduced this tax shortly after Gordon withdrew Canada's version of the same thing, supposedly under irresistible pressure from Eric Kierans at the MSE.[12] It seems remarkable that the anti-Kierans version of the Gordon budget–US guidelines story claims for itself, and denies to Kierans, the ground of economic nationalism. If the Pearson government's – or even Walter Gordon's – commitment to reversing American economic influence was so strong, why did Ottawa succumb in a mere 48 hours to the importunings of a few executives from a single stock exchange?

Conflicting Legacies

The Kierans Affair had two conflicting legacies. One was greater understanding of the workings of parent-subsidiary relationships and their effects on the Canadian economy and economic decision-makers. Kierans's principal speech on the guidelines drew attention to three facts that were soon to gain wider currency in more detailed studies such as the Watkins Report (1968) and Kari Levitt's *Silent Surrender* (1970).[13]

First, a subsidiary would tend to maximize not its own profits but those of the parent and this situation could create conflict between Canada's economic interests and those of the parent company concerning performance of the subsidiary. The parent could maximize its own benefit at Canada's "expense" by, for example, obtaining supplies for the subsidiary from other affiliates abroad rather than from Canadian sources, thus importing more goods and services than would a comparable, independent company.[14]

Second, intra-firm transfers among subsidiary, parent, and/or other international affiliates could profit the global enterprise without doing the same for its Canadian operations, or even by incurring losses on them, depending on the prices set by the parent firm for its purchases from and sales to other affiliates ("transfer pricing").

Third and finally, as documented in Kierans's speech, only about 5 per cent of the capital used in the expansion of foreign-controlled firms, including takeover of other Canadian firms, originated with the foreign firms. The remaining 95 per cent came from retained Canadian earnings, depreciation on Canadian assets, and borrowing from Canadian financial institutions.

The other legacy of the Kierans Affair may have undermined Kierans's ability to promote solutions to the problems that he outlined in his guidelines speech. His action provoked outright hostility in senior federal government ranks and great irritation from Jean Lesage. For example, Kierans recalls that "Pearson went 'ga ga'" over the first story that broke on the issue, and we have seen his argument with Louis Rasminsky.[15]

As for Lesage, it is hard to mistake the tone of mildly reproachful regret that pervades his written reply to Kierans's explanation of the letter. Lesage was not pleased to be relegated to the innocently injured party in his own government. Having explained that he had recently been questioned by the press about Kierans's actions, and about whether the cabinet had met or if the premier had been consulted, Lesage informed Kierans that he had told them "no." A reporter had then asked for his opinion on the tenor of Kierans's letters, and he explained to Kierans his reply: "J'ai lui repondu que, lorsqu'un Premier Ministre donnait son opinion, il engageait le Conseil des Ministres et que, dans les circonstances, ce dernier n'ayant pas été consulté, je ne pouvais pas exprimer d'opinion."[16]

The tone is consistent with the impression of Thomson, who closes his account with an air of anti-climax: "The incident was smoothed over when Kierans delivered a much more factual analysis of the United States guidelines to a Toronto audience on February 1, 1966; he took the precaution of clearing the text with the premier in advance. For Jean Lesage, the main result was to strengthen his view that Eric Kierans was not the reliable financial counsellor that he had thought he was recruiting three years earlier, but, rather, another 'star' that had to be watched closely."[17] Lesage, himself part of the Quebec and national Liberal establishments, here in effect represents a more widespread view of Kierans within that same elite. Kierans had won public popularity as a Canadian nationalist at the price of considerable notoriety within the very party that he would later attempt to win over to his agenda.[18]

In the end, though, Kierans did achieve recognition as an economic nationalist. Ironically, he was still disavowing this status in May 1966, in the aftermath of the guidelines incident. In replying to a letter that requested a copy of his Toronto speech, and also congratulated him on his nationalist views, Kierans wrote, "Incidentally, I am *not* a nationalist in economic matters."[19] Nevertheless, the vast, enthusiastic correspondence that he received, and the enormous interest shown by the anglophone and francophone media, clearly indicated that this direction could well be the route to national political prominence.

TRANSITION

Thus both the Kierans Affair and the 1967 QLF convention anticipated developments over the next two decades of Canadian politics. Kierans's role in Quebec City provided new avenues for his involvement in federal politics and stimulated his concern with national issues. First, the guidelines affair and the subsequent fight with Lévesque had quickly brought him into touch with both emergent nationalisms: English Canadians' desire to be less dependent on the United States, especially economically, and Quebecers' desire to be independent of Canada. These and related issues motivated him to enter national public life.

Second, the experience of governing tempted him to seek greater responsibility than was promised in opposition in Quebec's legislature. Joining a national government seemed more interesting in early 1968 than possibly, some day, being part of a future provincial government in Quebec. Federal politics might bring him the excitement of engagement – of being "where the action is" – that he had come to value so highly while part of the dynamic group around Jean Lesage.

Some observers seem undecided about when Kierans first formed his national ambitions – a question of some significance in interpreting what he may have really been up to during some of the episodes described above. Lesage thought that the guidelines episode was motivated by Kierans's desire to grab national attention, and at this point some members of the national press began to think of him in terms of national leadership.[20] All this notoriety, however, soon paled in comparison with the attention that he received for his part in Lévesque's departure from the Liberal party. "Eric Kierans has emerged as the new strong man of the Liberal party," wrote Clift again, in the aftermath of the 1967 convention.[21]

Just before the convention, Frank Howard had publicly noted Kierans's role in the fight against separatism and also the rumours of his interest in federal politics. "If he were able to create a genuine anti-separatist option in Quebec, his national potential would be greatly enhanced," Howard concluded.[22] Peter C. Newman had also been promoting the cause, in print and in person.[23] In sum, the question of when Kierans decided to enter federal politics seems beside the point; the Canadian media, especially anglophone, opened the way for him to seek the federal leadership. Thus, the opportunity was simply there, and increasingly obvious to everybody, including Kierans himself.

The Excitement of Governing

The reasons for Kierans's seizing that chance are more abstract and will be developed fully in later chapters. From the vantage point of the end of his Quebec years, however, three themes stand out, corresponding closely to dimensions of national life that almost define politics in this country and make it Canadian. They are independence from the United States, Quebec's place within Canada, and power – political power in general and economic power in particular, or what Marxists would simply call the "class question."

The centre of Canada's political life is where these three dimensions converge, or intersect. By 1967, Kierans, largely as a result of his service in Quebec City, was ready to move there: he had something valuable to say about each of Canada's national questions. Most important, he had some unique ideas about the interdependence of the answers to those vital questions.

The guidelines fracas and the confrontation with Lévesque had helped Kierans understand Canadian economic dependence and Quebec's relations with the rest of Canada, as well as connections between the two issues. Kierans had helped break the English-speaking hold on the government of Quebec; he was learning that foreign-controlled corporations could introduce alien economic and political priorities into the Canadian equation; and he was attacking the factors that encourage corporate concentration in Canada and the displacement of people's capitalism by managerial corporatism. Further, he saw social and economic reform as more vital and useful for Quebec than the dreams of intellectuals and professionals willing to gamble Quebec's economic future on independence. All these were signs of Kierans's notion of economic equity and social justice, as was his deepening appreciation of the priority of political considerations over economic enterprise and the distinctive angle that this provides on economic power and class relations in Canada.

Some political theorists would characterize this realization by Kierans as his recognition of the need to preserve the autonomy of Quebec in relation to the economic forces and vested interests constraining it from within and without.[24] However phrased, for Kierans this conviction was certainly reinforced, if not actually formed, by his wielding of economic and political power within Quebec for the achievement of specific ends defined by the government. The government in question was, on almost all important matters, a group of four to seven individuals, among whom Kierans was a prominent and highly valued member.[25]

Within this group (and along with it) Kierans learned that if governments know what they want to do, they can pretty well do what they want. Moreover, its freedom from the pressures of economic interests and powerful groups within society was so great that it came to be seen as arrogant, remote, and distant from everyday life – a truth that, to his credit, Kierans pointed out in several post mortems on the government's eventual defeat.[26] But no matter: Kierans had come to understand government as action, not administration. Moreover, he had experienced this as action on behalf of, and for the good of, the people in general; it was a matter of taking active and effective responsibility for the well-being of Québécois, and Quebec, as a whole.

Two of Kierans's favourite anecdotes convey his excitement, engagement, and pleasure in exercising power. One involves his first substantial contribution to public affairs – his assessment of the government's bargaining position in the negotiations over the BRINCO affair. The complex issue centred on the terms and conditions under which Newfoundland and the British Newfoundland Development Corp. (BRINCO) would export to Quebec, for further export to the United States, electrical power from the huge Hamilton Falls (later Churchill Falls) power project in Labrador.[27]

This issue vexed Quebec-Newfoundland relations for more than three decades, but it was particularly contentious in the early 1960s. When Kierans joined the government in late August 1963, he landed in the middle of both interprovincial bargaining and Quebec's negotiations with financial interests seeking to provide capital for such large-scale facilities as massive transmission lines from Labrador to markets in New York. Kierans first looked at these latter negotiations almost immediately after taking office.

This introduction to affairs of state made an indelible impression on the 49-year-old businessman and former professor of commerce. Twenty-five years later, he jotted down this brief recollection about his first collaboration with René Lévesque: "We spent three hours on a Sunday evening in August, 1963, going to Quebec on the CPR. René showed me the figures and working papers of the Brinco proposal by the Rothschild, Pitfield group, which I prepared to tear apart. (They were taking a 25% cut for no reasons that I could fathom)."[28] Kierans's BRINCO involvement thus saw his earliest effort to redefine relations between the government of Quebec and the national and international financial community, of which much was said in the previous chapter.

More pertinent here are the feelings that Kierans must have had as he joined in planning and executing some "new beginnings" in his province. His recollection of the trip with Lévesque confirms how enduring were those feelings, which were presumably an extension of those that Jamie Swift has suggested were there from his days at the MSE:

It was a clear day and Kierans was peering intently out of the plane window at the small farms dotting the river valley below, stretching in narrow strips back from the water. It seemed to the second-generation Canadian whose family had seen so much change that things were standing still in his native province, that they had not changed much since those farms had been laid out over two hundred years before. All of a sudden he plucked excitedly at his assistant's sleeve. 'Look down there, Charles,' Kierans exclaimed. 'I want to do something to really help these people get out of this situation. It just doesn't make sense. Look at those small farms. How can they make a living? Look at the possibilities here. We aren't using all the assets we have here in Quebec. We've been asleep too long.'[29]

Having realized such an ambition in his native province, Kierans readily imagined playing the same role in Ottawa.

The second anecdote concerns a trip to Val-d'Or, in the heart of one of Quebec's northern mining and logging districts. He was minister of health and determined to investigate at first hand practices in the town's hospital, which was run by an order of Catholic nuns. According to annual figures kept by the health department, the nuns were serving patients at 121 per cent of the hospital's rated capacity, presumably because they tended to keep patients on average seven to eight days longer than was normal for comparable hospitals. Confronted with these facts, the director, a gracious mother superior, revealed the reasons for the hospital's aberrant practices: "Over half our patients are Indians, Minister," she explained, "and they tend to have ailments, particularly respiratory illnesses, that simply require extended care and recovery." She also made it clear that these practices were not about to change merely because the minister wished to standardize, rationalize, and economize the province's delivery of hospital care.

The next day, the hospital put on a public lunch for the minister and invited the press and friends of the hospital. After the minister spoke briefly, the mother superior thanked him publicly for his personal concern for the welfare of the district's people and offered him a token of the community's gratitude. It was a large, black, plastic ball. It fact, as he learned momentarily, it was a large, black, plastic eight ball, which the director proceeded to place in front of the minister, with the crudely painted, white "8" facing the assembly. The minister thanked her for her thoughtfulness and bent over to turn the ball so that the "8" faced him. The mother stepped forward and put it back the way it was. The minister gave up and remained "behind" the eight-ball.

There is even a dénouement to this tale. Two weeks later, the local Liberal MLA brought Kierans a copy of Val d'Or's weekly paper and drew his attention to the birth notices. They reported the district's "new arrivals" since the minister's visit. Of eight boys born then, six had Eric as a first or second name. The MLA also wanted to know if Kierans had been to the community once before, and how long ago that was.[30]

Kierans, then, steadily felt the exuberance of personal involvement and effectuality at the centre of the Quiet Revolution. It was the product of a unique conjunction there of power, purpose, and affection, three elements of the relationships within the government and between the government and the people whom it served. It was a combination of elements that Kierans would never meet in politics again. His comparative alienation and ineffectuality at his next destination, Ottawa, largely explain the brevity of his years there. It is worth pausing at the point where he moved from Quebec City to Ottawa to look at the contrasts between the two governments.

"Styles" of Governing

Perhaps too much is made of "styles" of leadership and "tones" of government, but these expressions may be taken as short-hand for tangible and significant differences in the way in which governments conduct public business. To this extent, Kierans can be said to have been ideally suited for the style of the Lesage government and, especially, that of its most dynamic minister, René Lévesque. This cannot be said of the Trudeau government or, indeed, of the government of Canada. Anyone who has spent fifteen minutes speaking with Eric Kierans would not be surprised to learn that he was unable to fit in with "the Ottawa mandarins," or even with the cool, aloof rationality of Pierre Trudeau himself. Kierans was sharp enough; in fact, his deputy minister in Ottawa, Allan Gotlieb, formed the impression that Kierans was one of the few members of his first cabinet whom Trudeau respected as an intellectual equal. But Kierans was also gregarious, warm, exuberant, and about as far as one can get from the "arrogance of power."[31]

It is, therefore, at least an interesting coincidence that the single incident that did most to steer Kierans towards national politics was his argument over the telephone with Louis Rasminsky about the US guidelines, since Rasminsky is included among the mandarins profiled by J.L. Granatstein in *The Ottawa Men*. The men depicted in this study could not be more unlike Kierans in background, personality, and fundamental political assumptions, particularly their unquestioned centralism and disdain for the capabilities of provincial governments. According to these notables, Granatstein informs us, power must be at the disposal of "the only civil servants in the nation with the vision and skills to make Canada the kind of country it could and should be."[32] To those at the centre of power in Ottawa, "the provinces were in the hands of backward satraps, in charge of venal politicians and file clerks, their outlook limited by narrow geographical boundaries." Given Kierans's first-hand experience of an almost explosively dynamic provincial government, and given his innate suspicion of centralism of any kind, this attitude was almost certain to grate on Kierans and, as we shall soon see, did.

Judging from a highly regarded study of the subject, the hallmark of the government that Kierans was about to join was its concern with planning.[33] This, in itself, was unlikely to cause serious difficulties for him; after all, planning is a vital component in converting current investments into future profits, and Kierans had already known some of this kind of success with his own firm. More to the point, Kierans proved to be no mean government planner in the conduct of his own federal portfolios, giving creative leadership to the new Department of Communications and delivering a jolt of redirection and reorganization to the Canadian post office that was the match, in three short years, of anything that it has received in a comparable period, before or since.[34] This aside, the clash that was to come between Kierans's initiatives and the first circle of power in Ottawa was one between an individual minister and the planning systems that were beginning to preoccupy the federal government in the late 1960s and early 1970s.

The distinction just implied between planning and planning systems needs attention. "Planning" need mean nothing more, but be no less crucial, than being clear about "the relationships and relative priority of policies and programs," something that Kierans brought in abundance to his own government positions.[35] "Planning systems" can mean something entirely different, indeed opposite: "Planning systems that are unduly pluralistic, that fail to force choice, will squander political resources just as management control systems that have the same features will squander financial resources."[36] In short, planning does not help very much if the people doing the planning are not clear about, or keep changing, what they want. It is quite possible, of course, even likely, that people who want more than anything else to design a planning system will not have any idea of what else they want, or care about. In this case, the planning produced by the planning systems that such people design will not help very much either. Kierans ran into a lot of such people when he got to Ottawa, and he did not enjoy the experience.

The central difficulty that Kierans encountered in Ottawa – and it led to political disaster – was a product of cabinet "collegiality," the requirement that each minister consult his or her colleagues regarding new policy or program initiatives. This otherwise laudable procedure allowed central cabinet and bureaucratic organs, in the name of planning and "coordination," to qualify, if not totally undermine, individual ministers' responsibility. In fact, the compromised form of cabinet collegiality that had taken hold by the early 1970s combined the worst of two worlds for Kierans. Such "collective responsibility" as the Trudeau cabinet achieved was a product of the senior civil service, not the full cabinet acting in concert, so that Kierans was denied any true capacity to affect, at the cabinet table, the course of the government as a whole. He resented the resulting limitation on his role, especially with respect to economic policy, where he really wanted to have an impact. At the same time, this displaced form of collegiality intruded in ways that he could not accept on his own "individual responsibility" for his two cabinet portfolios. In the end, therefore, Kierans provided an object lesson in two observations made by Richard Van Loon about the perceived consequences of the Trudeau approach: ministers were not sufficiently able to take initiatives, while the prime minister and the central agencies gained dominance within the policy-making process without achieving adequate overall coordination.[37]

In fact, judging from the tone of his recollections of his Ottawa years, by the time that Kierans resigned from the federal cabinet he did not know whether to laugh or to cry at the absurdities to which the "central agencies" he had fought with for three years could succumb. He has one prized document that he feels sums it all up pretty well. Titled "Governing in the 70's," this thirteen-page (including appendices) memorandum to cabinet attempted to provide Kierans and his fellow ministers with an "assessment of the conditions the government will be facing in the years 1972 and beyond ... "[38] Apart from the generally incoherent babble that pervades this analysis – for example, "The lesson that one can draw from [Jacques Lusseyran's book, *And There Was Light*] is that there are many different ways in which to view the world and its problems, none necessarily less valid or coherent than another" – there is an almost grotesquely pseudo-scientific tenor to the entire document. This is perhaps best represented by an attempt to schematize the range of political challenges that the ministers must be prepared to face and, evidently, sort out in the years ahead.

Appendix 1 to the document therefore provides the individuals at the apex of power in Canada with a two-by-three matrix setting out "PROBLEMS GENERATED BY/IN PRESENT SOCIAL SYSTEM (SOCIAL, ECONOMIC, CULTURAL)." This general category of problems is divided into two subcategories: "PROBLEMS: DIRECT" and "PROB-LEMS *DERIVED* FROM DIRECT ONES, i.e. EXTREME REACTIONS." The second subcategory is further subdivided into "RE CONTROL OF SYSTEM';' and RE LEGITIMACY OF THE SYSTEM." The columns of problems are then horizontally divided into two categories, "Material" and "Psychic," a distinction that the document is at some pains to establish. An example provided within the matrix-cell for direct, material problems was "Wild Urbanization and Land Speculation." Meanwhile, an example in the cell for derived, material problems regarding control of the system is "Mafia Business," and one in the cell for derived psychic problems regarding control of the system is "Women's Lib. Movement." "Revolutionaries" are classified as an instance of derived, psychic problems regarding the legitimacy of the system.

It seems highly unlikely that Kierans had ever laid eyes on anything remotely comparable to this technocratic blather during his three efficacious years in the Lesage government: he had been ill-prepared – by business success, by the MSE, by the Quebec cabinet – for Ottawa.

PART TWO

The Centre Cannot Hold

CHAPTER SIX

Tax Reform and the Post Office

Only a fool, or an unforgivably sycophantic biographer, would try to make the case that Eric Kierans was a blazing success as a federal cabinet minister during his brief tenure, from 1968 to 1971. He can claim one major accomplishment as minister of communications – Telesat Canada, described in the next chapter – but he was a near-total disaster as postmaster general. In fact, Kierans's achievements in the government of Canada are scarcely significant enough to warrant attention, although in one crucial respect his time in Ottawa does illuminate the condition of Canadian politics and government.

While Kierans's successes in federal politics stand as little more than a footnote to his far more substantial contribution to the politics of Quebec, his failures in Ottawa are another matter, depending on how one reads them. If Kierans's failures and broad inconsequentiality in Ottawa were merely a matter of limited abilities or insufficient effort, the story would be simply banal, certainly uninteresting. However, if his failures say less about him than they do about the conditions and people that he met there, then they may contain a lesson about Canadian public affairs precisely because he brought to national politics some extraordinary strengths and worthy objectives.

The most telling single fact about Kierans's Ottawa experience comes at almost the end of the story, and it is just that he became disillusioned with and resigned from the cabinet as described in chapter 8. Ottawa could not hold him. In the introduction to this book, I argued that Kierans, like Tom Kent and in keeping with Charles Taylor's discussion of Hegel, was certainly hoping to be part of a strong federal government. Such a body would have been unswervingly committed to good, efficient government and determined to promote the interests of "the ultimate community," that is, Canada as a whole. What Kierans encountered instead, especially during debates on Kenneth Carter's proposals on tax reform and on Telesat Canada, was a cabinet that seemed unable to reach beyond, or even see beyond, the corporate, professional, departmental, and regional interests involved. The post office, too, brought to Kierans a series of lessons on the trials awaiting anyone who might attempt to hold the government – or the country, for that matter – to an all-encompassing view of national needs and interests.

THE CARTER COMMISSION AND THE CABINET COMMITTEE ON TAX REFORM

The Carter Commission's report on tax reform was tabled on 24 November 1967, about a month before Lester Pearson announced that he was stepping down as prime minister. Pearson's resignation, the ensuing leadership campaign, and the general election of June 1968 delayed serious undertakings towards tax reform until Pierre Trudeau's government was in a position to pick up the issue. However, in April 1969, a cabinet committee on tax reform was finally struck, and it met frequently from then until October of the same year. Edgar Benson, minister of finance, tabled the White Paper on Tax Reform on 7 November. Ten months of heated parliamentary, parliamentary committee, and public debate followed release of the White Paper, with the most powerful public opposition coming from the mining and petroleum industries and various provincial governments. In August 1970, Benson jumped ahead of the parliamentary hearing processes by announcing several key concessions to mining and petroleum interests, amounting to a two-thirds reduction of the tax increases against such firms that had been set out in the White Paper's proposals. A Senate committee report on the White Paper was released in September 1970, and that of a Commons committee appeared the following month.

The FLQ crisis in October then overtook this business of the government, along with much else, so that the actual tax reform legislation was not presented until the unveiling of Benson's budget of 18 June 1971. Further revisions were made to the tax legislation during 1971, and the final version of the tax reforms was not passed until December of that year. However, according to some observers, the final chapter in the Carter reform process was written not with these acts, but with the May 1972 budget of Edgar Benson's successor, John Turner. Turner's largesse to the business community effectively restored several of the long-standing tax breaks that the so-called tax reform process had so briefly and so meekly withdrawn the previous year.

In substance, then, the history of the Carter Commission's recommended overhaul of Canada's decrepit and incoherent tax system is a tale of the gradual erosion and dismantling of Carter's original reform edifice. Carter and his fellow commissioners and staff members had constructed a wholly new tax system built solidly around the concept of "comprehensive income" – the famous "a buck is a buck is a buck" – based on equity among individual taxpayers with comparable discretionary income and neutrality across sectors of the economy. In essence, it was a major, whole-hearted attack on what we have come to refer to as "tax expenditures" – special tax exemptions aimed to promote certain behaviour on the part of individuals and certain types of investment and production on the part of firms.

By nearly all accounts, the Carter Commission did an impressive job of designing a tax system whose exclusive task was to raise revenues for government in an equitable and non-distorting manner, rather than to act as an instrument of social engineering and industrial subsidization. If, say, one were to assign a score of 85 "points" out of 100 (the "perfect score") for the potential "equity and neutrality" attainable under the tax system recommended by the Carter Commission, one could then measure the effect of the politics following the release of its report by observing the gradual decline in points through successive stages of the policy making process. As measured on such an imaginary scale, the score for Benson's White Paper was about a 70, reduced further to 65 by the revisions announced by the minister prior to his budget. The budget itself made a score of 60, which was further reduced by Parliament's amendments to a 55. The Turner budget of 1972 further reduced the package to a failing grade of 45.

The Failure of Tax Reform

How did this happen? What accounts for it? What does it mean? Eric Kierans makes an important argument about the politics of the Carter Commission, to be reviewed in what follows. In outline it is this: neither the Pearson government on release of the report in 1967, nor the Trudeau government on its election in 1968, was very keen to give the commission's recommendations high priority. Both lacked enthusiasm partly because the commission had been a creature of the Progressive Conservative government of John Diefenbaker, and partly because the senior ranks of the Department of

Finance, along with some Liberal party insiders, still had vivid memories of the political fiasco occasioned by Walter Gordon's reform budget of 1963.[1] As a consequence of this caution, the Carter Report was placed in the hands of an ad hoc Cabinet Committee on Tax Reform, whose composition was deliberately kept unimpressive in both economic talent (with the notable exception of Kierans) and political clout.

The relatively weak membership of this committee and its duly adopted mode of procedure placed it more or less at the mercy of the "tax professionals" from the country's senior accounting firms and officials in the departments of Finance and National Revenue, who lacked real ambition to translate the report into large-scale, significant revisions to the Canadian tax system. Furthermore, once the committee had thereby produced a watered-down version of the recommendations in the form of the White Paper on Tax Reform, neither Edgar Benson nor Pierre Trudeau was inclined to do very much to stiffen the backs of cabinet when a barrage of complaints from vested interests began to descend on the government in response to the White Paper's release. Ultimately, therefore, the tax measures actually implemented on the basis of the Carter recommendations turned out to be but a sickly, pale reflection of the initial impetus from the commission.

There are several ways of corroborating the essential validity of this understanding of the Carter Commission and the general failure to give it full expression in legislation.[2] The most valuable insights from Kierans's distinct, inside view of the process have to do with, first, the capacity and determination of senior civil servants to deflect the movement towards significant tax reform; second, the Cabinet's inability to achieve progress on tax reform as a result of the prime minister's generally inconsistent and tentative leadership in economic matters; and, third, Kierans's own conclusions about the implications of corporate taxation in Canada for the country's major problems with unemployment, foreign control, and resource dependence. Also worth noting is the impact that all this had on Kierans's sharpening sense of alienation from national government and the Ottawa establishment.

Kierans argues essentially that senior officials of the departments of Finance and Revenue, especially Deputy Finance Minister Robert Bryce, hijacked the decision-making process. However, if the Ottawa mandarins prevailed in this instance, it must be recognized that this happened by default; the permissive condition was the absence of political will and leadership at the places where their presence was critically required – the desks of the minister of finance and the prime minister. There is still something surprising and even a little disturbing in the story of how some of the most strategic economic issues to confront a Canadian government since the end of the Second World War were handled at the highest level of decision-making. One of Kierans's starkly stated impressions is that few ministers ever read the report or could even have said accurately how many volumes there were to it. But Kierans's more profound complaint is over the manner in which the cabinet's tax reform committee met.

According to Kierans's answer to a question from Leslie T. MacDonald, who was doing research for a PhD thesis on the Carter Commission, it was

an absolutely ludicrous way of proceeding, but it was deliberately so done and was maintained throughout the whole process. And that manner was this: the cabinet committee met, as I say, the seven ministers plus about ten or twelve advisors from the various departments, principally Finance and Revenue, every Wednesday night at eight o'clock or virtually every Wednesday night at eight o'clock and met until eleven or twelve o'clock, and this went on for over a year until the publishing of the White Paper, and then it continued to resume immediately after [release of the White Paper]. But the procedure, now, was that you were handed a paper by the Department of Finance at eight o'clock on what was the subject to be discussed that night.

Les MacDonald: So you were not able to read it in advance?

Eric Kierans: No. Let's say death benefits, or something ... or insurance exemptions, or whatever it was, that was the paper handed to you, you discussed it as you were reading it, and then (I don't want to raise the hair on your head) officials from the Department of Finance immediately afterwards collected all the papers from the ministers and everybody else and put them back. Those I wanted to retain I retained just by being obstinate about it; but all this lent an air really of complete incredulity to the whole thing and I was just amazed that anyone could consider that this was an honest attempt to come to grips with the problems of tax reform.[3]

Kierans went on to tell MacDonald that, apart from these procedures, "there was no one on that committee with the exception of [the Finance Department's] Jim Brown and [Robert] Bryce himself who could really discuss the philosophy of what we were doing or could really integrate the overall objectives of what a tax reform proposal was."[4]

The superficiality of the deliberations is strongly suggested by some of the documents that Kierans was at such pains to take home with him. One of these, evidently prepared to aid committee members' discussion of numerous tax changes over two consecutive days of deliberations, set out 38 points that the government might be called upon to address publicly and would wish to be prepared to answer.[5] Examples of such questions are: "7. Is this system planned for conversion to a guaranteed annual income plan? If not, why not? ... 9. Why tax unemployment insurance when in most cases payments reflect a substantial cut in pay anyhow for the recipient? ... 17. This reform will drive out vital investment capital from the resource industries." These sorts of questions or topics were then followed by, typically, a small paragraph of three or four sentences or three or four phrases or sub-topics set out in point form. Hence, the documents contained close to 150 separate questions or points at issue, rendered in highly elliptical form and open to wide interpretation or further elaboration. If Kierans's description of the committee's procedures is accurate, these roughly 150 points would have been deliberated (to put it charitably, "scanned" might be more accurate) without prior preparation and with only three to six hours of meeting time to discuss them – on average, about one every three minutes.

Even allowing for other background documentation, verbal briefings by departmental officials, and subsequent meetings on central points, these documents lend credence to Kierans's complaint that the meetings were unbelievably superficial. There are few signs, even in abbreviated form, of the sophisticated, expert analysis and arguments presented in studies and discussion papers generated by the Carter Commission itself.[6] In any case, Kierans concluded that most of the cabinet members on the committee were either unable or disinclined to view taxation issues in terms that went anywhere beyond their personal finances or their own experience.

The upshot was that Kierans's own economic priorities with respect to tax reform, especially corporate tax reform, were defeated because he could not make a sufficient number of his colleagues come to appreciate why Carter's recommendations were so important. His colleagues either failed to see the relevance of the distinctions and arguments that he made, or, lacking independent understanding of the issues, they were reluctant to endorse the positions taken by one of their political colleagues against the advice and arguments of senior government experts. The final straw for Kierans, though, was when, despite these odds, he did save one or two key points out of the commission's work, only to witness their political defeat because of the highly cautious and tentative support lent to tax reform by the minister of finance: "There was one thing I guess that I got [through the cabinet committee process] that was put through really at my insistence, which was that there should be a review of the whole accelerated depreciation provision. The white paper comes out, and then in his first attempt to bring in the participation of outside bodies, Mr. Benson, in Vancouver, retracts all this and says that this was only the personal interest of one minister, and so on, and that he didn't think that they would be preceding with this."[7]

The effects on Kierans were predictable. As he told Les MacDonald, "It was a very disappointing experience for me and I must say that I became increasingly frustrated as we went along." Frustration led to depression, and Kierans began to wonder if he truly belonged in the government: "let's say it was a very distressing period in my life. It became quite clear to me that there was no way in which I could ever vote in the house if this was to be presented under any form other than that of simple tax changes, but to present this as tax reform was simply impossible and I was really making my position clear."[8]

Nevertheless, instead of resigning, Kierans decided simply to keep his head down and to refrain from public comment on the government's program. On the one occasion on which the prime minister had prevailed on him to defend the White Paper before French-language television – not many ministers were francophones and tax experts – he refused to speak about "les réformes fiscales," referring consistently instead to "les changements fiscaux," a subtlety duly noted by one especially observant journalist.[9] By the time Benson's tax legislation was before the House for a vote, Kierans had resigned from the cabinet over the broader issue of economic mismanagement, so he was in essence an "independent Liberal" when the vote was finally taken on tax reform. (He rose to vote against the government.)

The Absence of Political Will

All the published accounts of the failure of the tax reform process emphasize the power of vested interests to protect their economic position against attacks on their privileges within the existing system of taxation. The mining and petroleum lobbies come in for special attention, as do provincial governments as standard-bearers for the economic powers-that-be in their respective provinces. To this pressure, Les MacDonald has added the weight of the "tax professionals," who, regardless of their exact place of public or private employment, share a common perspective on tax matters shaped by their extensive commonality of interests with large corporations. However, while these accounts are certainly plausible and, in their own terms, powerfully persuasive, such accounts of the power of interest groups over public policy, while apparently true, may be beside the point.

Based on the impressions formed by two participants close to the centre of power in the Trudeau government from 1968 to 1971, it seems that the explanation for the failure of tax reform does not lie simply in the lobbying power of corporations and the economic elite. Instead, it appears that Pierre Trudeau's personal and political indifference to the whole issue, combined with the type of cabinet government that he put in place, had at least as much to do with the final outcome. The story is less one of the triumph of pluralism than of the absence of political will. In a sentence, tax reform failed because Pierre Trudeau and his minister of finance did not care whether it took place or not. Moreover, the type of cabinet government that Trudeau initiated neutralized the potential impact of the few in his cabinet who did care about it.

On the subject of political will, Les MacDonald's exhaustive account records his impression that there were many signs that the report of the commission was fated to become a political orphan, even on its release in the closing months of the Pearson government. One of the more conspicuous of these signs was that the report, unlike practically every other major royal commission report of the last fifty years, was never printed and released as a proper, type-set volume.[10] With 2,575 typed and mimeographed pages in six, plastic-bound volumes, it remained an "underground classic," suitable – as Kierans loves to point out – for graduate instruction in business taxation at the Harvard School of Business, but not deemed by the Pearson government or by senior officials of the Department of Finance to be of sufficient value for circulation – or even convenient availability – among the Canadian public.

Eric Kierans was to discover that, after 1968, cabinet ministers and senior officials of Trudeau's government were no more keen than Pearson's had been to promote widespread public appreciation of the elegant elementarity of the Carter reforms. This indifference, then, is one of the explanations for the failure of the recommendations. Other evidence is needed, though, to explain why the entire cabinet could not be swayed to promote tax reform. For this, it is necessary to consider the general composition of the cabinet and, more important, the manner in which the cabinet made decisions.

Decision-making in Cabinet

Kierans's disappointment over the Carter episode was only one important instance of his frequent annoyance caused by the fact that the cabinet's decision-making process did not give him an adequate opportunity to improve those economic policies that were brought forward. Kierans was quite aware that, as Allan Gotlieb put it, "he was one of the few members of the cabinet who could read a balance sheet," and Kierans felt strongly that this gave him a right, if not a duty, to try to plug the holes and correct the errors that he found in the proposals that other ministers brought to cabinet.[11] In this endeavour, too, he met with frustration because a pattern of cabinet deliberation had evolved whereby the minister responsible for the formulation and subsequent administration of a policy was generally given blanket approval by other ministers.

A heavy burden of justification rested on any single minister who might depart from this principle. This deterring effect was even more forceful when Pierre Trudeau himself showed signs of supporting the minister in question and appeared to be unimpressed by early objections raised by other members of cabinet. This pattern settled in after Trudeau had, briefly, tried out a process of "collegial decision-making" whereby ministers were expected, or at least encouraged, to take an active part in probing for weaknesses in the measures proposed by their fellow ministers. Ironically, in this earlier phase, Kierans had been one of the few cabinet members to take seriously Trudeau's preference for genuine dialogue. According to Allan Gotlieb, he had begun to use up some of his own political capital by pursuing with his usual bluntness and determination the shortcomings in his colleagues' efforts. But by 1970, on matters of taxation as well as the economics of a range of other policy initiatives, there was a presumption that individual ministers held the primary responsibility for policies emanating from their respective departments. This fact, combined with Trudeau's lack of interest in economic (as opposed to linguistic and intergovernmental) problems, made it increasingly clear to Kierans that his opportunities to contribute solutions to economic problems would be rare, if they arose at all.[12]

Just how bad the government's economic management could get is evident from one further episode which Kierans recollects as particularly galling:

This was a cabinet committee meeting on economic policy. On the agenda was a discussion of one of the chapters in [Consumer and Corporate Affairs

Minister Ron] Basford's Competition Act, an act designed to create an environment of fair competition and reduced concentration in Canada. The Department of Finance introduced, at the last minute, a resolution that, in effect, would permit large corporations to write off the interest charged, incurred, in buying other corporations, takeovers and so on, against existing profit ... This came into the cabinet committee on economic policy. And it was passed by everybody just like that. And I raised holy hell. Then I said to Marshall Crowe, who was the secretary of the committee. I said, 'Marshall, I can't stop you from preparing the agendas. But next time, will you please have the grace, at least when you have two conflicting things, such as a chapter in a competition bill seeking to diminish mergers, not to have on the same agenda paper a motion which is going to enable the government, by reducing its own tax take, to, in effect, finance the increase of mergers.'[13]

During the course of the tax reform process, Kierans became more and more frustrated with the capacity of Ottawa's technocrats to divert and trivialize the reform process to the point where it passed with scarcely a trace of the Carter Commission's initial design. There is something genuinely Weberian in Les MacDonald's account of the power of the "professional ethos" in the field of tax policy. These "intellectual agents" of big capital, essentially private and public accountants and taxation economists, were able to stall and smother, through the sheer force of bureaucratic inertia, just about all of the initial political impetus behind the Carter Commission's recommendations.[14]

Meanwhile, and ironically, the cabinet was under the sway of the most charismatic prime minister that Canada had seen since Sir Wilfrid Laurier, and possibly Sir John A. Macdonald himself. Surely the Carter Commission's tax proposals could have been saved, almost completely intact, if Pierre Trudeau had turned the full force of his considerable political leadership towards the fortifications of the mandarinate, even in the face of public campaigns and lobbying efforts of corporations and other vested interests. We shall never know for certain, though, because the attempt was never made. Part of Trudeau's charismatic appeal, in so far as it had policy substance at all, had been based on his commitment to the "Just Society," which presumably could encompass a truly equitable tax system. It was equally, if not more so, based on "participatory democracy," by which Trudeau presumably did not mean public policy coups d'états by the Mining Association of Canada, the Canadian Petroleum Association, and the Canadian Tax Foundation.

Similar frustrations led also to the resignation of Tom Kent as deputy minister in the Department of Regional Economic Expansion in the summer of 1971. In his memoirs, Kent expresses at several places his own growing frustration with the same two problems that plagued Kierans: the style of leadership and the inadequacy of economic policy. The substance of their complaints, on both counts, is remarkably similar. Kent points to "a chaos of too many decisions too little co-ordinated" as a pole towards which the Trudeau government was inclined.[15] And elsewhere, he gives examples of "the extraordinarily vacillating mix of inappropriate and incoherent policies that marked the Trudeau period."[16] He writes also of a failure to follow policy ideas through to their concrete realization in the structure and conduct of government: "He [Trudeau] was always interested in talking about ideas, but there were only a few that sustained his interest to be carried through into action. And in the centralized style of the Trudeau government, little got done without the Prime Minister's active involvement."[17]

Kent writes, finally, of Trudeau's determination to introduce "the order and system required for a rational process" of decision-making by centralizing power and enhancing the technical expertise available to cabinet. "The Philosopher King had arrived, trailing the paraphernalia of the 1960s fashions in 'scientific' management." Kent continues:

It was all a great nonsense. Studies were made. New agencies were set up to make more studies. There was a new jargon in which familiar issues were restated more portentously. But there were few ideas with practical applications. The 'rational' system could produce sound policies only if the options presented to decision-makers were derived from perceptive assessments of problems. Some were, some were not. The Trudeau system had more successes than, by reaction, it has lately been given credit for. But where it went wrong, it went terribly wrong. And that was so in the crucial matter of inflation and unemployment.[18]

Kent was therefore as determined as Kierans to advocate budgetary measures different from those that Trudeau was pursuing or accepting. With his own sense of futility beginning to show, Kent describes the major shortcomings in the policies with which Trudeau was willing to live: "I urged that the government should promptly act on most of the recommendations of the Carter Royal Commission on Taxation. In particular capital gains should be taxed exactly like income. In addition to its equity, that would weaken the speculative urge that was a major factor in bidding up costs and prices. In the same spirit, tax reform should end the legal laxity regarding the expenses that a corporation could deduct from its income for taxation."[19]

Kent adds that if he were giving the same advice now, he would suggest larger changes in corporation law and taxation to prevent the undermining of a competitive economy that results from the "paper entrepreneurship" of corporate concentration. All this, of course, describes Kierans's agenda "to a tee." It also shows that Kierans's perception of the uphill battle that he faced on economic issues was not all that exaggerated. But Kierans did not, because he could not, publicly formulate his economic program for the country until he left the government with which his differences on these matters were so great.

The Final Word

As for Kierans's part in the tax reform process, one passage written by Les MacDonald captures the essence of the story of systematic tax reform in Canada. It describes the dénouement of that story, when the bill implementing the Benson budget's tax provisions was approved by the House of Commons. On 17 December 1971, the final day of the debate, the House heard a speech from the prime minister, and later one from Eric Kierans, MP. MacDonald describes the scene this way:

Prime Minister Trudeau, one of the final government speakers on the [new tax] bill, read from a prepared text praising the bill as the crowning achievement of a decade of tax reform, during which 'For the first time in Canada a government has invited the population as a whole to participate in the formation of a major policy.' Opposition members, their opportunity to discuss the bill any further foreclosed, heckled the Prime Minister at every opportunity. However, a sense of the occasion had taken hold in the House following Mr. Trudeau's observation that the process had begun only a few months short of a full decade earlier with the appointment of the Royal Commission on Taxation. Then Eric Kierans calmly condemned the bill by setting it against what the Royal Commission had recommended.[20]

But Kierans's lessons in politics and government were not restricted to comprehensive tax reform. He also discovered, as postmaster general, that good policy from one minister, even the minister responsible, was far from enough to ensure good government by the cabinet.

POST OFFICE BLUES

Eric Kierans joined Pierre Trudeau's first cabinet in the summer of 1968 as postmaster general and minister of communications. He assumed these duties, especially those concerning the post office, with enthusiasm. Indeed, he seemed to be a man on a mission; he wanted to restructure the post office so that it could compete effectively with the private sector in serving the public. Kierans intended to carry out a series of modernizations and restructurings that would provide a sense of direction for the post office. He was not placing efficiency ahead of service, however. Rather, he wanted the post office to provide realistic services and to live within its means.

Kierans did not see his new charge as an institution operating in a vacuum. His strategy for it was designed to promote his ideas (and those of the Trudeau government, as he saw them) of a "just society," a point that he makes clear in a speech to the parliamentary committee considering an amendment to the Post Office Act: "A just society, Mr. Chairman, depends on a thriving economy, for only an efficient, expanding economy can afford the costs of rectifying injustices, improving distributions of wealth and incomes and hope to reduce the burden of poverty. The institutions of such an economy and such a society must be efficient and thriving. The post office is such an institution."[21]

In order to ensure an efficient and thriving institution, Kierans felt that he had to streamline operations, modernize, adopt emerging technological innovations, and mould the work-force into a more productive group. He was determined that the post office would be on the "cutting edge" of technology. He believed that he could transform the inefficient, patronage-ridden slug into a competent and productive organization which would benefit the entire economy by providing technologically advanced services efficiently.

Kierans took upon himself an enormous task in the face of much scepticism from others. For example, Clive Baxter of the *Financial Post* predicted: "What lies ahead would be a stunning management challenge under the best of circumstances."[22] Nevertheless, Kierans was confident. Moreover, he thought that he had a limited amount of time with which to work. As he told Baxter: "There in one clear message: we will have until 1975 to put our house in order. That is when we can expect the big breakthrough in many technical advances now on the drawing boards. The post office must be ready to compete by then. If it isn't we'll lose out to other systems."

Kierans reveals here that he was one postmaster general who did not have a parochial view of his bailiwick. He was determined to keep up with innovations in communications systems. As Baxter put it, "Kierans means ... that the post office will, if it feels it should, move into such areas as computer data transmission, telegraphs, and even telephone service, if this seems to make business sense." Transformation meant not only modernizing services and pricing them reasonably but also changing attitudes. In particular, it meant putting an end to worker-management friction. However, Kierans's biggest problem was turning the work-force into a skilled, modern group able to meet the technological changes that he could see coming. He considered the task urgent, saying, "There is no alternative."[23]

Transforming Operations

Kierans moved with break-neck speed, for a minister, in his efforts to transform the post office. He demonstrated a sense of direction and ambition that, it seems fair to say, was not characteristic of the government as a whole. In a "take-charge" and direct style, he seized the available tools of government and went about the task at hand. In September 1968, he assigned Kates, Peat, Marwick and Co. to do a study of the post office and make recommendations to improve it. However, Kierans anticipated many of the recommendations and implemented far-reaching policies, at a quick pace, even before the report came back to him. He began by invigorating the upper echelon, which one observer described as "filling [it] fast with high-priced, commercially oriented, senior managers."[24] The drive for efficiency also included plans to rationalize the price structure and mail delivery systems, decentralize operations into four regions, close uneconomic outlets, and end the blatant patronage that was associated with several aspects of operations.

Postal Rates

One of Kierans's first priorities was to establish more realistic prices for services. Increasing postal rates was always unpopular, and few had dared to do it. Kierans inherited a pricing structure that was outdated and irrational. First-class rates had not been altered since 1954, and second-class rates since 1951. Third- and fourth-class rates Kierans raised unilaterally. However, raising first- and second-class tariffs required parliamentary approval. This was achieved in October 1968, and new rates went into effect on 1 November. First-class rates (for mailing normal letters) went to 6 cents; second-class rates (for mailing newspapers and magazines) also went up. Before this revision, second-class rates were being subsidized by almost 80 per cent – that is, newspapers and magazines carried postage that amounted to only 22 per cent of what it cost to deliver them. Of the projected post office deficit of $100 million for 1968, the second-class mail subsidy accounted for $47 million.[25] Other rationalizing moves included closing the Post Office Savings Bank (accomplished 1 January 1970), introducing a postal code for greater efficiency, and, as of 1 February 1969, reducing delivery to five days per week for urban areas.

These moves, although practical steps towards greater efficiency, irritated a lot of people. The halt to Saturday delivery, for instance, was very unpopular and received a rough ride in the House of Commons. The higher rates also upset consumers. As Swift points out, a Committee for Fair Postal Rates was started by voluntary and non-profit organizations such as the Boy Scouts and the Consumers' Association.[26] The press also complained – not surprising, considering that second-class rates on their products had been hiked. In general, the media felt that postal subsidies were "in the interests of a free flow of information."[27] In an editorial entitled "No Voice," the *Globe and Mail* also decried the lack of consumer representation in the post office decision-making process and the sacrifice of service to consumers for the sake of efficiency: "With the Saturday cut-off of deliveries, they will suffer a 17 per cent loss in service. The decision to cut daily mail sortings from two to one will undoubtedly decrease the service they receive by at least another 17 per cent."[28]

Kierans seemed to consider these criticisms mere whining, saying simply, in response to complaints from MPs concerning the end of Saturday delivery, that "all efforts to reduce costs or improve efficiency will undoubtedly be received unfavourably by the people who are affected."[29] He was also suspicious of the motives of the press on becoming consumer advocates. The *Financial Post* paraphrased him as saying, in response to the swelling ranks of critics, that "part of the blame lies with publishers who are annoyed at their higher second-class rates and so are egging their editors on in criticism of the post office and its minister."[30]

All these policy changes were undertaken for the sake of efficiency, controlling the deficit, and, Kierans thought, fairness. Raising rates would make users pay for service, instead of being subsidized by all taxpayers who in the end would have to cover the deficits. Even Kierans's plans, however, were merely to bring the post office's deficit under control, not necessarily eliminate it. As he said in the House, "the post office deficit, while it has always existed, is in the process today of reaching critical as well as chronic proportions. A deficit such as the $130 million envisaged next year is simply insupportable. Unless controlled it will escalate out of sight."[31] Kierans, though, may have invited an excessive amount of grief in attempting to eliminate the deficit on the operating budget while at the same time increasing spending on new technologies. He discovered what he deemed to be an unconscionable amount of "fat" in operations, and he was determined to reduce it as far as he could. This led to intense resistance both from within the service and, outside it, from the communities that it served.

Eliminating Postal Stations

One deficit-reducing measure was elimination of the smaller, inefficient post offices, deemed to be of relatively limited usefulness. This was carried out on a significant scale. Between June 1968 and April 1970, 990 post offices were closed throughout the country. Although the reduction was done on business grounds, it was politically explosive. In fact, this decision more than any other may have doomed Kierans's later policy initiatives because it seriously undermined his support within the caucus and the cabinet. A patronage network had built up over the years as part of operations; as Swift summed it up, "The postal system had long been a source of patronage for the Liberal party. The job of postmaster-general had traditionally gone to a Quebec political operative whose job was to make sure the party faithful were happy."[32] As for rural MPs, the staffing of small, rural outlets was a good way of returning favours.

Closings, however, were essential from an economic standpoint. Moreover, Kierans insisted that they were to be carried out not arbitrarily, but according to objective criteria, uniformly applied. As he said in the House of Commons, several conditions were required to close down a post office. An outlet was to be shut down when it served fewer than 30 families, when the income was less than $1,000, when administration costs amounted to $2,000 or $3,000, and when it was possible to introduce a rural service.[33] All offices that met the criteria for closing were reviewed, however, and not all initial decisions to close individual offices were carried out.

The rural initiative was generally unpopular. Opposition MPs used to badger Kierans for lists of the number of post offices closed, and how many were scheduled for closing, often by constituency – a practice that began to resemble calls for a body count of soldiers during a war. Gradually, the closings undermined Kierans's political support among Liberal MPs and even made Kierans a powerful enemy within the cabinet, Allan MacEachen, whose primary if not exclusive concern was the government's standing with the public.[34] Ultimately, as demands mounted for Kierans's resignation as postmaster general, "not the least of the pressure for Kierans's scalp came from backbenchers, particularly from Quebec, who resented the loss of their traditional Post Office patronage rights."[35] The closings made good economic sense, but they helped deprive Kierans of the political support within the cabinet and the caucus that he would later need during the even more contentious Lapalme affair.

However, to keep this growing tension among Kierans, Parliament, and the rest of the cabinet in perspective, it is worth noting that Kierans eventually won recognition, even praise, for his willingness to "buck the trend" politically for the sake of some basic principles and concern for governmental efficiency. For example, Jeffrey Simpson's *Spoils of Power* almost singles out Kierans during the Trudeau years as a minister determined to wrest politics away from the pattern of "greasing the wheels" that emit the loudest squeaks: "One important patronage reform, largely unheralded at the time, did mark the first Trudeau government – Postmaster-General Eric Kierans placed the appointment of post-masters under the public service commission. Kierans, a minister who believed in applying the principles of business efficiency to the post office, eliminated at a stroke one of the federal government's oldest bastions of local patronage, one that had served and bedevilled ministers since Confederation."[36]

I would argue, of course, that Kierans's principles along these lines also motivated the other decisions, covered in the present chapter and the next, that he made while a minister – only to be "bedevilled" even more. It is consistent with the thesis of these two chapters – though, of course, no proof of it – that Kierans should stand out in Simpson's book as an exception to a malaise of Canadian politics that Simpson characterizes this way: "What bedevils contemporary Canada is that because the demands of clients are unremitting, the patron's [i.e., the government's] desperation to respond never slackens, not because there is widespread evidence that widespread spending will buy them any political benefits – for bushels of evidence suggest the contrary – but because there is a fear of political reprisal if their answer is no."[37] Kierans certainly paid a political price for his determination to say no, and he paid it within the Trudeau government.

Crown Corporation?

An even more ambitious aspect of the drive for efficiency was Kierans's push to turn the post office into a crown corporation. This episode is not the most dramatic test of the ministerial effectiveness of Eric Kierans. However, it was important for three reasons. First, the government's abandonment of the crown corporation initiative helped to move Kierans closer towards resigning as postmaster general. Second, the episode indicates the differences between Kierans and his cabinet colleagues in their approach to government. The cabinet's approach was more easy-going than that of Kierans; it was content to muddle through rather than face the storms associated with extensive structural changes. Third, it underscored Kierans's own lack of political support within the cabinet. The two latter reasons were soon to become noticeable.

As with all of Kierans's other initiatives, the plan to create a postal crown corporation was not an end in itself; it was just another part, albeit an integral one, of the scheme for making the post office more business-like. This particular structural change was to provide a form of financial independence that would, in turn, make modernization easier. As Stewart-Patterson explains it, "Once the Department of Finance had given money to a corporation, it would not be as easy to grab it back. Postal management, for the first time, would be able to count on the size of its purse."[38]

Matters got off to a good start, it seems, as Kierans had little trouble getting cabinet approval for the idea of a crown corporation in 1968. However, he was always sceptical about the commitment of federal bureaucrats to the idea. Kierans felt pressed by his officials into consenting to a study on the feasibility of establishing a crown corporation, but this doomed the project by delaying it. By the time that a report was submitted and approved, in 1970, momentum had evaporated. "Too many other events had filled the intervening two years, ones that would abort the fetal Crown corporation almost as soon as it had been conceived," Stewart-Patterson tells us. There were also time constraints: "The debate on any postal bill would be sure to tie up business in the house for months, and there were plenty of other problems on the government's agenda." The plans for a crown corporation simply collapsed.

It has been common to portray Kierans as politically naive – that is, to say that he had no sense of what was likely to alienate the electorate – or paid no heed to what sense he did have of it. This is only partially true. Kierans was not ignorant of the political ramifications of his policies; however, his commitment to efficiency, and his determination to act on it, overrode his desire to be popular.

Where Kierans was genuinely naive was in believing that he could expect support from his cabinet colleagues in the face of popular discontent with his policy measures. In short, Kierans may have overestimated the political will of his associates. When concrete realities were encountered, the cabinet lacked both will and coordination – a limitation that Kierans failed to anticipate. Moreover, there was a clash of personalities within cabinet that was both personal and professional. All these elements were poised to combine into the political disaster over the trucking of mail in the city of Montreal.

Swift and Stewart-Patterson detail how Kierans had managed to antagonize some very important cabinet members.[39] Kierans had frequently irritated some of his cabinet associates and Liberal backbenchers with his zeal and his commitment to reform. Clive Baxter alluded to this situation following Kierans's resignation, writing that as far as many of Kierans's colleagues in and out of cabinet were concerned, he had been trying to do too much, too quickly, and what was needed was a period of calm.[40] "Many members complained that Kierans's hard-driving approach to reform had annoyed the public and was costing the Trudeau government heavily across the country." Kierans's most noticeable shortcoming, then, was that he was not really a "team player." This would have been evident in any portfolio that Kierans might have held, but it did help to make him unpopular within the cabinet over the postal foul-ups.

This particular trait might have been overcome, however, had there been a clear cabinet agenda. Most new governments assume office with a sense of purpose and direction. But political plans often disintegrate once confronted by signs of public resistance. This seems to have happened to the first Trudeau cabinet. The resulting lack of clear government direction, combined with the personality conflicts within the cabinet, provided a setting in which Kierans's strengths were not assets. Kierans's sense of mission and his belief that effective government is more important than favourable public opinion were qualities more suited for leadership than collegiality. He had shown this as part of the very small group who took charge of the government of Quebec, where circumstances allowed for a rare opportunity to engage in both.

The Lapalme Affair

The Lapalme imbroglio, precisely because of the mess that it became, provides a good opportunity to sort out these elements and to rate Kierans as postmaster general. Lapalme was a direct consequence of Kierans's plan to place post office affairs on a more business-like basis and to run it in the service of the national interest rather than for the benefit of particular interests. He wanted, in short, in a single stroke, to eradicate patronage in the awarding of contracts and to lower input costs. The Lapalme strike thus demonstrated, in combination, Kierans's commitment to economic efficiency, his seeming disregard for his public standing, and his unwillingness to give way graciously to some of the powerful members of the cabinet. It also highlighted the lack of political will and coordination, as well as the personal and political conflicts, within the cabinet.

While the incident is probably the event most closely identified with Kierans's troubles as postmaster general, it was not an isolated case. Neither the initial decision that fostered the affair, nor the public reaction and political fall-out from it, were unique during Kierans's tenure as the head of the post office. Lapalme did not arise out of a singular incident but was rather part and parcel of Kierans's approach to governance and a reflection of his fundamental political attitudes.

The Drive for Efficiency

The original decision concerning Lapalme was inextricably tied to Kierans's drive for efficiency: "One of his moves was to review the way the post office handed out contracts to private businesses, including those for local [mail] transportation in major cities."[41] In the past, local transportation contracts in Montreal had not been given on the basis of open, public tenders. They were given to one company on a yearly basis. Between 1952 and 1968, Rod Service Ltd. had received the local transportation contracts. The firm's employees unionized in 1965, establishing le Syndicat national des employés de Rod service (SNERS), in affiliation with la Confédération des syndicats nationaux (CSN). Labour disputes began almost immediately. There were strikes every year from 1966 to 1969. The combination of the closed tendering system with the high-cost, low-productivity SNERS agreement made local transportation very expensive in Montreal compared to other major Canadian cities. The cost of collecting mail in Montreal was $7.46 per hour, whereas in Toronto it was $6.11, and in Vancouver, $6.39.[42]

The mail collectors were not affiliated with a postal union and were not technically employed by the post office. However, as Swift put it: "The drivers saw themselves as postal workers and even wore special uniforms on the job. They knew their employer's contracts were just one-year deals and that their jobs ultimately depended on the Post Office."[43] This point is essential. The drivers held the post office responsible for their livelihood and were no more averse than most workers to striking and contemplating violence when their livelihoods were threatened.

Lapalme entered the scene in the spring of 1969. In late January of that year, Rod Service had asked to withdraw from its contract with the post office. The post office toyed with the idea of taking over mail collecting itself or establishing a crown corporation for the purpose. While it was reviewing its options, it was also negotiating with G. Lapalme Inc. to take over local transportation in Montreal. The union, for its part, refused to be absorbed by a "special Crown corporation or agency." Moreover, according to Swift, the CSN "immediately reminded the government that they [the government] had just helped negotiate a collective agreement under which they would have to assume all Rod's obligations and recognize the CSN as the bargaining agent for the drivers. The postal authorities, wary of the militancy of the drivers' union, were reluctant to recognize the CSN inside the Post Office, where there was already a collective agreement with the Council of Postal Unions."

In April 1969, G. Lapalme Inc. was awarded the mail delivery contracts in Montreal. Lapalme agreed to hire workers from Rod Service and to uphold the agreement with SNERS. As Swift explained it, Lapalme was a shady outfit that came into existence solely because "the possibility of a postal delivery contract arose." Moreover, its set-up, essentially a shell corporation, made it look like a front for the post office: "Pay cheques were paid by the Treasury Board through the Royal Bank; the Lapalme brothers each received $480 a week."

Regardless of the new arrangement, Kierans still wanted to hold open, public tenders, as specified in the Post Office Act, in order to bring the costs of delivery in Montreal down to a level comparable to the other major metropolitan centres. One point must be remembered: Kierans in 1969 won cabinet support for the tendering system.

The Desire for Job Security

The move to public tenders, though, was a radical break with tradition in the awarding of Montreal's delivery contracts. As the Goldenberg Commission later reported, Kierans did not execute this transition in a haphazard manner. One paragraph of its report makes it clear that Kierans had given his cabinet colleagues, Lapalme, and the Lapalme workers advance notice of his intentions:

In 1969 the Government decided upon a major change in policy. By letter dated September 25, 1969, the Postmaster of Montreal advised G. Lapalme Inc. that its contract was expiring on March 31, 1970; that the Postmaster-General would call for public tenders for contracts for the transport of mail pursuant to the provisions of the Post Office Act; and that such contracts would be for periods of five years. Lapalme was invited to tender and to advise its employees before October 1, 1969, of the new policy and of the termination date of the existing contract.[44]

The entire process appeared to have been carefully thought out. The Lapalme workers were to be given advance warning of the move to public tenders, the successful bidders were to be selected in January 1970, and the new contracts would come into effect on 1 April 1970. The transition, however, was far from smooth. Because of the high costs of its operation, which was a result of the agreement with SNERS, G. Lapalme Inc. decided not to bid for the new contracts – it simply could not compete with companies not encumbered by expensive union agreements. The workers at Lapalme were to be notified of the decision on 30 December 1969.

Kierans had been informed of the possible consequences of Lapalme's decision: "We can expect that upon receipt of advice to the effect that their work will be terminated with the end of the contract, the employees of G. Lapalme Inc. will endeavour to use coercion to maintain their employment. Thus we must prepare for either a strike or a slowdown commencing Tuesday, December 30th."[45] As they began to fear for their jobs, the Lapalme employees did resort to violent actions and work disruptions, and their obstructing tactics were causing a backlog of mail to pile up in Montreal.

In hindsight it seems evident that in this particular government-labour dispute – unlike more recent confrontations, such as those between the air traffic controllers and the US government or the coal miners and the British government -the advantage was tilted so far towards the union that there was no way that the government could emerge from the feud without losing face. First, despite the extensive violence employed by the Lapalme workers and their supporters to disrupt postal delivery, there was considerable public sympathy for the drivers' concerns over job security.[46] This unlikely situation was the result of the lack of public respect for the post office and the aura of incompetence surrounding it: matters had reached the point where, regarding any dispute or controversial decision, the post office was automatically deemed to be in the wrong. This, to some extent, was Kierans's fault, in that he failed to convince the public of the need for restructuring operations and raising rates. He thus allowed public support for the post office to sink to a new low.

Second, and nothing to do with Kierans, radical political developments were taking place in Quebec. The union "treated the dispute as a cause célèbre for Quebec nationalism. *Les gars de Lapalme* were not in it for the money, separatist circles insisted, but were out on the streets because they wanted to keep their union a Quebec union."[47] Moreover, according to the famous FLQ manifesto, the current postmaster general was one of the Quebec people's capitalist oppressors.[48]

Third, the press reacted strongly to the Lapalme situation. The terms of the post office's tenders did not specify that the winners of the trucking contracts must absorb the displaced workers, and this did not go down well with the press, especially in Montreal. Suddenly the post office, according to the media, had "moral obligations" to workers whom it did not, technically speaking, employ – a point echoed in the Goldenberg Report.

The press felt that there should have been conditions placed on the tendering of the delivery contracts, especially to protect older workers with useful experience. An editorial from the *Montreal Star* (19 March 1970) exemplifies the general mood of the press: "This has been a mess from the start, largely because the human factor was ignored ... Mr. Kierans, in effect was filling, at least in mannerism, the role of a traditional labor buster."[49] Kierans was thus strongly criticized, mostly for insensitivity. But the criticism was not limited to him; the government as a whole was chastised for bungling the affair – that is, for not controlling Kierans. As the *Star*'s editorial pointed out, "Mr. Kierans was permitted to ride roughly over the drivers in their concern for employment during the transition period."

In sum, Kierans was portrayed as insensitive and unduly intransigent, although some of the criticisms seem a little unfair. For instance, the tenderers were informed that wages for drivers had to be in line with the industry standard. Also, Kierans assumed that the drivers would find work with the new contractors. After all, the companies would need drivers and the drivers would need jobs, so it made sense that the two should come to terms. But no specific guarantees were made to the Lapalme drivers by either the post office or the Department of Manpower – Kierans advised the drivers to register with Manpower and apply for "their" jobs with the new contractees. Kierans realized, further, that some jobs would be lost, regardless of who took over the contract. G. Lapalme Inc. employed 459 drivers, but Kierans himself admitted that the new delivery companies could get by with 350.

Providing specific guarantees in the tendering of contracts represented neither a lapse of reason on Kierans's part nor an attempt to "bust" the union. In response to an MP's question on 15 April 1970 about why the post office failed to guarantee the drivers' jobs and certify the union, Kierans replied, "why in hell should you ask for tenders if you are going to put in this type of condition; and who is going to submit quotations in response to tenders that contain such conditions?"[50] Kierans was, in effect, trying to nurture the tendering process, which he believed was essential for running a cost-effective postal operation. Excessive constraints might have scared off potential tenderers, he argued, thus preserving the current, and clearly inefficient, status quo. Earlier the same day in the House, in reply to a charge that he was a union buster, Kierans had insisted, "I am as pro-union as any man in this chamber but I am not one of those who is willing to say that at all times, under all conditions and in all places a union is eternally right. A union, just like a business, large or small, can price itself out of a particular market. This appears to be what the present union is doing."

The whole Lapalme affair is confusing. To at least one observer, the real struggle seemed to be not over the preservation of jobs but over the status of the union.[51] Since the existing union forbade the drivers to apply for jobs with the companies that won the contracts, it is difficult to see what difference it would have made if the government had "guaranteed" the workers' jobs. (The certification of the union would also need to have been guaranteed.) Nevertheless, as a result of public attitudes, political developments, and media interpretations, the incident turned into a political problem at the highest level.

This is not to say, necessarily, that Kierans fumbled the ball. Indeed, it is difficult to point to any one particular decision and say, "There, this is where Kierans made his mistake." Every decision that he made was rationally sound, with economic efficiency the overriding goal. The trouble over the incident, therefore, cannot be attributed to ministerial ineptitude. The *Montreal Star* (12 February 1970) seems to have acknowledged this point: "the present conflict is principally the result of two contradictory desires, both of which are commendable in themselves. The drivers want job security. The post office wants to ensure the efficient delivery at a lower cost by contracting the delivery of mail through public tenders to independent firms."[52] Kierans, along with his credibility, was swept away by circumstances beyond his individual control.

Ottawa's Response

Kierans tried to weather the storm by taking a tough line. He refused to negotiate with the union because he felt, since the post office was not the direct employer of the drivers, that it was not his place. The task fell to Bryce Mackasey, the labour minister, whom the union had asked to mediate the dispute. But while Kierans wanted to remain tough, the cabinet's resolve began to soften. As we have seen, Kierans had previously made some enemies within the cabinet, but now Jean Marchand, who had been president of the CSN, came to oppose Kierans outright because he disagreed with his position.[53] The cabinet, including Pierre Trudeau, which had originally approved the move to open public tenders in Montreal, gradually backed away from Kierans's position. Adverse public opinion and possible political repercussions frightened Kierans's cabinet colleagues, even though the government was still in the middle of its mandate and presumably safe from electoral sanction.

Kierans decided, therefore, to resign. However, on a direct appeal from Trudeau, he reconsidered his decision and agreed to stay on as postmaster general. As part of this understanding, Kierans was expected to accept and implement the recommendations of a report to be prepared by H. Carl Goldenberg. The report (late March 1970) illustrated perfectly the truism that hindsight – in this case, Goldenberg's – is 20/20 vision. It reiterated the criticisms being bandied about in the press and by Kierans's cabinet adversaries: "the invitation to tender made no reference to the hiring of present personnel. In my opinion this was a serious omission. Although the Post Office was not their direct employer, its change of policy would directly affect the livelihood of the Lapalme employees. The Post Office was therefore under a moral obligation to seek to protect their employment as far as possible."[54] As previously mentioned, though, Kierans believed that providing adequate job protection would probably have scared off new bidders for the contracts, making the whole tendering exercise pointless.

Goldenberg questioned whether the new contractors would be able to provide efficient service: "I am not in a position to pass proper judgement on their bids but, on the basis of contemplated wage rates and the attitude of labour relations disclosed to me, I am of the opinion that they will be unable to fulfil their commitments within the fixed price and, at the same time, maintain industrial peace. Moreover, in the present climate of strife, none has yet been able to organize properly to commence service on April 1st." This conclusion is based on overly pessimistic guesses. The transition from Lapalme to the new mail delivery companies could have been very rough indeed. However, given that the new contracts were to last for five years, there was no way to tell whether the delivery firms could rationalize their operations, overcome the labour problems, and live up to the terms of the contract. Goldenberg, though, implies that it was wrong to allow one of them the opportunity to make the attempt.

Goldenberg's contention that service would be faulty because three of the four firms were not in existence prior to the awarding of the contracts is also debatable. Of the four firms seeking the contract, only H. Lapalme Transport Ltd. existed previously; the others – Moses & Duhamel Inc., Courrier M. & H. Incorporé (which won two contracts), and Ménard and Desmaris – did not. G. Lapalme Inc. had not existed before winning the contract formerly held by Rod Service, and it had managed to get the job done – that is, until the labour problems began. Furthermore, there were now five private mail delivery contracts in Montreal, where there had in the past been one. Therefore, mail collection was not at the mercy of the competence, or lack of it, of any one outfit. Also, the companies might have been able to learn from each other, imitating each other's successes and avoiding each other's mistakes. (Once again, the method in Kierans's madness turns out to be avoidance of monopoly in the interests of efficiency.)

Finally, Goldenberg seemed to write off as understandable the violence employed by the Lapalme drivers to underscore their disapproval of the situation. Although he insisted that the violence "must not be condoned," he went on to say that, as things then stood, "the Lapalme employees lose their status and rights as employees under their collective agreement on the expiry of the agreement and of the Lapalme contract of March 31st. This has created a state of fear, insecurity and demoralization which has led to destruction and violence." Goldenberg, then, recommended that "the Post Office should assume operation of the postal transport service throughout the city of Montreal and that the Lapalme employees should be integrated in the Public Service of Canada in the order of their acquired seniority having regard to adjustments in requirements, the necessity of which is admitted."[55] The report made no mention of certifying the union. Its conclusions, therefore, did not end the demonstrations; however, the recommended solution did require additional government spending. Cancellation of the replacement contracts alone cost over $820,000.

Good Intentions, Bad Consequences

The decision made by Kierans to move to public tendering for mail collection in Montreal was sensible from an economic standpoint. Apparently the cabinet agreed, allowing the process to move ahead. However, once the trouble started, Kierans and most of the rest of the cabinet seemed no longer to understand one another. Kierans continued to let economic rationality – plus his deep-seated aversion to potentially corrupt abuses of the government's procurement of services – guide his judgment. Meanwhile, some of his cabinet colleagues were more taken with emotional arguments – the government's ostensible moral responsibility to the drivers – and were worried about negative public reaction. Moral responsibility and economic efficiency often seem impossible to reconcile, as they may have been in the Lapalme case. However, governments are elected to make tough decisions in the interests of the whole public, not to serve the special needs of a few.

Kierans's handling of the Lapalme incident was made to look more error-ridden than it really was, especially by the media and in the Goldenberg Report. His good economic intentions did indeed produce bad consequences. However, this was caused not so much by ministerial failure as it was by political failure on the part of the cabinet, which had quite simply failed to give Kierans the support that he needed in order to see the dispute through to the end that they had all, in the beginning, resolved to seek. Such support, of course, was impossible, given the intensity of opposition to Kierans's intransigent position on the key issues. Kierans's central political failure was, thus, his refusal to give ground to the ultimately overpowering political forces lined up against him on this issue, from the corridors of Parliament to the streets of Montreal.

Kierans's intransigence during the Lapalme affair had political consequences for the government and for Kierans himself, and they can be counted only as a costly mistake. Kierans's final defense must be that he refused to be political – a strange posture for a sitting MP and member of cabinet. However, apart from raising the interesting question of whether or not Kierans was ever, in fact, a "politician," the affair equally draws attention to the most appropriate way to characterize the "heart and soul" of the first Trudeau government. It does this because of the connections between "les gars de Lapalme" and the FLQ – the same gang of thugs who, as we shall see, proceeded to terrorize the government along with the rest of the country in October 1970. Kierans, unlike his cabinet colleagues during the spring of 1970, refused to let acts of violence intimidate him into conceding the political agenda of their perpetrators. This was, of course, exactly the stand taken against the FLQ by the prime minister, which all the ministers were called on to support in the fall of 1970. Even here, of course, the government eventually compromised. Perhaps Kierans had learned something from Lapalme, after all.

CHAPTER SEVEN

Telesat and the National Interest

Kierans was appointed minister of communications – as well as postmaster general – when Pierre Trudeau took office in mid-1968. By the spring and summer of 1970, he was preoccupied with creation of the world's first domestic communications satellite. The story of Kierans's efforts there is revealing. First, it provides a clear example of his exercise of ministerial responsibility. His new department, Communications, had been authorized to supervise financing of Telesat Canada and launching of Canada's new telecommunications system, and Kierans took a more active and positive interest in this aspect of his mandate than in any other that arose during his period of office. Second, precisely because of this direct involvement, combined with the federal government's role in the venture, the Telesat project is a rich source of insights into Kierans's political philosophy – that is, his ideas about the theory and practice of government and the relationship between the public and private sectors in Canada. Third, the decision to acquire Telesat's satellite hardware from Hughes Aircraft Corp. of California, rather than from RCA Ltd. of Montreal, was the most politically charged decision that Kierans made as a federal minister, with the possible exception of his awarding of the mail contracts already reviewed.

Telesat's procurement of an American-built satellite pitted Kierans's view of the national interest against a vociferous and powerful array of particular, vested interests. In this respect, it represented yet another version of the kind of politics that surrounded the recommendations of the Carter Commission and, in its own way, the Lapalme strike. Thus the Telesat decision involves an issue that was central for Kierans during his years in Ottawa. Is there a national interest? Is there something that transcends special interests and represents more than the sum total of particular interests that stand to win or lose as a result of action taken by the state? Telesat Canada's procurement of the Hughes Aircraft satellite does not represent merely a confrontation between Kierans as custodian of Canada's interests and everybody else in pursuit of their own, special interests, although this simplistic interpretation is not without merit. A detailed examination, however, will clarify Kierans's distinct role in the creation of Telesat Canada and the launching and operation of the Anik satellites.

Several of the most significant features of Telesat Canada through the 1970s and most of the 1980s stemmed from Eric Kierans's determination not to permit the government to be deflected from the core national interests involved in the Telesat decision. His leadership on this issue accounts for the fact that Canada preceded the United States in deployment of communications satellites for national, domestic use. Moreover, because of Kierans's vision and commitment, Telesat Canada is a good, early example of a "mixed enterprise." It was a creature of neither the government, like a fully fledged crown corporation, nor of the private sector, as in the "carriers' carrier" that telecommunications companies would have controlled themselves.

Of course, these two features of do not exhaust the national priorities bearing on the system that finally did emerge. Kierans took several national concerns as starting points, and he did not abandon them when they proved controversial. For example, a series of government decisions and investigations in the 1960s had concluded that Canada's geography and demographic composition gave it an unusually strong interest in emerging space-based systems of telephone, television, and data transmission. Satellite technology was economically indifferent to both magnitude of distance and ruggedness of terrain, and it allowed nation-wide "coverage" of signals from specific, central locations. Consequently, government pronouncements on the subject, including speeches by Kierans as minister, highlighted northern development and national dissemination of French-language broadcasting as goals that could be advanced through space-based telecommunications. The latter concern was intensifying in the light of increasing French-Canadian nationalism and the prospect of direct Quebec-France cooperation in satellite communications.[1]

Consensus also existed on two further aspects of satellite communications: Canada's communications system must be subject to purely domestic political control, and the project should be carried out in a way that promoted domestic scientific and industrial development.[2] It is perhaps ironic, therefore, that acquisition of the satellite 'hardware' for the new communications system produced a conflict between these two priorities. Kierans's approach to this issue played a critical role in resolving it.

Exclusive control of satellite telecommunications and broadcasting within Canada was gravely threatened by almost any delay in deployment of a Canadian system; maximization of scientific and industrial spin-offs almost certainly meant delays. This straightforward, yet stark, impasse seems to have escaped many of the participants at the time (and observers since). Many characterized the issue as a simple (and, as such, fairly obvious) choice between a Canadian-built and an American-built piece of space-based hardware for Canada's new telecommunications system. However, in practical terms, this was in fact a choice between hardware built in the United States now and hardware built in Canada later – possibly so much later that the first operational system to provide access to satellite communications for domestic use would be owned, operated and controlled by US firms. This prospect implied that telecommunications services would be made available to Canadians as marginal extensions of American services. It implied also that if Americans became the first, they might easily remain the only, providers of these services.[3]

In short, time was a crucial dimension and can itself be seen to consist of two distinct but interdependent considerations. First, an American system might precede, and hence pre-empt, a Canadian one by physically occupying or otherwise tying up available geostationary orbiting positions and/or by absorbing all Canadian-based demand for such services, especially in the commercial sector. Second, any reduction in the likelihood that the Canadian system would precede the first American system would make Telesat Canada less attractive to the telephone companies and general shareholders.

Unfortunately, the issue for Eric Kierans and his cabinet colleagues did not present itself in exactly this form. Instead, they had to decide whether the satellites themselves should be built in Canada by RCA Ltd. of Montreal or bought from Hughes Aircraft Corp. of California. The issue became one of "jobs, jobs, jobs" – in Quebec, in aerospace and other technologically sophisticated fields, and in future export-oriented industries. So posed, it attracted a wider and more determined group of players than it might otherwise have done. These ranged from the Science Council of Canada to the International Brotherhood of Electrical Workers, with an array of cabinet ministers, MPs, corporation presidents, and editorializing journalists in between.

HUGHES V. RCA LTD.

As we have already seen, the origins of Telesat go back as far as the Pearson government. In June 1969, the government made a preliminary commitment to two Canadian companies, RCA of Montreal and Northern Electric of Ottawa.[4] It offered preliminary contracts, a letter of intent, and a promise that the companies would have a good chance to receive the prime contracts for the satellites and accompanying ground stations.[5] Kierans apparently had no objection to RCA's primary role in provision of Telesat's first satellites. In fact, as the first president of Telesat remembers it, "Kierans wanted RCA; we all wanted RCA. The problem was that RCA couldn't give us a firm price or a firm delivery."[6] This assessment conveys the weaknesses that "did in" RCA's application between June 1969 and 31 July 1970, when the production contract was awarded to Hughes Aircraft.

While most accounts of the Telesat decision make it sound as though Hughes stole the production contract from RCA, the documentary record suggests that, rather, RCA lost it, by default. In fact, the reasons are already discernible in the cabinet's original authorization (in May 1969) for the minister of communications to open talks with the company immediately.[7] These discussions were intended to lead to awarding of a "directed contract" for supply of spacecraft and ancillaries. Furthermore, direction was to be given to RCA with respect to possible subcontracts, such as Northern Electric for transponders and Canadair and SPAR Aerospace for participation in selected sub-systems. RCA was also to be instructed to "optimize use of US technology by undertaking negotiations with Hughes Aircraft Co., Los Angeles," for competitive bids on several sub-systems. Project definition was to take three months and was to end with specifications for a ceiling price, target date, and a profit and penalty formula. All this was to be determined before any large subcontract was to be placed in the United States. Finally, RCA was to be required to give certain guarantees of management performance, including "investing the project manager with an adequate level of authority and also a direct channel to management support from the vice-presidential level."

Three parts of this cabinet instruction to Kierans foreshadow some of RCA's later difficulties. One is the reference to the potential involvement of Hughes Aircraft; another is the provision concerning a ceiling price and target date. A third, more ominous, is the implication of some concern in cabinet about either the management capability at RCA in Canada or the relations between RCA and its American parent. However, none of this began to surface until the spring of 1970: RCA completed project definition in March of that year and submitted its first proposal the following month.[8] (Kierans had ushered the act incorporating Telesat Canada through Parliament; third reading had passed 27 June 1969. David A. Golden had become president on 1 September 1969, and a provisional board of directors had been named on 12 September. Last but not least, Canada's still-awaited first domestic satellite had been given a name, ANIK, on 13 November 1969.)

The project received its first serious jolt on 20 April 1970, when Telesat's new board took exception to several features of RCA's first proposal. The board was particularly concerned about RCA's provision for two six-channel satellites (plus one spare) for $63.5 million, on a thirty-six-month delivery schedule starting 1 July 1970. The board's reaction to this timetable was no doubt coloured by its receipt that day (20 April) of an "unsolicited proposal" from Hughes Aircraft to provide satellites costing a total of $28.1 million, on a delivery schedule of eighteen months.[9] There followed a contentious wrangle over which of the two firms would finally be awarded the production contract, initially marked by a series of revised proposals from RCA, whose evolving details would only confuse this story unnecessarily.

By 4 June 1970, however, the competing firms had both offered modified proposals. The differences amounted to a trade-off between "Canadian content" and "total cost," with some additional concern about RCA's ability to deliver on time. RCA submitted costs of $42.1 million, with Canadian content guaranteed at 55.0 per cent and estimated as high as 64.3 per cent. Hughes's "all-American" proposal was to cost $28.0 million, and an alternative proposal set a slightly higher total cost of $29.7 million, with Canadian content of 11.7 per cent. At this point, and in the face of these figures, Telesat's board requested permission from Kierans to reject the proposal from RCA in favour of the one from Hughes. The debate grew in volume and shrillness through June and reached a crescendo the last week in July.

CABINET CRUNCH

We can find the essence of this debate by simply "lining up" the parties that stood either for or against RCA's campaign to reverse Telesat Canada's decision in favour of Hughes.[10] Perhaps RCA's most powerful supporters were the executives of affected Canadian electronics and aerospace firms, "who made direct private representations to make their case, largely on behalf of RCA." The Electronics Industry Association of Canada also argued for a national satellite program with maximum Canadian content and presented its position to cabinet on 3 July. The International Brotherhood of Electrical Workers demonstrated outside Parliament in support of much the same position. *Le Devoir* and the *Montreal Star* struck the editorial themes of Canadian nationalism and the drift of economic activity from Montreal to Toronto, issues echoed by the chair of the Montreal Urban Community.

The Department of Communications' Space Branch and its Communications Research Centre, the Department of Industry, Trade and Commerce, and the Science Council of Canada all lent active intragovernmental support.[11] At the cabinet level, the RCA coalition was strongly led by Jean Marchand. Marchand – minister of regional economic expansion, head of the Quebec caucus, and one of Prime Minister Trudeau's closest confidants – was especially concerned about the potential loss of Montreal industry to Toronto. His position won sympathy in cabinet, to varying degrees, from Jean-Luc Pepin of Trade and Commerce, Bryce Mackasey of Labour, and Joe Greene, Herb Gray, and Bud Drury.

Facing off against this quite formidable team were representatives of the Toronto-based financial community, who pointed to the need to acquire the satellite at the lowest possible cost if private-sector financing of Telesat Canada were to proceed without further delay.[12] Toronto's *Star* and *Telegram*, noting RCA's American parentage, also argued that only a company with Hughes's experience could build the system without such delay. Finally, there was "a bureaucratic-level group led by Telesat Canada, especially its President, David Golden." There were others who may not have endorsed Hughes outright, but who were not firmly in the RCA camp, either – notably the *Globe and Mail* and the *Financial Times*, which argued for formation of a new government-industry consortium to construct the satellites, consisting of RCA, Northern Electric, SPAR Aerospace, and the Communications Research Centre of the Department of Communications.

The imbalance on the side of RCA is striking. This fact was not lost on the cabinet, where Eric Kierans remembers the balance of forces to have been even more heavily tilted towards RCA: "RCA had 27 friends in a cabinet of 28."[13] Even if this is a slight exaggeration, significant questions arise in the face of the cabinet's very strong support for RCA. How and why did RCA obtain practically unanimous favour, even after ministers had been shown hard evidence that RCA was unlikely to meet any of the most vital national interests at stake? How did Eric Kierans turn the decision around, despite extremely long odds? Why was it so hard to get the government to do the right thing, and what finally made it do that?

The decision-making processes of the industrial democracies are gradually losing the capacity to protect broad national interests from the erosive effects of the promotion of particular interests.[14] It is becoming commonplace for private groups to undermine the national good. The public interest regularly seems to get trampled over in an onslaught of private interests, all of which attempt to protect or advance their particular fortunes in the name of, but at the expense of, the public good. (The classic exploration of this development in American politics is Theodore Lowi's *The End of Liberalism*.) Telesat Canada's procurement of its first satellites provides an example of the working of such forces.

The Hughes Aircraft option was not only much more likely than the RCA option to protect several of Canada's most vital interests in satellite telecommunications, but it was also cheaper. Moreover, those who supported RCA over Hughes apparently did so not despite the higher expenditures associated with it but because of them. RCA's proposal had one attraction that Hughes's did not: it represented government spending on industrial production and public and private research in Canada, and it was precisely this characteristic that provided RCA with a strong and active group of business, political, and bureaucratic supporters. Every supporter of RCA had some sort of financial stake, direct or indirect, in the government spending that it would generate: the Montreal newspapers and politicians, including cabinet ministers; potential subcontractors and their local supporters; the Canadian science, research, and development community; and, finally, the woolly headed nationalists, who seemed to believe that "buying Canadian" must be universally observed at all costs, even when the "Canadian" producer is an American branch plant.

Eric Kierans resisted the pull of comparable returns to his own political standing as a Quebec and Montreal politician. He insisted, instead, on giving top priority to the basic national interest at stake – namely, getting Canada into space telecommunications as early, reliably, and cheaply as possible. He provided his colleagues with overwhelming evidence of Hughes's almost unchallengeable superiority in meeting this priority, not to mention compelling evidence confirming RCA's near-incapacity to do so. As a result, this episode demonstrates precisely how much economic and technical reality the cabinet was prepared to ignore in order to satisfy clients and constituents. On this score, it is especially important to review in some detail the case that Kierans placed before cabinet in support of Telesat Canada's selection of the Hughes satellite.

This case against RCA had principally to do with higher cost and lesser reliability. A cost comparison shows that the RCA option was more expensive, partly because of its higher demand for Canadian technical and industrial employment. The whole issue could be described, in fact, as a difference of views about the extent to which the higher expenditure was justified by Canadian industrial development. Much of the paper circulated through cabinet, at any rate, addressed the issue in these terms. For example, Jean-Luc Pepin, minister of industry, trade, and commerce, wrote a memo to cabinet outlining his department's view that the "implications of the award to Canadian industry" were to confirm that Canada has confidence in its own industry; allow satisfaction of future domestic needs; ensure that Canadian industry is "in the business," allowing development of future export sales; employ some 500 highly skilled engineers, scientists, and technicians; strengthen Canada's systems management capability; and permit "follow on" increases in Canadian content. This memo added that "spin-offs in export sales" had already begun, pointing to SPAR and STEM as examples.[15]

A cabinet memorandum from the minister of labour was even more emphatically preoccupied with jobs.[16] This brief and somewhat belated document set out Bryce Mackasey's primary reason for favouring the grant to RCA. As he saw it, it would create 120–140 new jobs in Quebec, in addition to the 250 already in this industry in the province. Furthermore, 45 professional and 30 support positions would be created in the rest of Canada, while RCA outside Quebec would hire 30 professionals, 30 non-professionals, and 15 others. Within ten years, Mackasey submitted, the industry would employ 900–1,000 people across Canada. He made dire forecasts of the job losses associated with cabinet's refusal to overturn Telesat's decision. Upholding Telesat would mean dismissal of 100 professionals and 140 support staff in Quebec, and another 30 workers outside the province. Even worse, the eventual result "might be" the shutting down of an entire section of RCA, with the loss of "100 or so" professionals. This could in turn result in 200 more professional and 800 other jobs being lost. (Eric Kierans's copy of this memo shows signs that he was completely incredulous over Mackasey's data; most items were underlined and scored with exclamation points and question marks.)

Finally, members of the cabinet received detailed assessments of the significance of failure to exploit the "Research and Development" potential of the Telesat contract. One such document concerned the resulting dissipation of Canada's aerospace design expertise and the "backing up" or "bottlenecking" of this country's science and engineering graduates:[17] "the credibility of Canadian design capability rests largely on the existence of a Canadian satellite program ... Without it, it is debatable whether a facility for the design of space craft components could be competitively maintained." Would the savings represented by the cheaper Hughes option support space-related research in other areas? The document stressed that the significant consideration was whether or not alternative programs would conserve the very specialized facilities and competence that had been systematically developed over several years. Also, would Canadians reap the benefit from past government involvement in satellite R&D? Contraction of RCA's aerospace units would flood the market with 380 scientists and engineers – "a substantial fraction of one year's University output of physicists and engineers" and exceeding "one year's output of grads from those University groups working on space research." These programs would be redundant, the document claimed, if there were nowhere for these graduates to go.

Jean-Luc Pepin communicated the concerns of his department, Industry, Trade and Commerce (ITC), on R&D in similar terms, but with greater emphasis on the importance of domestic procurement to Canada's future international trade position in a growing industry.[18] In an appendix to this memo, the department presented an estimate that the total domestic and foreign market for Canadian aerospace production in the 1970s would be $97 million if the award were made in Canada, and $21–24 million if Americans got the award. ITC advanced another concern as well: "The proposed procurement represents a major new step by Canada in a high technology area. It is not considered possible that we can realize any significant technological and general international benefit unless we carry out a major portion of work in Canada. ... Such technological steps and long range advantages necessitate investment in people and facilities." ITC (one suspects, somewhat slyly) acknowledged the financial advantage made available to American producers by the US military budget as well as that of the National Aeronautics and Space Administration (NASA) in this area.

As a consequence, a new Canadian satellite built in Canada would cost more, albeit less than it might have without previous government and private funding of the Alouette and ISIS programs. The ITC's position emphasized several more specific implications of an award to US industry, predicting that it would increase US industrial capabilities in domestic satellite systems. It would also show lack of confidence in Canadian industry.

Moreover, the ITC's memo continued, since the remaining work in Canada would "not be sufficient to maintain the present level of industrial competence," engineering firms would shrink and disperse, thus preventing future satellite developments. It would not permit, even with the Canadian work promised, development engineering or sales to foreign countries. It would produce an initial loss of 250 workers in Quebec, possibly more, and perhaps even cripple RCA's Commercial and Defense System Division, reducing it to 1,500 employees. Finally, it would deny high-technology jobs to Canadian graduates. "Under PAIT, DIP, IRDIA the department has provided $9.4 million to Canadian Aerospace and electronics air industries." Moreover, under existing programs the department could, if required, "contribute on a cost-sharing basis up to $10 million of the $20 million non-recurring costs of a Canadian designed satellite."

UPHILL BATTLE

Eric Kierans thus had quite a fight on his hands. But fight he did, right down to the point of a threatened resignation and a direct personal appeal to the prime minister. The key components of his campaign were several carefully presented memos to cabinet, a direct appeal to the editorial boards of several newspapers, a "one-on-one" approach to Pierre Trudeau, and a final finesse of his leading opponents in the government, as related at the close of this account.

The cabinet memoranda from Kierans speak for themselves. One sets out a comprehensive yet reasonably succinct "final word" from Kierans to his cabinet colleagues. It points to the disadvantages that Telesat Canada and Canada's telecommunications system would face should the government indeed persist in regarding acquisition of the ANIK satellites as little more than a barrel of pork. It appeals to cabinet to advise the minister of communications on the minimum level of Canadian content that it deemed acceptable as a condition for the awarding of Telesat's satellite contract.[19] It invited the cabinet to choose from the following alternatives: "HA – $28.0 million with no Cdn content[;] – 29.9 million with 11.7% Cdn content[;] RCA – 42.4 million with 55–64% Cdn content." It informed the cabinet that the board of Telesat Canada recommended the Hughes satellite in view of its lower cost, greater capacity, and "increased opportunity for the corporation to achieve communications viability."

The memo also predicted minimum capital requirements at $90 million, with revenue required to break even at $18 million. It set out the minister's recommendations to inform Telesat that Hughes was acceptable as is – that is, declare that it met Canadian requirements. Alternatively, the cabinet could inform Hughes that its design, including participation by Northern Electric Co. met Canadian requirements, as is or with conditions. Or, it could inform Telesat that neither of Hughes's proposals was acceptable and suggest to Hughes that it consider building an RCA-designed satellite, with an opportunity of participation by SPAR Aerospace and United Aircraft of Canada as subcontractors. However, if the cabinet rejected all three of these options and confirmed Canadian procurement, Kierans's memo suggested, then to strengthen the economic viability of Telesat the government should provide it relief from customs and sales taxes, provide development assistance of $15 million from industrial assistance programs, and purchase $30 million in equity in Telesat Canada.

The memo provided the chronological background leading up to Telesat's decision in favour of Hughes, along with a summary of the grounds for that decision – first, Hughes's price was lower; second, the capacity of the Hughes satellite was higher; third, "the risks of developing a new design of satellite are less with the more experienced contractor." Telesat's board had calculated that even the lower-cost Hughes satellite required almost $90 million in capital. At this level, the corporation would not be commercially viable unless additional revenue were forthcoming. The 12-channel Hughes satellite would have three additional channels for rent, RCA none. Therefore Hughes permitted 40 per cent more revenue and a profit margin of 10 per cent. Kierans's memo declared that the board had reported to the minister that it could not reconcile the objective of the corporation as a "commercially viable operation" while at the same time "making maximum use of Canadian industry" through the RCA acquisition.

In the light of later developments, though, one argument of Kierans's was especially noteworthy. He emphasized that RCA's bid was not alone in promising future Canadian participation in space-related manufacturing or the export sale of aerospace technology. Kierans made use of two arguments urged on him a few weeks earlier by Allan Gotlieb, his deputy minister.[20] Hughes itself was prepared to transfer technology – especially electronics – to a Canadian contractor (Northern Electric). Hughes also promised to provide product mandates to Canadian subcontractors – that is, to incorporate Canadian-built sub-systems in the satellites that it sold to Hughes's American and world-wide customers.

Kierans also made the point that the only possible cost of a decision to go with Hughes would be the inability to build complete spacecraft in Canada. The foreign sales possibilities for complete communications satellites in competition with American industry were never very convincing, he argued. Instead, consideration of foreign sales had always emphasized Canadian sub-system capacity. As Gotlieb had suggested, "Rather than pressing for an already advanced technology in the 4 and 6 GHz bands, Canada should proceed [as a subcontractor] to the next generation of communication and broadcast satellites." In sum, Ottawa should use government programs to build new technology in advanced sub-systems and promote development of advanced techniques in new and expanding fields of satellite use, such as satellite broadcasting.

When Kierans made these points in cabinet, he did so with reference to the special lengths to which ITC seemed prepared to go in order to buttress RCA's claims to superior R&D content, suggesting that RCA would be prepared to promise anything, provided that it could do so with the public's money. Moreover, he asked, what other industry was about to do without the $10 million that ITC had promised RCA to help with its R&D? "Or has ITC ten million too much cash?" he asked, rhetorically, in his memo. "Or does ITC intend to ask for supplementary estimates?" Unqualified concern over Canadian content and R&D placed at risk the cabinet's entire rationale behind formation of Telesat Canada as a mixed enterprise. The indefinite terms of RCA's bid with respect to both final cost and date of delivery severely reduced the attractiveness of Telesat to potential investors.[21]

Such a course, Kierans pointed out, would leave the government to explain and correct several consequences. Specifically, it would have to postpone the public equity offering for the crown corporation, thus threatening the 1/3, 1/3, 1/3 shareholding formula; open new negotiations with RCA on the exact terms of a new contract; leave everything to sit until 1973–74; and incur increased costs and risk. Elaborating on the last point, Kierans continued: "There is no means of estimating the cost of a possible new arrangement which may be negotiated with RCA or another Canadian agency. The range of bids is from $42–63 million. These would mean additional government cost of $14–35 million, as well as another $30 million in capital since no public offering will be possible in these circumstances. Finally, the position of the carriers is not known."

If Eric Kierans had been tutored in political science, and had thereby been impressed by Graham Allison's rational policy model, he might have been willing to leave matters there.[22] Instead he campaigned to alter the climate of public opinion. He knew that he needed to counter the bias of the coverage being given the issue in most of the media and so attempted to convince the editorial boards of major Canadian newspapers, which were generally unsympathetic to the Hughes option. In this campaign, he adopted two main tactics. He put Frank Howard on the job of supplying the media with material calculated to counter their tendency to focus only on the "jobs in Montreal" or the "Canadian R&D" story line. According to Richard Gwyn, Howard also played a key role in "counterleaking against leaks by Drury and Mackasey."[23] Howard did a "good job of manipulating the media, about which he felt very guilty, giving the press the 'right squibs and the right time' and many leaks: a brilliant performance."

Kierans also paid personal visits to some editorial boards in Montreal and Toronto. This effort won strong praise from some of the partisans on Kierans's side of the debate. For example, David Golden, then president of Telesat, has expressed his gratitude to Kierans for his willingness to "go to bat" so publicly on behalf of the corporation.[24] He felt that Kierans's action had quite a positive impact on the public's perception, and eventually the government's perception, of the appropriate priorities bearing on the satellite acquisition. Moreover, Kierans himself feels that his visits did alter the stances of at least some papers.[25]

In the event, Kierans's efforts did produce one of the more interesting anecdotes of the whole debate. Among the editors whom he visited was Claude Ryan of *Le Devoir*, who had complained fairly vigorously about Kierans's supposed insensitivity to the aspirations of the Québécois towards better employment opportunities and his lack of concern for the drift of economic activity out of Montreal, which the predicted demise of RCA's industrial and R&D capacity was hardly likely to stem. Kierans told Ryan that his department had checked the list of 140 personnel that RCA claimed would be laid off: "Only one of them is a francophone, Claude," Kierans remembers saying, "and he sweeps the floor." This and other rejoinders to Ryan's principal criticisms began to do the trick, and Ryan began to soften a little. Nevertheless, towards the close of the discussion, Ryan remarked that this was all very well, but "Mr. Kierans is a very bad Minister." "And why is that, Claude?" asked Kierans. Replied Ryan: "Because a good Minister would have provided me with this information before I had written my editorials."

Meanwhile, back in Ottawa, none of this effort was producing much discernible change where it mattered – in the minds of the prime minister and the rest of the cabinet. This left Kierans with only one more "play" – to put his cabinet job on the line. However, he did this in a way that included the finesse alluded to earlier. He placed his threatened resignation in the context of the mess that the government would be letting itself in for if it refused to do what he insisted it must. One might have expected a sober, even sombre summary of arguments used to date and a lofty appeal to the national interest. However, Kierans made a somewhat more base appeal to his colleagues' instincts for political survival.

As Kierans describes it, the turn-around was finally produced by fear of embarrassment. In an exclusive meeting with Pierre Trudeau, Kierans asked the prime minister to contemplate how much credibility the government would retain if a satellite built by RCA Ltd. of Montreal "flamed out" on the way to its geo-stationary orbit – a not implausible outcome, given RCA's technical immaturity in the satellite field.[26] What if this dramatic failure were to happen after Kierans himself had resigned over the cabinet's rejection of a satellite built by Hughes Aircraft, as originally recommended by its own appointed board at Telesat? This prospect finally changed Trudeau's position, and after the prime minister had changed his mind, it was not long before the rest of the cabinet followed suit. And so Canada's national stakes in domestic satellite telecommunications were served by the government of Canada after all.

Of course, the matter may not have been quite as neat as this retelling of it by Eric Kierans would suggest, although it appears from the record to be essentially accurate. The ground had been well prepared for introducing doubts about RCA's competence to deliver a working piece of space hardware. The cabinet itself had expressed concerns about the relations between the management of RCA and its American parent, RCA Inc. Moreover, documents from the Department of Communications suggest that RCA was simply not competent, either technically or managerially, to do the job within acceptable levels of risk. Perhaps the most convincing of these documents will suffice to stand for all the rest, since it constitutes unmistakeable evidence that RCA Inc. itself had almost no confidence in the ability of its Canadian subsidiary to actually do the job. As late as the first week of July 1970, less than three weeks before the cabinet finally confirmed Telesat's decision against RCA, the parent firm, to all intents and purposes, withdrew from the competition.

RCA Ltd. in Montreal had sought written confirmation from its parent corporation for a $39-million bid to Telesat, which would have reduced the disparity between RCA Ltd.'s most recent bid and the competing bid from Hughes. A memo to Kierans from his deputy minister describes his latest meeting with the president of RCA Ltd.: "Despite earlier 'green light' from parent, the President of RCA told [President Houlding of RCA Ltd.] to withdraw latest RCA bid. The only proposal the parent company would back was on a 'cost reimbursement basis,' during development stage, followed by a target price with incentives. They would forego profit, but would provide no guarantee whatever as to cost performance, patents and delivery."[27]

As if this were not enough to destroy RCA's credibility as a prospective contractor, there was further evidence of a severe personal failure of nerve on the part of the Canadian firm's chief executive: "Throughout the conversation, Houlding appeared to be shaken, apologetic and deeply disturbed. He emphasized that the reason behind the parent decision was an unwillingness to compete with the leading and most experienced U.S.A. manufacturer of commercial satellites [Hughes] on any basis whatsoever, except the elimination of all risks." To drive the point home, however, by the time that Kierans was taking this whole matter to cabinet, he had further arguments and evidence that the bid from RCA should not be taken seriously:

The fact that their incentives were of little significance to them and that they subsequently withdrew their fixed price proposal would justify one in thinking that they were not very sure of their own ability to fulfil the contract. I have had a very embarrassing experience with this company involving a price increase on a contract from $4.5 million to approximately $13 million. It was my conviction that a little more engineering and a little less political activities around Ottawa would have materially contributed toward a lower price and a better product. [The] Company has been making some extremely wild claims which from a technical point of view leave a lot to be desired.[28]

Even if all these departmental memoranda were not included in the cabinet documentation prior to the final decision, it seems likely that "the word would have got around" concerning the simple incompetence of RCA to do the job expected of it, and, even failing that, one suspects that Kierans himself would have made this type of evidence known verbally to Trudeau and his colleagues. Kierans's decisive reference to a "flame-out" of the satellite was probably taken by some of his colleagues not entirely on its own terms but rather as a graphic way to signify the more general technical deficiencies of the RCA option.

AFTERMATH

However one accounts for the force of Kierans's "coup de grâce" against the RCA bid, it is clear that it came at the end of a long, difficult, and, until the last minute, extremely one-sided struggle. It does seem fair to characterize the episode as a conflict between the national interest and a host of more particular special interests and to argue that the former prevailed over the latter only because of some extraordinary effort and commitment on the part of one minister in the government. Moreover, there is yet another angle from which to see whether Eric Kierans was the main line of defence of the true national interest on this issue. This is to inquire how the national interests identified at the beginning of this account have fared since Kierans quit the government and left Telesat Canada to the un-tender mercies of interest-group politics.

Only two points emerge clearly enough to deserve attention, but they are of interest. First, the "mixed enterprise" formula has been gradually compromised since Kierans left office. Events have gradually worked in favour of the "carriers' carrier," as opposed to the "state instrument" view of the corporation. The cabinet and the Canadian Radio-television and Telecommunications Commission (CRTC) have not sustained, in the short tradition of the first minister of communications, the effort to keep Telesat Canada out of the grasp of the TransCanada Telephone System and other corporate interests.[29] Second, the "Kierans approach" to R&D was also proved subsequently to be right, or at least much closer to being right than most other players were prepared to accept at the time. In brief, there were real pay-offs to the strategy of giving priority to sub-system development through participation in future Hughes contracts instead of subsidizing RCA's plan to "reinvent the wheel" at its Montreal plant. The strategy paved the way to the subsequent success of SPAR Aerospace (later of "Canadarm" fame, among other accomplishments), and it may have given a boost to Northern Telecom in the same manner.[30]

The objection could be raised that nothing in the above argument proves that the Hughes award was the only or even the best way of meeting these objectives, or the best or only way of guaranteeing that Canada was "the first with the best" in domestic satellite communications. In the event, Canada was precisely this: ANIK was completed by Hughes and launched in April 1971, well before any comparable American system was ready. Whether RCA, too, might have served this crucial dimension of the national interest we shall never know, although most available evidence would seem to support the doubters.

CHAPTER EIGHT

From Minister to Critic

Kierans had indeed prevailed, at the end, in the story of Telesat. The bitterness, however, was hard for him to stomach. Having brought himself to the brink of resignation a second time in the Trudeau government, he found it difficult to carry on as though nothing had happened. For a couple of months after the resolution of the Telesat issue, Kierans pondered his departure from the cabinet. It is sometimes said that politicians and officials in government can be bitten by the bug of "finally winning one"; but for Kierans, the one big victory was Pyrrhic, not addictive. He had had enough, and by the autumn of 1970 he gradually became determined to go. However, his resignation did not take place until the following spring. The delay was the result not of prevarication but of the October crisis and the invocation of the War Measures Act. After that tumultuous period, Kierans prepared to leave government and then launched a new career as a public intellectual – and scathing critic of the government that he had left.

TRUDEAU TAKES A STAND

Kierans's part in the deliberations and decisions of the government during the course of one of Canada's deepest peacetime traumas – the kidnapping of British diplomat James Cross and the kidnapping and murder of Quebec cabinet minister Pierre Laporte – provides little beyond what has already been said, often with eloquence and acumen, in existing studies of these events.[1] The principle of collective government responsibility and the rule of cabinet secrecy must be fully respected on an issue of such deep controversy and heavy substance, and Kierans has declined to place on the record any detailed impressions of the government's conduct during the crisis. He has said, though, that he "does not disagree with anything" that he read in Donald Jamieson's diary of the event published in *Saturday Night* magazine in 1988.

This source, then, provides some clues as to where Kierans stood on some of the central issues surrounding the October crisis, such as whether or not the cabinet acted on the basis of concrete evidence of an impending insurrection – which Jamieson clearly felt it did not. It seems clear that Kierans suspected that the massiveness of the federal governments's response to what it did know had much to do with the perceived weakness of Robert Bourassa, at the head of a fractured Quebec cabinet, as well as Pierre Trudeau's determination to prevent success for the FLQ from undermining the federalist position in Quebec. Kierans has expressed admiration – which runs counter to Denis Smith's strong and profound criticism of it – for Trudeau's personal conduct of the government's responses during the crisis. According to Richard Gwyn, Kierans described the prime minister's performance as "Very cold, very tough, totally determined. He never lost his cool, he was always in command. It was very, very impressive."[2]

If this is enough to suggest that there is some ambivalence in Kierans's outlook on the crisis – some concern about possible over-reaction in the substance of Trudeau's approach sitting uncomfortably with strong admiration for its form – it is of some interest to understand how this might be. The most likely explanation lies in the fact that this was one of the few occasions on which the cabinet of Pierre Trudeau consciously acted on behalf of – indeed, acted *as* – the Canadian state. Eric Kierans no doubt would have loved to have seen similarly decisive, though appropriately scaled down, "state" action during the early phases of the Lapalme affair, which in some respects represented more widespread and conspicuous violence and disorder than the October crisis. (This lends some irony to the fact that Kierans was one of the few Canadian politicians – as opposed to business people – singled out for personal vilification in the FLQ manifesto, which also included the "guys at Lapalme" on its list of alleged victims of the "aggression organized by high finance and the puppet governments in Ottawa and Quebec.")[3]

Perhaps because Kierans had felt let down by the cabinet's cave-in during the Lapalme affair, his sole public defence of its use of the War Measures Act stressed the importance of firm and confident government action in response to anarchic threats to public order. In a speech delivered at the peak of the tension, Kierans maintained that the politics of Quebec and Canada had to halt the recent "drift into the self-fulfilling prophecy of terrorism":

Stopping this drift was also the government's intention last week when it temporarily invoked the War Measures Act to protect the democratic institutions which are the only acceptable instruments of peaceful social change in our country. By its action the government demonstrated that Canada is not in the classical pre-revolutionary stage where the authorities are so consumed with self-doubts that they are incapable of action. Not to have acted would have indicated a lack of confidence in the democratic institutions through which the people of Canada chose their leaders.[4]

Kierans's conclusion to this speech makes this theme – and the possible parallel with the Lapalme strike – even more conspicuous: "Until it can be shown that violence will not work, there will be continued violence. That is what the War Measures Act was meant to do; that is *all* it was meant to do."[5]

One suspects that Kierans may also have been as impressed with Trudeau as he was during the crisis because of the contrast between Trudeau's conduct during that episode and his lack of leadership with respect to economic policy. Jamieson contrasts Trudeau's actions during the October crisis with his general failure to give leadership to his cabinet colleagues: "He never articulates his own philosophy on any issue or gives the cabinet a frank declaration of his views on most subjects. He makes no serious effort to establish a communion with his colleagues or to shape a strong shared commitment. Contrary to the impression given by newsmen, he does not dominate the cabinet, nor, on most issues, does he exert leadership from the beginning of the discussion. In cabinet, he is essentially a listener."[6] Jamieson is led to these observations by puzzling over a different contrast: he found it difficult to reconcile the Pierre Trudeau of the War Measures Act crisis with the more familiar one, especially with respect to his normally high regard for human rights.

Thus, like Kierans, Jamieson saw a large disparity between Trudeau's determination and decisiveness during the October crisis and his general indifference to the requirements of governance. One could, of course, argue that determination and decisiveness are intrinsic to successful crisis management, but it seems more likely that what moved Trudeau to such unequivocal application of the full power of the state was his view of FLQ terrorism as an all-too-predictable extension of his real enemy, French-Canadian nationalism. In his earlier writings, Trudeau had closely associated this nationalism with both racism and totalitarianism, and both of these have been historically associated with terrorist political tactics.[7] The invocation of the War Measures Act dramatizes the almost total singularity of Trudeau's political agenda.

As we have seen, Kierans had recently experienced Trudeau's general indifference to the requirements of good government and the frustration that it could create for anyone with a more inclusive agenda and a deep sense of the more conventional needs that governments must meet in serving the national interest. Despite his bitter frustration over this dimension of the Telesat debate, however, Kierans further put off his intended resignation for the duration of the FLQ crisis, out of fear that, regardless of its declared motives, any minister's resignation would be bound to stir up a lot of misunderstanding and possibly even further instability.[8] Likewise, by the time the Cross/Laporte crisis had passed, the Telesat story was close enough to a successful conclusion that it seemed reasonable for Kierans to wait a few more months and be present at the launching of Canada's ANIK satellite, the culmination of one of his few successes in Ottawa. But, as Allan Gotlieb has observed, Kierans really spent his last few months in the cabinet "writing his way out of it."[9] Kierans was preoccupied with a paper on economic policy that he was determined to get before the public. He could write this piece, though not publish it, as a member of the government. In due course, ANIK went up, Kierans got out, and the paper came down – all in the spring of 1971.

THE PRESSURES OF PARLIAMENT

It is no accident that Kierans's address of June 1971 to the Learned Societies was a careful and comprehensive critique of Canadian economic policy. This speech, given at Memorial University in St John's, Newfoundland, indicates the degree to which he felt that his potential contribution on this front had been passed over, or at least under-used, in Ottawa. At times his chagrin and disappointment boiled up into positive resentment. This resentment had been fuelled for three years by the flack that Kierans had to take in the House of Commons – a forum in which he seemed destined to display only his troubles and shortcomings, never the strengths and passions that he ultimately invested in his speech at Memorial.

A careful reading of Hansard shows that Kierans's portfolios, particularly as postmaster general, generated a lot of specific questions regarding the provision of postal services to particular ridings.[10] To Kierans, it must have seemed at times as though every MP in the country saw himself or herself as the sacred guardian of his or her riding's mail service. Granted, while mail delivery may not be the stuff of high politics that lured Kierans into running for office, it is quite undeniably the backbone of old-time Canadian politicking. Kierans, then, was charged simultaneously with the challenging task of leading the post office out of the gloomy shadows of nineteenth-century patronage politics, along with the more intellectual task of ushering Canada's communications policy towards the sunlit uplands of twenty-first-century technology.

The records of parliamentary debate indicate that it was not the idea of updating the postal system that so rankled opposition MPs: few were prepared to defend the performance of a department that was losing more money each year than some departments were given to spend. Rather it was the visible and tangible effects of the new austerity in the post office that led to the many grand and disparaging soliloquies which, for the most part, Kierans suffered resignedly. It was the politically difficult decisions to end six-day delivery, close money-losing depots, and raise postal rates that precipitated the most vociferous attacks in parliament.

Seldom a day passed that Kierans was not forced to expand on the nature of and rationale behind reductions in service from Kamloops to Cape Breton. This rather mundane duty he carried out with tireless efficiency, and while he showed little interest in giving the opposition any more information than was specifically requested, he would also not hesitate to reiterate the seriousness of the commitment made by his government to carry through on the policy that it had undertaken. To some extent, then, Kierans began to seem the very personification of the cool, deliberate, and rational decisions that were being made, under his stewardship, within Canada's postal system.[11]

The postmaster general's job had always been rather tedious and thankless, as there was seldom much credit to be won for overseeing a highly visible yet perennially money-losing public service. Opposition MPs wasted no opportunity to remind Kierans that his portfolio had a high turnover, possibly to undermine his confidence, but more likely to associate his name and reputation directly with the increased costs and decreased services that all Canadians were to experience in one form or another. Whatever their motivation, it was he, and he alone, who bore the brunt of the continual attack on the government's plans for the post office.

It was undoubtedly with some degree of relief that Kierans was eventually able to report to the House of Commons that a commission had been appointed to study the feasibility of turning the post office department into a crown corporation. This move would have both rationalized procedures and removed a perpetual thorn from the government's side. Both of these effects could hardly have suited Kierans better. In fact, on one occasion, when a member asked

Kierans if his program for automation of the postal service "will proceed to the extent of dispensing with the office of Postmaster General," Kierans shot back, "I would enjoy it."[12]

When constructive criticisms or tangible alternatives were actually offered on government policy, Kierans was perhaps a little condescending in his warm reception of them, but he did seem genuinely interested in responding with thorough and informative answers. It was only as Kierans's term wore on that he allowed himself to get caught up in the more intense partisanship of the House, and even then it was usually through a provoked response to particularly long-winded and pontifical remarks from a member opposite. When he was suitably aroused, however, Kierans showed no hesitancy in unleashing a fairly acerbic wit, well fortified with allegories that may well have left less formally educated members behind.[13]

It is unfortunate, in the light of this sort of repetitious verbal fencing, that the nature of Kierans's portfolios affords only rare glimpses of the man's potential as both a defender and a creator of public policy. There are indications that he held well-conceived and highly principled notions on the issues of the day as well as on the broader questions of appropriate long-term policies. When Kierans was able to address economic policy, he did so with a didactic zeal that better approximated the relationship between professor and students than that between government minister and loyal opposition. Similarly, the prepared policy statements that Kierans read to the House often had a spontaneous, even effusive quality that revealed a consistent moral outlook.

One particular debate not only displays Kierans as a parliamentarian but also foreshadows more significant events and contains deeper meaning. Kierans was taking advantage of an opportunity to speak about the topic closest to his heart, economic policy – in this instance, a debate on the "unpegging" of the Canadian dollar. The tone of the exchanges between Kierans and such opposition members as George Hees is crucial. Kierans did sound at times to be giving the House a lecture on the political economy of exchange rates and international trade.

Perhaps partly for this reason, opposition members went out of their way to discredit Kierans's competence, particularly through heckling him over the state of the mail service. For example, as Kierans was trying to say that "We should resist, even when we cannot prevent, the introduction of such policies as the tariff protection suggested by the people opposite," Hees interrupted with, "Stop reading and tell us about the Post Office, Eric."[14] Later during the same speech, when Kierans stated that "Floating rates will work only if they are really floating and not if they are manipulated in the way they were in 1960–62," an honourable member interjected, "You look after the floating mail."

The parliamentary record, with its constant criticism of changes in the mail service and repeated needling of Kierans himself, provides a perspective on Kierans's ultimate resignation from the cabinet. It suggests that his stated reasons for leaving Parliament may not have been his only ones. Kierans claims credit (I think fairly) for resigning on a matter of principle, in particular out of frustration with what he saw as the government's neglect of economic policy. However, his resignation should also be placed in the broader context of the blows to his reputation and credibility brought on by his single-minded (and largely single-handed) defence of Canada's national interest in achieving cost-efficient postal services.

Kierans saw himself as a potential minister of finance. It was bad enough to discover the degree of resistance to that idea in the upper levels of the Liberal party and the civil service; but the last straw must have been personal ridicule in the House even while he was attempting a small contribution to more general debates on economic policy, his real interest in politics. Kierans, of course, simply had to learn to "roll with the punches" of parliamentary debate, but it must have taken its toll, especially as opposition members (and occasionally editorialists) often buttressed their criticisms of his speeches or policies on other topics – particularly economic ones – with references to his very unpopular actions as postmaster general. When Kierans attempted in the House to condemn inflationary tendencies inherent in Social Credit's economic policies, the proverbial "Hon. member" heckled, "Tell us something about stamps."[15] This phrase could almost serve as an epitaph to Kierans's failure as a federal minister.

In the end, the single overriding impression of Kierans that one gets from Hansard is of a minister who was, at least in the beginning, convinced of both the economic and philosophical strengths of the policies that he was called on to defend. This sense of conviction, while not necessarily rare in political circles, certainly helped Kierans to weather the unrelenting criticisms and insinuations regarding the purpose and consequences of the policies that he promoted. It was a characteristic that he also displayed in the biggest battle that he ever fought in Ottawa – his selection of Hughes over RCA to construct Canada's first communications satellite. He won that battle, and, if the subsequent story of Canadian industrial policy is to be believed, so did the country.

Many Canadians might therefore be entitled to wish that he had not lost so many others.

LETTER OF RESIGNATION

Apart from "economic policy forays" in the House of Commons and, later, his speech of June 1971 to the Canadian Economics Association, Kierans also recorded his opposition to the main pillars of the government's economic policy in his letter of resignation from the cabinet on 28 April 1971. There was little scope for a full explanation of his reasons for that opposition, although one sentence anticipated his imminent speech at Memorial University: "Tax concessions that force the pace of our raw material exports or favour the over-employment of capital, which we have to import, at the expense of labour which is in surplus would not be consistent with long-run Canadian growth and employment objectives."[16]

The prime minister's reply was brief. It referred to the concern for the economic future of Canada that Trudeau claimed the two men shared: "While your own views have not always prevailed in the frequent discussions the Cabinet has had on this subject, they have nevertheless added a dimension that has helped provide the broad perspective within which our decisions have been made." Kierans would have been mindful of his failure to persuade Trudeau that he deserved to be appointed, if not minister of finance, then at least minister for some department such as Energy, Mines and Resources with responsibilities bearing directly on Canada's economic performance.

A SPEECH AT MEMORIAL

In June 1971, after his much-delayed resignation in late April, Eric Kierans delivered the single most important paper of his life to the annual conference of the Canadian Economics Association.[17] In it he developed initial insights and data that were to inform a whole series of his publications through the 1970s, including most notably his report on resource policy for the province of Manitoba, to which this discussion turns in the next chapter. It also caught the eye and stirred the interest of a body of Canadian political economists, who followed its lead into a radical reconsideration of Canada's economic position through the 1970s and beyond.[18] In short, the paper at Memorial University staked out, in one highly concentrated piece of readily accessible analysis, all of the economic arguments with which Kierans has been identified since. It therefore marks his transition from politician to public intellectual. Kierans was never to hold government office again, and in that sense his days as a political actor were over. However, the address was actually the beginning of a new career, one of holding the country's other political actors to account. The public man had embarked on a new mode of giving effect to his sense of responsibility to the country.

All this began with a speech to a gathering of Canada's main-stream academic economists. It was, quite simply, a block-buster. Despite its academic style and reasoned, closely argued analysis, it was in fact a release of all the pent-up frustration that Kierans had accumulated vis-à-vis Trudeau's economic policies of the previous three years. It pulled few punches and showed several signs that its origins lay in its author's experiences as a member of government. For example, these were the paper's opening sentences:

On August 26, 1970, the Minister of Finance wrote to the provincial finance ministers and treasurers, proposing a modification to the [taxation] White Paper proposals that would permit metal mining companies to deduct $4 from mining profits for every $3 invested in new facilities for the processing of mineral ores to the prime metal stage or the expansion of existing mining facilities. With such a promised windfall, an upsurge of new investment plans in the industry could be predicted. In the event, capital expenditure plans for 1971 have risen by 62 per cent, from an estimated $435 million in 1970 to a projected $706 million. The possible tax-exemption value of the deduction of $4 depreciation for every $3 spent therefore amounts to $235 million more than the $706 actually invested. How much of that $706 million would have been invested in any event because of a strong and increasing world demand for natural resources is another question. It is sufficient to say that the metal mining industry can contemplate a profit horizon extended by $235 million, unclouded by the gruesome approach of federal revenue officers.

Kierans pointed out that on 3 December 1970, the minister of finance made a similar budgetary move to assist manufacturing and processing enterprises, now permitted to value new investment in machinery, equipment, and structures at 115 per cent of their actual cost as a base for earning capital cost allowances: "Mr. Benson noted that his new instrument of fiscal policy would increase significantly the net return on capital investment, encourage new capital projects, and speed up (bunch would be the better word) the implementation of capital outlays planned for the future." As a result, $500 million of corporate profits earned by companies making such investments would be freed from corporate tax. However, investment intentions for 1971 in manufacturing already amounted to $3 billion, causing Kierans to wonder again what greater surge in capital expenditures the minister could count on in response to "his gift."

Use of this sort of fiscal instrument was not new to Canada, said Kierans. In fact, he provided a litany of the accumulating tax breaks granted industry by a series of finance ministers. In March 1949, Douglas C. Abbott introduced a form of accelerated depreciation whereby a company could deduct two-thirds of the cost of equipment with an estimated life of fifteen years in the first five years, whereas formerly an allowance was granted on the basis of actual wear and tear of assets used in earning the income subject to tax. Similarly, on 15 April 1955, the budget of Walter Harris ushered in the strongest investment boom in Canada's history, to that point, by making "a permanent part of our law" special tax provisions for oil, mining, and gas industries. Harris also introduced the practice of permitting corporations to report depreciation to shareholders on the basis of actual wear and tear but to record depreciation to tax authorities on the basis of maximum tax advantage under regulations. Profit as recorded on the books of corporations began to diverge sharply from income reported for income tax purposes. On 20 December 1960, Donald Fleming announced double depreciation rates in the first year for investment in new products or in designated areas, and on 20 June 1961, he announced a further new incentive in the form of a 50 per cent increase in the rates of capital cost allowances applicable to new assets acquired prior to 31 March 1963.

Finally, Kierans told his audience, in April 1962 the minister of finance offered "a new series of tax gimmicks," extending tax exemptions to the oil, gas, and mining industries and allowing corporations to pad their costs and reduce their tax liabilities by recording on their tax returns 150 per cent of the actual amounts spent on research, "the 'in' concern of Canadians at the time."

It is difficult not to be cynical or critical of the officials who prepared the budget addresses in those years that had the Minister proclaim in his exuberant and optimistic fashion that these measures designed to expand the capacity and improve the efficiency of Canadian industry would turn the economy around. The problem was not to expand capacity; capacity was already there, built up during the great investment boom of the late fifties. With unemployment at 7% and excess capacity, economic policy dictated an expansion of demand. But tight money choked off domestic demand and drove up the exchange rate so that manufacturers could not, with their newly built plant, effectively penetrate export markets either ... Canadians never did get the advantage of the productivity inherent in their increased capital stock by the longer [production] runs and lower costs that expanded demand, domestic and export, would have given them. The capacity was there, both physical and human, but the demand was shut off by a monetary policy that worked in the opposite direction to the fiscal incentives. Operating at less than capacity, the inflexibility of excess investment in plant and equipment and overhead costs had to be worked off and prices remained sticky and even rose during the period.

Characteristically, Kierans closes this passage with an aside concerning one of his persistent themes, the excessive and misguided influence of the Ottawa bureaucracy: he expressed sympathy with "Mr. Diefenbaker's intuition that somehow, somewhere, he was not getting the best advice from his officials."

Kierans provided more data to show that in Ottawa an idea, once adopted, dies hard. That idea was to boost physical investment at whatever cost to the treasury, and all would be well. Walter Gordon's budget did the same thing, experimenting with tax incentives to encourage Canadian ownership and regional development, which forced a 60 per cent increase in capital expenditures between 1963 and 1966. Meanwhile, social investment (essentially housing) levelled off and began to decline as interest rates rose and monetary policy tightened. "Canada exchanged investment in housing for investment in machinery." Kierans went on: "The fixed costs of the new excess investment were again charged to less than anticipated sales causing prices to remain high and rising. Excess and wasteful capacity, deliberately created by government subsidies to bunch investment decisions and to create short-lived booms, means high cost plants and in an oligopolistic tariff-protected economy, the consumer pays these costs and is robbed of the benefits of the new optimum scale as the government, fighting the inflation caused by its own policies, reduces the level of total demand."[19] Kierans's main point, of course, was that in 1970–71, Canada appeared to be once again on the same road.

Expanding demand through cuts in personal income tax was eschewed in favour of promoting an investment boom in the private sector by offering allowances to the mining, petroleum, and manufacturing industries. Kierans then introduced his main theme – the way in which unemployment and foreign ownership were the product of this misguided approach to Canada's economic problems. With a nod, one suspects, to the audience facing him, he continued this way: "Some of you have again called for investment stimulants or incentives. I am completely opposed to them as providing a solution to Canada's long-term chronic unemployment problems. I also believe that they have contributed more than any other single policy to the concentration of American ownership that now exists in Canada. In other words, it is not what the Americans have done to us but what we have done to ourselves." On unemployment, Kierans argued that tax concessions to stimulate investment distort the choices made by economic actors between labour and capital as factors of production. If the choice between factors is not neutral, Kierans stressed, the production path chosen will be inefficient.

Kierans also outlined seven other "structural distortions" that result from government subsidies for the employment of capital and the resulting over-investment that they stimulate. These incentives

1) contribute to the 'stickiness' of prices, as higher-than-otherwise fixed costs reduce the ability of firms to modify their methods of operation in response to fluctuations in demand.
2) place a drag on the economy's capacity to respond to changing wants and preferences, while new products carry a share of the costs of obsolescence, since depreciation allowances confer greater benefit on the long-lived asset than on equipment with a shorter life.
3) favour large capital-intensive firms within an industry as compared with smaller firms, as well as favouring mining, manufacturing and petroleum industries over other industries, such as service industries, who employ less physical capital and more working capital.
4) promote the substitution of capital for labour, as already discussed.
5) add an impediment to the entry of new firms into an industry, as existing firms have a stream of profits that make the tax breaks valuable to them, where new firms may take years to arrive at a comparable position.
6) assuming public expenditures remain the same, force increases in personal tax rates, indirect taxes or the across-the-board corporate tax rate to make up the shortfall in revenue.
7) apply precisely to those industries where foreign ownership is most concentrated, and help finance the expansion of foreign control of the Canadian economy with Canadian funds.

To avoid these distortions, while providing some incentive for new investment, Kierans recommended an economic strategy reminiscent of the views that he first expressed as president of the Montreal Stock Exchange in the early 1960s:

If the quality of living in Canada is to improve, an increasing proportion of total income should be used to satisfy the social and private needs of Canadians as consumers, not as investors. This expanding demand, with a money supply growing more evenly than in the past, will provide all the incentive that private investment needs. And it will be responsible and profitable investment, responding directly to the growing and more permanent elements of demand as foreseen by investors themselves rather than the premature investment decisions that are forced on them by the bribes of tax deductions and result in increased capacity that may or may not be suited to the changing consumer needs and values over the longer run.

By contrast with this economic common sense, we have this vivid encapsulation of the government's grand economic strategy of the post-war period:

When private investment is used as the lead horse in promoting a boom in a high-consumption economy, instability is doubly magnified. The inflationary effects appear long before a high employment level is reached and governments cut back on their expenditures while social needs remain unsatisfied and the central bank slams on the brakes to reduce consumer demand. The cart, that is investment, has been put before the horses of social and private demand and even the businessmen, for whom the government has done so much, have their confidence shaken as they close down the shiny new plants, which they built at government insistence, for the lack of demand. Idle capacity is no more capable of satisfying real social needs than planes put in mothballs.

Having thus set out his critique of past government performance and the essence of his alternative approach, Kierans drove home this matter by means of a set of six tables (reproduced here) designed to reveal just how deep a hole Canadian governments had been digging themselves into for the past twenty-five years. Table 1 compares the book profit of corporations (as reported to shareholders) with their taxable income for the years 1965–68. (Kierans had reminded his listeners of an earlier point about the policy of the Dominion Bureau of Statistics towards corporate financial statistics, developed as a consequence of the extensive use of taxation allowances.) He drew his audience's attention to 1968 as an example: book profits reported to shareholders that year had amounted to $8,350 million while taxable income amounted to $5,021 million. Taxable income thus represented 60 per cent of book profits in 1968, and comparable proportions for the other three years ranged between 56 and 59 per cent.

More important, though, were the reasons for the differences. These Kierans listed simply as non-taxable Canadian and foreign dividends, excess of capital cost allowance over audited depreciation, exempt mining income, depletion, and gains on capital assets.

Kierans went directly to the distorting effects of such taxation allowances, particularly among industrial groups. Hence, Table 2 presents a comparison of book profit before taxes and taxable income, by selected industries, aggregated for the years 1965–68. Taxable income as a proportion of book profit ranged from a high of 90 per cent for "Retail trade" to a low of 5.7 per cent for "Mineral fuels." Kierans drew his conclusion with powerful language: "If foreign ownership dominates the mining and petroleum industries, our tax system has clearly invited this concentration. We have not only extended a warm invitation to foreign capital, but we have told it where to go. If you want to invest in the service industries, we say, you will have to pay taxes on 87% or 90% of your profits. On the other hand, in metal mining you will only have to pay on 13% and in petroleum on 5.7% of your profits. The invitation says in effect, 'come and gut us.'"

But Kierans had more evidence about distortions. Table 3 shows that, for all industries taken together, the larger the firm, the smaller the percentage of book profits subject to tax. In effect, the big get bigger and the small, at best, stay small. Table 4 reveals that tax policies also tended to encourage corporations to retain earnings at the expense of both taxes to government and dividends to shareholders, compared with the likely distribution of corporate income under a strictly neutral tax regime (that is, taxes 50 per cent, dividends 25 per cent and retained earnings 25 per cent).

Tables 5 and 6 set out one last complaint against the Canadian tax system. This concerns deferred taxes. Accounting practices define deferred taxes as "Reserves for Future Income Taxes," but they are understood best as the difference between the capital cost allowance claimed by corporations as a charge against income permitted by tax regulations and depreciation in the form of actual wear and tear on capital assets, as seen by management and auditors and as reported to shareholders. Kierans sees deferred taxes as interest-free loans from government to big business. The amount of these loans is not trivial. Their total value ($931 million in 1966; $495 million in 1968 – see Table 5) represents the extent to which current costs are inflated and profits are reduced for tax purposes.

Deferred taxes are not very productive, either, according to Kierans. Future costs are charged against current income which results in companies spending excessively on often-unproductive factors. Table 6 shows how the total amount of these "loans" had accumulated over 1965–68, reaching an aggregate of $2,778 million by 1968; taxes on corporate profits of over $5 billion thus remained unpaid.

Table 1
Comparison of book profit before taxes and taxable income ($ million) –
all corporations, 1965–68

Year	Book profit	Taxable income	$\dfrac{Taxable\ income}{book\ profit}$ (%)
1965	6,787	4,000	59
1966	7,385	4,100	56
1967	7,521	4,198	56
1968	8,350	5,021	60

Source: Annual Reports, Corporation Taxation Statistics, Dominion Bureau of Statistics (DBS), 1965–68.

Table 2
Comparison of book profit before taxes and taxable income ($ million) –
by selected industries aggregated for 1965–68

Industry	Book profit	Taxable income	$\dfrac{Taxable\ income}{book\ profit}$ (%)
Metal mining	1,707	222	13
Mineral fuels	795	45	5.7
Other mining	374	120	32
Manufacturing	12,745	8,052	63
Construction	993	643	65
Wholesale trade	2,066	1,802	87
Retail trade	1,620	1,445	90

Source: CALURA, Report for 1968.

Table 3
Book profits and taxable income ($ million) by size of corporation (all industries),
1968

	< $1	$1–$5	$5–$25	> $25
Book profit	809	1,007	1,265	4,145
Taxable income	612	701	810	1,960
$\dfrac{Taxable\ income}{book\ profit}$ (%)	76	70	64	47

Source: Unpublished CALURA data, analysed by Gordon F. Logan, program officer, Treasury Board, Ottawa.

Table 4
Distribution of net profit ($ million) before taxes, all corporations, 1965–68

Year	Taxes	Dividends	Retained earnings
1965	2,225	2,672	2,393
1966	2,252	2,721	2,863
1967	2,208	2,925	2,417
1968	2,593	3,101	2,581
1965–68	30%	37%	33%

Sources: Taxes: DBS National Accounts (taxes actually paid do not include deferred taxes).
Dividends and retained earnings: DBS, Corporate Financial Statistics, 1965–68.
Note: This table comprises the total corporate population in each year, but the number of companies differs from year to year as corporations enter and leave.

Table 5
Comparison of capital cost allowances and depreciation ($ million), 1965–68

Year	Capital cost allowance*	Depreciation†	Difference‡
1965	3,259	2,573	686
1966	3,851	2,920	931
1967	3,976	3,173	803
1968	3,930	3,436	495

Sources: DBS, Corporation Taxation Statistics.
* Permitted by the tax regulations as a charge against income.
† Actual depreciation as seen by management and auditors and as reported to shareholders.
‡ Amount by which current costs are inflated and profits are reduced for tax purposes – represents future costs charged against current income which result in a padding of the accounts.

Table 6
Liability for future income taxes ($ million), all corporations, 1965–68

	1965	1966	1967	1968
Reserve for future income taxes	1,472	1,864	2,301	2,778

Sources: DBS, Corporation Financial Statistics.

The amount of $2,778 million represents government loans to business for one specific purpose, to invest in plant and equipment. The loans carry no interest charge whatsoever. This is tax relief extended primarily to capital intensive industries such as mining, oil and gas, and in manufacturing to the larger, capital intensive firms.

The monetary implications are considerable. This 'Bank of Deferred Corporate Income Taxes' with loans of $2,778 million to big business at a zero interest rate compares with the impact of the Industrial Development Bank with loans outstanding in 1968 of $371 million to small business at high interest. It can also be compared to the business loans outstanding of all the chartered banks in Canada which amounted to $7,567 million at the end of 1968.

The government by lending back taxes due is a bigger lender to business than any single chartered bank and the rate of interest is zero. Not only does this lessen the dependence of the largest firms on the banking system, it also reduces the pressure to market new equity issues in Canada. The firms, benefitting from these loans, are immune to monetary policy and changes in the interest rate affect only the customers of the I.D.B. or the chartered banks.

Kierans further predicted – correctly, as we now know – that, short of a massive economic downturn, the size of this account would continue to grow. The practice was encouraging what we now think of as corporate "paper trading" and was probably contributing to the take-over of Canadian firms.

The above review does not exhaust the issues raised in Kierans's speech, but it certainly represents the general weight of the argument. One further point was that if such tax concessions were ended, the across-the-board corporate tax rate could probably be reduced to 40 per cent of profits with no loss of revenue to governments, but with the added benefit of the elimination of inefficient distortions in the allocation of resources. But, having dwelt this long on his argument, we should sum it up in his own words:

Canadian experience in using the tax system to achieve swift growth has not been a happy one. The choice of factors of production has been distorted. Favouring capital favours not only those with capital, foreigners, but regions where capital normally locates, adding to concentration and inflation in high growth areas. All industries have not benefitted equally nor the small and medium size firms within industries. Investment decisions have led to overcapacity for businessmen, like householders, with surplus funds at zero interest rates tend to use those funds prematurely. Social investment, if the taxes had been paid, could have been more productive and beneficial. The private investment booms certainly added to the inflationary pressures and instability, and subsequent monetary policy limited severely government expenditures and investment. It is distressing to see tax policy again operating in 1970–71 to increase capacity and ignoring the demand forces that tax cuts would generate.

Kierans's paper thus presents an early and integrated discussion of subjects that were to occupy much of his public speaking and academic and popular writing for the next fifteen years. Two points, however, are of immediate interest. One is the support for Kierans's views in other studies of post-war Canadian economic policy. The other is the part that these concerns played in his resignation from the Trudeau government.

Kierans's main complaints about Canadian economic policy cannot be widely supported from the work of Canada's academic economists. The policies that Kierans took to task were, and continue to be, derived from Canadian economic orthodoxy, and mainstream academic and government economists have not been inclined towards his kind of criticism of the very policies that they have implemented or sanctioned. However, some Canadian political scientists – a few of whom would prefer to call themselves 'political economists' – and some left-wing economists have produced work that supports much of what Kierans had to say.

There is, for example, a close fit between Kierans's main points and the arguments presented by David Wolfe.[20] The principal similarities have to do with the government's absolute priority of "maximum growth of the economy," its belief that "the best way to achieve this goal was through the encouragement of increased investment in the economy," and the fact that to Canada's economic policy-makers "this could only mean providing public inducements to private investors to bring about the desired outcome." Wolfe provides the early history of accelerated depreciation rates, "accompanied by a host of other incentives designed by the government to stimulate economic expansion," all of them focused on the balance sheets of private firms. He also reviews the use of capital cost allowances and "deferred depreciation."

The strongest support for Kierans in Wolfe's discussion, however, is on the connection between post-war taxation policies and expanded foreign control of the Canadian economy:

The two key government policies of selling off wartime production facilities at reduced prices and of permitting accelerated depreciation allowances were both instrumental in encouraging a high degree of foreign participation in the growth of the Canadian economy. A large number of government plants were sold to foreign enterprises and the accelerated depreciation allowances, which provided one of the fastest rates of tax write-off in any western economy, were a strong incentive to foreign investors. However, the import control policy, instituted in 1947, represented the most direct attempt by the government to induce foreign manufacturers to locate in Canada. In the minds of the government's economic policy-makers the primary goal of the controls was 'import substitution.' The Emergency Exchange Conservation Act was designed to encourage the substitution of domestically manufactured products for imported consumer goods, frequently through the establishment of a branch plant in Canada by the foreign manufacturer.[21]

Wolfe says that there can be no doubt that it was the government's explicit goal to provide "an attractive inducement for encouraging increased industrial expansion and foreign investment in Canada." Growth was the objective, business investment the means; "the origin of the investment capital, whether from domestic or foreign sources, was clearly a subsidiary question, if it was raised at all."

Wolfe argues, paralleling Kierans's analysis, that capital cost allowances and deferred taxes provided a substantial portion of the "total expansion funds" of foreign-controlled enterprises in Canada. In sum, Wolfe and Kierans have focused on similar aspects of Canada's economic policy to arrive at almost identical conclusions about how those policies helped increase dependence on the United States. Both critics would presumably agree with yet another observer's summation of the relationship between the economics and politics of foreign control: "Economic growth in Canada since the Second World War has depended significantly on inflows of foreign investment, direct and portfolio, but these same capital flows have helped to shape an economy characterized by high levels of foreign ownership in some of its most dynamic sectors, and by regional balkanization and closer economic ties between some of its constituent parts and the U.S. than among them. As the Canadian economy has expanded, the structural constraints on the capacity of the national government to direct and regulate it have similarly grown."[22] Eric Kierans, of course, had long believed that the constraints on the Canadian government's capacity to reduce substantially the nation's economic subordination to the United States were not nearly as constricting as most of the Ottawa establishment was inclined to accept. The cool reception in Ottawa to policy ideas based on that perspective finally persuaded Kierans that he had no place in the government. Indeed, as events soon revealed, he was on the verge of leaving the Liberal party.

Kierans set out for Prime Minister Trudeau his opposition to the government's economic direction in October 1972, in the midst of a general election campaign. He wrote to inform the prime minister that, because of the government's economic shortcomings, he intended to vote for the NDP candidate in Mount Royal, Trudeau's riding: "If I were to vote for you," Kierans wrote, expressing his dilemma, "it would mean that I accept and approve courses of action which I firmly believe will worsen our present problems."[23]

Parts of this letter show that economic times were quickly changing and, with them, some emphases in the agenda facing economic policy-makers:

When I resigned from the Cabinet, I expressed my concern over the economic policies of the government and the determination to challenge them in public debate. It seemed like tilting at windmills, at the time, but President Nixon's dramatic reversal of American policy on August 15th, 1971, made people all over the world more sensitive to economic issues and anxious about their own policies. Nowhere has this questioning and critical analysis of long-established policies been more prolonged than in Canada. And yet, there have been very few answers.

We continue to build our policies on the twin pillars of resource exploitation and subsidizing capital expenditures. As you know, I have been completely opposed to both elements. They do not provide the framework on which a free and independent Canadian society can be built. And yet, they have been confirmed by your own commitment to build a $10 billion corridor to the Arctic [to accommodate at least one major pipeline], by the statements of several ministers, notably Donald Macdonald's estimate of a $50 to $70 billion investment requirement during this decade in the energy sector alone and by the Minister of Finance's 2-year depreciation allowance for capital installed after his May 8th budget.

It is my firm belief that these policies will lead to the rising value of the Canadian dollar during the seventies, will damage severely the competitive position of our manufacturing, forest and agricultural industries, will confirm the rising secular rate of unemployment and will increase substantially the degree of foreign domination of the Canadian economy.

Kierans made his frequent complaint about tax concessions to corporations as a means of "forcing the pace of private investment" and set out some of the statistics concerning deferred corporate income taxes, or interest-free loans, in recent years. (He estimated that the amount of such loans to corporations at the end of 1972 would be over $4.5 billion.) More disturbing, Kierans insisted, was the distribution of this government largesse among different classes of firms. According to figures for 1969, reserves for future income taxes stood at $3.2 billion, distributed among 207,424 corporations reported on by Statistics Canada. Slightly over eight-tenths of one per cent (0.8 per cent) of all firms, that is, the 1,710 largest firms in the country, received $2.8 billion of this money, or 89 per cent of it. Meanwhile, the smallest firms in the country – 159,864 of them with assets of less than $250,000 – divided up four-tenths of one per cent (0.4 per cent) of these interest-free loans from the government.

According to Kierans: "Since foreign controlled firms dominate the upper brackets (see Gray Report) and Canadian firms are the conspicuous majority in the small and medium size groupings, our tax policy contributes to increasing foreign ownership. Secondly, it favours and forces size and concentration. To the best of my knowledge, this has never been Liberal policy." Kierans raised another central concern that, while not entirely new, was coming to the forefront in his economic thought and would remain there for the rest of the decade: "It is, however, the government's obsession with resource exploitation that completely baffles me." He cited the "Pigovian" theory (after Cambridge economist Arthur C. Pigou, 1877–1959) that it was the "clear duty of Government" to act as the trustee of unborn generations, as well as of its present citizens. This meant that it must watch over and defend with legislation "the exhaustible natural resources of the country from rash and reckless exploitation." Kierans continued:

There has been no recognition in Canada of this principle, that a nation should husband its resources so as to leave an amount for the use of future generations, at least since 1955 when Walter Harris made resource incentives and tax exemptions a permanent feature of our laws. We have turned over our natural wealth to any and all who would exploit it in return for hazardous and temporary bursts of employment and pitifully small percentages of royalties and taxes.

The principle seems to be that we have this warehouse of natural resources and must cash them in before they are rendered obsolescent by technological change. With the cash, presumably we can finance the technology that will produce the substitutes for the natural resources themselves. One may well ask if we are not simply rationalizing our own greed.

In any event, that possibility is not open to Canadians. We have knowingly alienated our own lands, lands that were turned over to us by the British Crown when we assumed responsibility for our own government.

Kierans illustrated this failure by pointing to the current government's "fixation" with development of the Mackenzie Delta and construction of a pipeline corridor down the Mackenzie Valley. He pointed out that, compared with American policies applied to the oil and gas deposits on Alaska's North Slope, Canada had failed to call for competitive bidding on leases to exploit the Mackenzie Delta, thereby forgoing the opportunity to reap anything like the almost $1 billion of public revenues that Alaska had taken in. Ottawa had also proposed a royalty rate of a mere 5 per cent for the first three years and 10 per cent thereafter, compared with royalties of 21–22 per cent in Alaska.

Can we even recover the $10 billion that you contemplate spending on the corridor to the Arctic? If the royalty rate were 10%, it would require the sale of $100 billion of our resources to justify the venture. Otherwise, the cost would be borne by the taxpayers.

When I contemplate these sums, I can understand the demands of those who call for nationalization of our resources. Only they are wrong. This wealth belongs to the Canadian people and one cannot nationalize one's own possessions. It is government which has given away the 90%–95% of the people's wealth. Neither you or I would handle our own estates in this fashion.

Kierans noted the incompatibility of depending heavily on resource development for economic growth while attempting to spur expansion of manufacturing exports and enhancement of new technology within Canada. Huge capital inflows and balance of trade surpluses in energy and raw materials, he argued, inevitably increase the value of the dollar, reducing Canada's competitive position in world markets for sophisticated manufactured products. "The simple fact is that we cannot build an industrial policy on top of the policy of resource exploitation that we are presently pursuing." The selling off of Canadian assets gives only the appearance of sustainable economic growth.

The letter contains harbingers of a shift in Kierans's criticism of Liberal economic policy towards resources and the proposed Mackenzie Valley pipeline and a closer and more tangible association with the NDP and its nationalist, democratic socialist wing. One passage in his speech at Memorial University had criticized

Canadian policy-makers' failure to recognize that Canada is an ideal supplier to the United States, Japan, and Europe: "It is ridiculous for Canada to sell at bargain prices the advantages (rents) of long-term supply, location, transportation, political stability and security of access."[24] Ottawa was wasting potential revenues through extraordinary tax concessions to resource industries, which would anyway continue developing Canadian resources. Kierans now believed, as caught by a phrase in his letter to Trudeau, that Canada's resources were the property of its people.

Kierans's identification and association with left-wing nationalism were beginning to go much further than voting for an NDP candidate. He had already written the foreword to *Louder Voices*, a book by NDP leader David Lewis that took up the cause of a more neutral tax system in many of the same ways and for most of the same reasons that Kierans had set out in his Memorial University address. He later produced a major policy review for the NDP government of Manitoba.[25] He was even, for a brief and somewhat bizarre moment, considered as a possible new leader of the NDP itself.[26]

Nevertheless, Kierans's key identification with the Canadian left lay more in the very close overlap between his views and those of such prominent left-wing spokesmen as James Laxer and Mel Watkins, gurus of the left wing of the NDP (the so-called Waffle Movement). Time and again through the 1970s, Kierans was to share the spotlight of the media, and sometimes the same public platform, with Mel Hurtig, Jim Laxer, and/or Mel Watkins in driving home his opposition to "giving away" Canadian resources and building an enormous pipeline through the Canadian Arctic so that American consumers could have access to Alaskan natural gas. An earlier chapter on Quebec politics raised the suggestion that Kierans had worked in such close unison with René Lévesque, and had such sympathy with most of his complaints about the overcentralization of Canada, that one might begin to wonder why Kierans was not himself a Quebec separatist. One could similarly note Kierans's sympathy with the views of prominent, left-wing Canadian nationalists and wonder why he did not join (or lead?) the Waffle Movement's campaign to take over the NDP and convert it into a political instrument for the radical reconstitution of Canadian economic policy and Canadian-US relations.

Careful consideration of the theoretical dimensions of this question will form part of the conclusion of this study; for now, it is enough to return to the closing words of his letter to Trudeau, written at precisely the time when Kierans was taking these new policy departures. "I remain a Liberal," he declared. He continued, "Like others – and how many Pauline Jewitts can we afford to lose? – I hope that you will command a full scale Liberal party conference on Canada's economic future. We need desperately this debate on our problems, the search for new solutions to our changing circumstances and the formulation of new policies that will guide this nation in the seventies. Governments, and especially bureaucracies, are not always sensitive to change and that is why we have political parties. The Liberal party is a powerful party. We should use it for thought, new insights and judgement."[27]

An entrepreneurial, liberal spirit himself, Kierans could not bring himself to believe that the bulk of Canadians, even as they became increasingly nationalistic, could ever be persuaded to become socialists – just as he had believed that the bulk of Quebecers were individualists and entrepreneurs at heart and could never be persuaded to become social-democratic separatists. He therefore sought to revitalize and redirect a political party that could hope to win a majority of supporters from among the Canadian people. He wanted, in a phrase, liberal nationalism (or nationalist Liberalism). And what he wanted most was to use such a popularly based liberal nationalism, in the form of a regenerated Liberal party of Canada, to shake up the Ottawa establishment and to wrest control of economic policy from the upper levels of the bureaucracy which was, as he put it mildly in his letter, "not always sensitive to change."

There is published evidence for this interpretation in the closing words of his introduction to David Lewis's *Louder Voices*, whose subtitle, "The Corporate Welfare Bums," served as the NDP's main slogan in the 1972 election campaign:

The tax policies criticized in this introduction are not policies that have emanated from the [Liberal] party itself. Most members would abhor these special privileges, exemptions and concessions as much as I do. They originate in that most stagnant of all Ottawa bureaucracies, the Department of Finance. It is time that the party itself came to the rescue of the government, with new ideas and policies designed to resolve the problems our country faces.

But until that time comes, many of us will follow Mr. Lewis's efforts to inject some realism into this electoral campaign with a great deal of respect and considerable admiration.

Further evidence that what Kierans wanted most was to turn the Liberal party around on economic questions is available in one of his anecdotes from this period. I once asked him about his contacts with Harry Johnson, perhaps Canada's most prolific economist, who occupied positions simultaneously at the London School of Economics and the University of Chicago. Their relationship had been characterized for a number of years by a form of mutually respectful, public sparring over the pros and cons of foreign investment in Canada and related issues. Kierans answered my query about Johnson by sending me this note, attached to a copy of the October 1972 letter to Trudeau already reviewed here: "Apropos of Harry Johnson. Elizabeth [Johnson] and he dropped in on the Sunday afternoon following the date of this letter [to Trudeau]. They were on their way to Ottawa and the letter was then in the mail. I showed it to him and gave him a copy. He said that the first two pages were the clearest summary of Canada's policies that he had seen. He was looking forward to the storm breaking (it was during the election) and the fun that he would have with the mandarins saying 'that Kierans is dead right!' "[28]

The compliment from Johnson was extremely gratifying to Kierans, as was Johnson's prediction that it would create a storm in Ottawa's inner circles. The letter, after all, had presented pretty much a distillation of his speech at Memorial. Kierans might then also have recalled the response to that speech from someone who stood – and still stands – very near the centre of those Ottawa circles, Sylvia Ostry, then chair of the Economic Council of Canada. "I've heard so much about that paper you gave at the Learneds," she had said to Kierans a few weeks after he had returned to Ottawa from Newfoundland, "I hear Jack Weldon wrote it."[29]

Apart from the scabrous suggestion that Eric Kierans might have presented to an academic conference a paper written by anybody else, Ostry's remark carried a hint of plausibility, as all taunting jokes must. Jack Weldon was a long-standing friend and colleague at McGill University's economics department. He was also active in the NDP, a role that included some consulting work with Ed Schreyer's new government in Manitoba. And so Jack Weldon, who had nothing directly to do with Kierans's Memorial paper, had a great deal to do with Kierans's next contribution to the debate over national economic policy. Weldon prevailed on Schreyer to commission Kierans to write a report, for the Planning and Priorities Committee of Manitoba's cabinet, on natural resource policies in the province.

PART THREE

The Unretiring Voice

CHAPTER NINE

Whose Resources Are They, Anyhow?

Kierans's 1973 report on Manitoba's resource policies marks perhaps the culmination of both his thought and his political career to that point. He had been shocked, as minister of revenue for Quebec, to see data showing that the province's income from its resource industries was exceeded by its expenditures in support of those industries. Much of the Manitoba report is devoted to the argument that provincial governments must ensure that exploitation of resources takes place on terms that ensure the maximum benefit for the people of the province.

We have seen as well how Kierans, in his speech at Memorial University, showed how Canada's taxation policies heavily favoured large, resource-producing firms over smaller companies and those in service and manufacturing industries. Data to exactly the same effect are also produced in the Manitoba study, in relation to its major mineral producers. We saw in the previous chapter that Kierans's final falling out with Pierre Trudeau and the Liberal party of Canada was motivated most strongly by his determination to promote rethinking of the country's excessive dependence on primary industries. The Manitoba report examines the proper role of provincial governments in that task. We saw in earlier chapters that Kierans, especially during his years in Quebec, experienced both the creative energy of entrepreneurship and direct accountability to the wider community in which it prospers. Kierans's Manitoba study is regarded by some as a textbook in public entrepreneurship.

In sum, Kierans's examination of resources in Manitoba bears the unmistakeable imprint of the author himself. He had grasped more profoundly than any other Canadian academic or politician at the time the failure of Canada's approach to the use of its resources and the significance of that failure.

The Manitoba government released the report in February 1973.[1] Almost immediately Premier Ed Schreyer publicly repudiated its major policy recommendations – a reaction noted with evident satisfaction by Hedlin Menzies and Associates in a massive critique of the report (over twice as long as the report itself) commissioned by the Mining Association of Manitoba soon afterward.[2] Despite this early, inauspicious response, the report affected provincial and federal resource policies, the attitude of the media to such issues, the political actions of the mining industry, and – as reviewed in chapter 1 – the academic study of resource policy in Canada. The Kierans Report also increased the political salience of resource rents in Canada and may have affected governments in their "choice of instrument" for capturing a greater share of these rents.

Each type of effect stemmed from one of the central thrusts of the report. First, the document was concerned throughout with the economic rents accruing to the owners of natural resources and the idea that the people of Manitoba, not the province's resource producing firms, were the proper beneficiaries of these rents. The report gave extra impetus to the idea that the people of Canada, by virtue of their residence in their respective provinces, own the country's resources and have a right to a share of the wealth that they generate. Second, the report argued that crown corporations were better instruments (compared to royalties, for example) for capturing resource rents, particularly when such corporations converted the basic raw material into a saleable primary commodity. Third, and underlying both of the first two, the report undertook an uncommon economic analysis of the firms in the industry in order to reveal their high degree of corporate concentration and very low effective rates of taxation.

RESOURCE OWNERSHIP AND ECONOMIC RENTS

Chapter 4 of the Kierans Report contains its most extensive elaboration of the theme that Canada's resources are the property of its people. However, the same perspective pervades the rest of the study, and Kierans made the point powerfully early on:

A government is above all responsible to the people for using all their resources efficiently and wisely in accordance with the priorities the people have set. If their credit and capital are squandered, if their labour is not employed and if their resources do not yield the highest possible returns, the government must answer. It is not a question of capitalism or socialism.

It is simply searching for the better way. In any event, one cannot nationalize what one already owns and it is clear that the province owns its own resources. What must be determined is the manner in which one can gain the highest return from that wealth, both now and in the future. This is not a matter of questioning the rights or sanctity of private property. The issue of proprietorship has long been settled. It is public.[3]

From this perspective, Kierans's principal complaint was that the resource industry had swayed governments to dispose of the property of Canadians too cheaply.

Accordingly, chapter 4, "The Manitobans," argued that for too long governments of the province had been satisfied to obtain *employment* in return for the ceding of resources to mining firms, whereas their real responsibility lay in realizing, on behalf of the people, the *wealth* that their resources were capable of generating. The chapter opened by observing how industry had promoted the misleading impression that the province could choose to obtain either revenues or jobs from its resource base.[4] However, his main complaint was the ease with which the industry seemed able to dampen the public's desire for higher returns from their resources by raising uncertainty in their minds about the level of activity that the industry would be willing to maintain under higher tax and royalty regimes. Implicit in the industry's arguments, Kierans claimed, "is the assumption that mining activity will be undertaken by the private sector only under terms and conditions acceptable to it or *there will be no development whatsoever.*"[5]

Thus the apparent suggestion is that "any attempt to improve the returns to the people of a province will result in decline and an end to economic growth. Tax reform in the resource area is made to seem like tempting fate and inviting ruin." Given that public investment in resource extraction would also create jobs according to the same "multiplier" effect as private investment (whatever the real rate of that multiplier might be), Kierans insisted that the price of resource development by private firms – public revenues driven down by threats of a "capital strike" by the industry – is simply too great: governments will have to develop their own resources. "If the private sector is unwilling to recognize that appropriate taxation rates are simply the recognition of and payment for the privilege of vesting resources in private hands ... then development will have to be carried on by government."

The rest of chapter 4 elaborates on this preoccupation of governments with generation of resource-based jobs. It criticizes governments' fixation on encouraging the upgrading of resources within the province before export, especially by means of tax incentives to the mining industry to increase investment in refining and processing. Several tables reveal that refining is not a particularly profitable phase of mineral-based industries: its returns are often far below those of the more basic enterprise of converting the "dirt and rock" into a saleable commodity. Indeed, Kierans argued, some of the "surpluses" available from the primary phase of production can be frittered away by the creation of excess refining capacity or by artificially high returns to capital and labour in the refining sector.

However, Kierans was even more disturbed over the opportunity cost of tax incentives for processing and refining – that is, the public investments that the province might have made in its more general social and economic development if, instead, it had captured a larger share of the original surpluses itself and directed them to these other priorities. Chapter 4, accordingly, was also designed to show just how large these potential public revenues in the form of rents on resource production really were. Kierans made this point most dramatically by comparing the current distribution of surpluses among the province's major resource firms, the provincial government, and Ottawa. Using data on income and taxation for the province's three largest mining firms (International Nickel Co. of Canada [Inco], Sherritt Gordon, and Hudson Bay Mining and Smelting – which together accounted for over 95 per cent of total mining output in the province), Kierans explained:

The value of metals produced in Manitoba by the three corporations during the three years 1968-70 amounted to $676.1 million. The book profits before taxes of the big three totalled $192 million. This constitutes ... the difference between the value of the minerals produced and the costs of that output. The profit generated amounted to 28.4 cents of every dollar of metal produced from Manitoba resources.

Of this 28.4 cents, the people of Manitoba received 2.3 cents as payment for every dollar of resources produced, i.e., $15.6 million in taxes on profits of $192 million from an output of $676.1 million.[6]

He pointed out that the firms also paid federal taxes of about $15 million. He concluded: "By turning over the management of their resources to the private sector the government of Manitoba has given up all but $15.6 million of a total flow of profits of $192 million in 3 years."[7]

Kierans left his most powerful argument to the end of chapter 4. Reading it, one begins to see why the mining industry might have feared the potential appeal of Kierans's views and why (as discussed below) it tried so hard to discredit them:

The annual sale of Manitoba resources is composed of two elements, the costs of production and the surplus. If the surpluses were to remain in Manitoba to be invested in whatever sector would yield greater benefits to the people and the economy, the value of the depleted resources would remain. This is what would happen if the resources were developed by crown corporations. When the surpluses are withdrawn to be invested elsewhere, there is a net consumption of Manitoba resources. Manitoba is poorer although some corporations will be richer. The natural wealth of Manitoba has been converted to their advantage. The costs of developing Manitoba resources, wages and salaries, will have been paid largely to Manitobans but the value of the converted resources, the difference between costs and selling price, become[s] the property of the giant firms and increase[s] their power and influence. The converted wealth will be invested according to their global objectives not the needs of Manitobans.[8]

Clearly, these views were not likely to receive the enthusiastic endorsement of Canadian mining companies.

In fact, the industry based its objections to the report's policy recommendations concerning resource rents on two inconsistent grounds: first, the rents did not exist; second, they were better left in the hands of private enterprise than collected by governments. The arguments that it brought to bear on the former point were informed mostly by economic theory and industry data opposing those used by Kierans; the arguments on the latter used corporate capitalist ideology and sought to undermine the popular appeal of Kierans's recommendations by discrediting him.[9] At least, this is the unmistakeable impression left by the industry's major broadside against the report – the critique of it that the industry commissioned from Hedlin Menzies and Associates. The implicit dialogue between these two documents thus provides an instructive object lesson in the political economy of natural resources.

The Hedlin Menzies report took Kierans to task on three main fronts. First, he had "misappropriated" Ricardian notions of rents obtained by the owners of a fixed stock of land and applied them misleadingly to mineral reserves. The latter, unlike the stock of land, exhibit sufficient "expandability" to ensure that, in ways fatal to Kierans's argument, apparent rents or "super profits" are, at best, "quasi-rents." Second, Kierans had ignored the extent to which "ownership" of Manitoba's resources had in fact been legally transferred to the private firms through the sale of mining leases.

Third, Kierans had combined his inadequate grasp of both these issues into a misunderstanding, if not misrepresentation, of the proper way to evaluate the prices at which the province transfers its resources to private developers; the prices paid historically have reflected a realistic bargain between the two parties, given the overall attractiveness (read "worth") of Manitoba's resources to firms operating in a global market for such resources.

Concerning the distinction between "rents" and "quasi-rents," at issue between Kierans and Hedlin Menzies is the notion that owners of an asset in fixed supply can enjoy unearned income from that asset as demand for it increases, creating a shortage of supply relative to the new level of demand and, hence, a higher price. This notion of unearned income is reflected in the (surprisingly similar) definitions of economic rent set out in the two reports.[10] Each document places a different construction on virtually the same passage from John Stuart Mill's *Principles of Political Economy*, but each proceeds to take off in opposite directions from Mill in relation to policy.

Kierans quotes at length the following argument from Mill to stress the unearned character of rent income and to show that such income should rightly go to the society at large, not to individual "landlords":

Suppose that there is a kind of income which constantly tends to increase, without any exertion or sacrifice on the part of the owners: those owners constituting a class in the community, whom the normal course of things progressively enriches, consistently with complete passiveness on their own part. In such a case it would be no violation of the principles on which private property is grounded, if the state should appropriate this increase in wealth, or part of it, as it arises ...

Now this is actually the case with rent. The ordinary progress of a society which increases in wealth, is at all times tending to augment the incomes of landlords; to give them both a greater amount and a greater proportion of the wealth of the community, independently of any trouble or outlay incurred by themselves. They grow richer, as it were, in their sleep, without working, risking, or economizing. What claim have they, on the general principle of social justice, to this accession of riches? In what would they have been wronged if society had, from the beginning, reserved the right to taxing the spontaneous increase of rent, to the highest amount required by financial exigencies?[11]

Hedlin Menzies responded by quoting a portion of the same passage and, a little further on, by extending the same paragraph from Mill beyond the text presented by Kierans. It did this in order to lend credence to its main theme that, while rents may indeed exist, as a practical (and political) matter their capture by government on behalf of society as a whole is fraught with complications. Hence it argued, Kierans "should have continued to quote the remainder of Mill's paragraph," where Mill recommended making an initial evaluation of land and then, "after an interval had elapsed, during which society had increased in population and capital, a rough estimate might be made of the spontaneous increase which had accrued to rent since the valuation was made ... and in laying on a general land-tax, which for fear of miscalculation should be considerably within the amount indicated, there would be an *assurance of not touching any increase of income which might be the result of capital expended or industry exerted by the proprietor.*"[12]

From this concern of Mill that governments capture rents, but purely rents, accruing to landlords, the Hedlin Menzies report proceeded to make the interesting observation that a similar concern might have explained Kierans's preference for public ownership of resource firms, rather than taxes or royalties, as instruments for the public capture of resource rents. Crown corporations, unlike taxes and royalties, avoid the need to distinguish rents from other profits, either conceptually or in practice, because their earnings directly constitute public income.

Thus Hedlin Menzies used Mill's thoughts on economic rent to establish two concerns with Kierans's approach. First, how do governments capture income currently going to private operators in the form of rents without touching any increase of income that might result from the efforts, technology, or capital spending of the mining firm?[13] Second, how do governments design taxation or royalty regimes that take into account the fact (directly acknowledged by Mill with reference to mining activity) that individual mines "vary in fertility," while the output of all mines sells at a common price regardless of the relative fertility of the mine from which it is derived?[14] If mineral prices are equivalent to the cost at the least productive mine, and all more productive mines thereby earn an economic rent, it follows that rents will vary from mine to mine, according to their relative costs.

Thus a royalty rate, rent charge, or tax rate on property values set at the same value for all leases is not an effective method for capturing economic rents, as it will inevitably affect mining output. Flat royalty rates, applied equally to all properties without regard to their respective richness, will capture some of the economic rent from the most profitable operations, but they will also force reduced output from any marginal mines or ore deposits. Finally, to the extent that rents vary across mines as a result of the relative richness of different deposits, then the rents earned by a given mine can also vary over time, owing to variations in its richness relative to other mines. While its own characteristics of quality and accessibility will be whatever they are, its potential economic rent may go down as better sites are developed elsewhere, or up as competitive sites are depleted and only more costly ones can be developed to replace them. (Most economists would say that the simplest answer to this problem is a tax on profits, although intra-firm transfers and the status of returns on capital complicate this approach, as well.)

It is for this reason that Hedlin Menzies took the Kierans Report to task on another of its principal recommendations. Kierans felt that because Manitoba's resources were the property of its people, the government of the province should act to reassert those rights of ownership by imposing a "property tax on reserves" held under existing leases by private firms and forcing them, at some point in time, to "repatriate" their resource holdings to the crown.[15] Hedlin Menzies, objected that, contrary to Kierans's view, private firms in possession of existing leases on resource properties do in fact own the resources present on the land covered by the lease, provided that the firm meets all obligations (such as rental payments) specified in the lease.

In other words, the province of Manitoba, as landlord, does lose ownership of its property after it signs a lease with a private developer, which for its part automatically and instantly becomes the owner of any minerals mined during the term of the lease.[16] From this perspective, Hedlin Menzies observed that there are really only two possible constructions that one can place on Kierans's complaint that the province is receiving very little income from its leasing arrangements: "It is possible, of course, that the province, by signing the existing long term leases, made a major error of evaluation of the strength of their position. However, it is perhaps equally possible that the modest direct returns to the province represent the best that could be obtained with adequate development of the province's natural resources in competition with those of the rest of the world."[17]

With this line of argument, Hedlin Menzies went to the heart of the debate and, willingly or not, also uncovered one of the central weaknesses of Kierans's analysis – his inattention to the problem of the marketing of resource-based goods and the bargaining power that control over such markets places in the hands of the major firms in the industry. Before delving more deeply into this issue, though, let us review the criticisms – generally less academic than those of Hedlin Menzies – directed at Kierans by the Mining Association of Canada.

INDUSTRY AND GOVERNMENT
REACTIONS

The Mining Association of Canada (MAC) regards Eric Kierans the way we must imagine the New Bedford Whalers' Association felt about Moby Dick. This antagonism was clear in the MAC's reaction to the Kierans Report, and it has lingered to the present day. Even in 1986, the MAC's managing director assessed the report and its author with clear antipathy during an interview on the subject conducted thirteen years after its release, suggesting at one point that parts of the report could have been written only by a man who did not value his integrity.[18] Such resentment of Kierans probably stemmed from his ability to place the industry on the defensive in public. Especially on public ownership of resources, Kierans's thinking threatened to increase greatly the number of Canadians prepared to accept that they were being "ripped off" by major mining firms. Kierans was frequently labelled a "Marxist" and "socialistic" by mining company officers and industry trade journals for his arguments on this score.

Thus, a story in the *Northern Miner* (8 March 1973) informed its readers that the president of the Manitoba mining association had referred to the Kierans Report as "a communist document, foreign to any Canadian thinking on the mining industry."[19] According to the same story, the president of Sherritt Gordon (speculating more precisely about the report's "foreign" origins) had said that the whole thing "sounds like Uganda," that the province "will have to make up its mind whether it wants jobs or full taxes," and that the report came from "someone who can't run a post office." For their own part, the editors of the magazine suggested that "The disgruntled Liberal whose extreme socialistic views led to his resignation from Pierre Elliott Trudeau's Cabinet seems to have found his home in the bosom of Premier Ed Schreyer's New Democratic government in Manitoba ... The report reeks with a frighteningly childlike naivete in its approach to the mining industry."[20] These themes reverberated through the pages of the *Northern Miner* for some weeks and are echoed in somewhat less strident tones in other industry publications such as the *CIM Bulletin* and the *Canadian Mining Journal*.[21]

Meanwhile, the *Winnipeg Free Press* reported that reactions to Kierans's report reflected "feelings ranging from bitterness to outrage to personal attacks on Mr. Kierans."[22] One such reaction, reported separately in the same issue of the *Free Press*, was that of Ed McGill, Progressive Conservative MLA for Brandon West, who claimed that "the political rape of the economy of Manitoba is about to take place and warned that the extreme left wing of the NDP has taken the reins of party fortunes in the province whether Mr. Schreyer likes it or not."[23] Editorially, the *Free Press* added its own voice to the mining industry's view that Kierans "subscribes to the theory, dear to all socialists, that the state can do everything better than can private individuals or corporations."[24]

Despite the tone of these reactions, perhaps the most dramatic of the industry's rejoinders came in the form of a debate on television between Kierans and Alf Powis, president of Noranda, which even the best friends of the mining industry concede that Kierans won. It was waged as a battle between the "resources are ours" theme of Eric Kierans and the "flight of capital" theme of Alf Powis. Powis took pains to get across at least two main points against Kierans's views that appeared about the same time in his own corporate magazine, *Horizons Noranda*. First, "repatriation" of mining leases "amounts to confiscation without compensation of existing mining and concentration operations." Second, for the mining industry, the "super-profits" so strongly attacked by Kierans

are the exception, not the rule, and yet the myth persists. The policies recommended by Professor Kierans would lead to a mis-allocation of the taxpayers' money, and to the immediate stagnation and ultimate decline of the mining industry. In fact, the mere existence of these recommendations creates uncertainty which, if not soon dispelled, will lead to the same result. And it is doubtful whether anything of comparable value – in terms of tax revenues, employment, export earnings, etc. – can be created to take its place.[25]

Disappointed with the results of this and other experiences of public debate on these issues, the industry began to take a longer-term view of consolidating its credibility with the public. It increased advertising in the media and expanded support for the study of the role of resource industries in the Canadian economy. Shortly after the release of the Kierans Report, the MAC undertook a major media campaign under the banner slogan, "Does Anybody out There Give a Damn If the Mining Industry Is Taxed to Death?"[26] According to the former managing director of the MAC, the public relations budget of the association swelled during the 1970s, to over a million dollars per year.[27] Finally, the industry became a major impetus behind creation in 1973 of the Centre for Resource Studies at Queen's University.[28]

However, the more immediate challenge confronting the mining industry upon release of the Kierans Report was, of course, to protect the "bottom line" of firms in the industry. The fear was that the government of Manitoba and other Canadian governments could embody the report's analysis and recommendations in major policy reforms. Numerous changes in provincial and federal resource taxation did take place during the following decade. This result could be seen as evidence that Kierans had inspired Canadians to pressure their governments into raising royalties and taxes on extractive industries. This conclusion, though, might be to confuse coincidence with causation; too many other forces were pushing in the same direction to permit any inference that Kierans and his report alone occasioned this shift.

A stronger argument can be made that Kierans and his report helped move Canadian governments towards adopting crown corporations as primary instruments of resource policy. Kierans also popularized the concept of resource rents and made Canadians familiar with the size of rents available on some of Canada's most prevalent resources, just when the increase in oil prices in 1973 pushed up the prices of a variety of resources.

It would be misleading, though, to dismiss entirely the suggestion that the Kierans Report had something to do with changes in resource taxation in Canada. However, if it did indeed have this effect, it did so despite the expressed intentions of its author. The Kierans Report definitely prefers crown corporations over royalties and taxes as means for public capture of proper returns on the sale of natural resources. (In fact, in a highly unconventional variant on this notion, Kierans recommended competitive crown corporations – plural – providing yet another demonstration of his distrust of monopoly, public or private.) It is thus surprising and a little ironic that one of the few commentators not to have missed this point is (again) Hedlin Menzies. It quotes Premier Schreyer to the effect that the Manitoba government considered it "too drastic or radical" to bring existing mining operations under a form of nationalization or public ownership and criticized the premier's response to Kierans's policy recommendations:

It would appear ... that the Kierans Report will be used to justify a policy of increased royalties and taxes based on the conclusion that the public currently receives an insufficient reward out of the so-called excess profits estimated to be created by Manitoba metal mining.

It should be appreciated that this type of policy response was strongly rejected and criticized by the Kierans Report itself. The Report viewed such action as a weak compromise approach which at best would be exceedingly complex to work out, and at worst would show that 'the political authority admits that it cannot restrain or contain commercial interests.'

In many ways, it is inconsistent to claim that the Kierans Report analysis is 'excellent,' and then proceed to reject the central recommendations which flow from this analysis.[29]

Yet this is precisely what Schreyer's government proceeded to do. In one of several press releases concerning the report issued on 2 March 1973, the premier is quoted at length concerning his own assessment of the advice that his government had received. Without once referring to any form of nationalization or public ownership, the premier reacted as follows: "Terming the report 'an invaluable contribution to the Manitoba government's ongoing resources policy review,' [the premier] said that while the government was in no way committed to the adoption of any or all the specific recommendations, it was committed 'to make certain that the people of Manitoba will be guaranteed a fairer return from the development of their non-renewable resource wealth in the future.'"[30] All this proved to be the case, as Manitoba was one among several provinces to increase mining royalties and taxes in the spring of 1974.[31] On crown ownership, however, Manitoba attempted little: in 1975 provision was made to allow the government the option to participate up to 50 per cent in any new mineral exploration involving costs of over $10,000 per year.[32]

While the idea of crown corporations as primary instruments of provincial resource policy did not go far in Manitoba, the basic concept did diffuse widely across the country during the next ten years, extending as well to federal operations. Writing in 1982, Marsha Chandler estimated that 49 per cent of existing provincial crown corporations were created in the 1970s.[33] Another study estimates that a similar proportion of all 66 federal and provincial "agencies and other governmental corporate interests participating directly or indirectly in mineral ventures" were created after 1973.[34] A recent study of provincial crown corporations shows that 67 per cent of all such enterprises in mining were created between 1970 and 1980, while in oil and gas the figure was 92 per cent. Moreover, the proportion of the total assets of these corporations acquired during the same decade was 92 per cent for mining and 85 per cent for oil and gas.[35]

GENERAL IMPACT

As with the proliferation of taxation and royalty changes during the 1970s, of course, the fact that public ownership spread rapidly after release of the Kierans Report may be a matter more of coincidence than of causation, as again there were many forces pushing in the same direction. Not the least of these was the provinces' use of the crown corporation in their conflict with Ottawa over shares of resource-based income. The federal government terminated the deductibility of provincial royalties from corporate income tax in 1974. Because provincial crown corporate revenues were not subject to federal taxes, this change made public ownership an even more attractive method of provincial rent collection. There are, in any case, no reliable measures of the extent to which a public policy change, or a series of related changes, can be traced back to a single source of inspiration; no more can the currency of a particular topic of academic analysis, or an approach to it, be confidently attributed to a single study or its author.

In any case, the decade that followed the report saw numerous governments in Canada adopting a variety of new policies to capture the rents available from resources under their jurisdictions – including Manitoba, which stressed changes in royalty rates, which Kierans had expressly argued against, rather than the competitive crown corporations which he had specifically proposed. The other governments adopted one or another (or a combination) of these approaches. To what extent was the Kierans Report responsible for the rather substantial shift in Canadian resource policy during the decade following its release?

The short answer seems to be that the report is best regarded as a necessary, but not sufficient condition for the observed changes in policy. There were, however, several other important conditions: the "winds of change" that for over a decade had been sweeping across the former colonial world as new and highly nationalistic governments asserted their independence against the neo-colonialism of international resource enterprises; the perception, most famously disseminated by the Club of Rome, that the world's stock of a wide range of natural resources was dwindling as the demands of population and economic growth pressed against a fixed supply of raw materials; some actual shortages of deliverable supplies of several commodities, with the inevitable (at least in the short term) upward pressure on the prices of available supplies; and, perhaps most crucial after the autumn of 1973, the dramatic and (to most observers) apparently irreversible triumph of the organization of oil-exporting countries over the world's most powerful industrialized nations.

Moreover, these world developments seem to have made it possible for Canadian governments at both levels to invade the formerly sacred ground of the country's mineral industries, even though the politics of the Carter Commission and Edgar Benson's White Paper, for example, had previously demonstrated the strength of the industry's defences against political pressure for significantly higher taxes on their incomes.[36] In fact, these background conditions appear so powerful, especially in combination, that it seems more plausible to argue that they themselves were enough to account for the post-1973 policy changes in Canada, leaving little residual significance for Kierans's report or his part in the policy debate that followed it. What, then, can we conclude that the Kierans Report did contribute, in and of itself, to resource policy changes in Canada?

Politically, the single most potent notion in the report was that of unearned income, or "super-profits." While some of the permissive conditions outlined above did allow several prominent Canadian resource industries to accrue such "super-profits" during the 1970s, by themselves these expanding profits would not necessarily have attracted the attention of Canadians to their presence, struck Canadians as problematic, or generated a clearly defined program for distributing this newly expanding resource wealth more equitably. These are things that the Kierans Report accomplished. In the mind of the average Canadian, Kierans's hallmark idea that "you cannot nationalize what you already own" might not have extended naturally to include a particular nickel mine in Sudbury or oil well near Leduc – these assets, after all, represented in part investments of capital and knowledge by dedicated, responsible companies – but it could, and in these abnormal times did, extend to the windfall profits that such firms began to earn – and "earn, as it were, in their sleep" – during the 1970s.

The Kierans Report was thus perfectly timed to provide governments and publics in Canada with a clear case against the basic injustice involved in corporations' obtaining, rapidly and increasingly, unearned wealth from resources provided by nature's bounty and the sweat of nobody's brow. This attitude, pervasive in Kierans's discussion, was the most fundamental of his contributions to Canada's debates on resource policy. It stands far above, and in a sense subsumes, everything else that he had to say about other major themes.

Kierans, then, may have single-handedly redefined Canada's national consciousness on the subject of resources. His role here was perhaps similar to that which (according to Karl Deutsch) a small group of strategically placed historians can occasionally play in making a vast number of historical facts applicable to some current public issue. Simply by being at some "bottleneck point" between what there is to be known about their nation's history and particular, new political developments, they can give certain historical details new salience.[37] On this model, Kierans gave timely political relevance to an idea from the history of economic thought – Ricardian rent. At any rate, such an interpretation is consistent with the assessment of insiders to the politics between the mining industry and Canadian governments during the 1970s.

Both the former and the current managing directors of the MAC are wont to refer to the 1950s and 1960s as "the good old days" and the 1970s as "the bad old days" and to view Eric Kierans as an important factor in the transition.[38] George Miller, now president, has described Kierans as "a compelling voice you had to listen to." His distinctive quality may have been "that he backed up his views with something that passes for analysis." He was more influential than Mel Hurtig or Mel Watkins, "who had not thought to publish a report with a bunch of numbers in it." John Bonus, Miller's predecessor, credits Kierans with "introducing a philosophy which was revolutionary at the time ... the concept that since these resources belong to the provinces they can do what they like with them. The private sector can get something out of it because they're working at it and they developed the resources, but they're not going to get anything like as much as they did in the past." Finally, even Alf Powis admits the power of his opponent in changing government attitudes towards taxation of the mining industry: "Certainly Kierans contributed to the mood across the country that you could take anything you wanted from the mining industry. It did us very serious damage. I wasn't amused at the time, but I always liked the guy ... But I still regard him as a very destructive force."[39] Interviews with government insiders convey similar impressions of the "turning point" quality of Kierans's role.[40]

Interviews with these government insiders shed some interesting light on the otherwise anomalous feature of the whole story of the Kierans Report. Despite the report's apparently heavy impact on other provincial and federal policies during the 1970s, the government in Manitoba proved very reluctant to pick up on its main recommendations or, in Mark Eliesen's less delicate description, "ran from it like Napoleon from Moscow." The most obvious explanation for this lies in the timing of the report's release. The Schreyer government was well into the fourth year of its mandate and an election was clearly in the offing. The government had survived without any major catastrophes and was in good standing with the public, even though it had just come through a bitter fight with the insurance industry over public automobile coverage and may have used up its political capital on the issue of public ownership. Any move even hinting at nationalization of companies such as Inco and Sherritt Gordon must have seemed highly imprudent politically. The left-wing Waffle Movement was very active and visible within the Manitoba party, and the party establishment was concerned to avoid the appearance that NDP governments would be bent on widespread nationalization and might actually be the "socialists" that their opponents accused them of being, rather than the "democratic socialists" that they advertised themselves to be. By this logic, and as events were to prove, the Conservative government of Alberta would have an easier time creating an Alberta Energy Company than an NDP government of Manitoba would have creating a "Manitoba Mining Company."[41]

The major multinational oil companies in Canada proved ultimately able to resist the "obsolescence" of their "pre-NEP" bargains with the Canadian government, achieving significant rollbacks of the most objectionable elements of that policy even before the political eclipse of the Liberal federal government that had devised it. So the mineral industry in general seems to have weathered quite well the political tempest of the 1970s that Eric Kierans helped to stir up.[42] Yudelman's summation of the more recent developments in government-industry relations in the mineral sector is revealing: "The 1970–78 dominance of distributive issues was gradually supplanted in 1978 by a concern for the health of the industry which generated the revenue and employment in the first place. Governments and the industry became aware again of their positive mutual interests. There was a new determination to lay down a stable taxation and general mineral policy regime in which the industry might re-establish its strength."[43] Apparently, somebody had begun to "care that the mining industry was being taxed to death," about as much as the MAC had hoped.

There may be, however, a more substantial and instructive explanation for the apparent decline in the political salience of resource rents. This explanation would begin with Manitoba's reluctance to nationalize its mining firms (à la the Kierans formula) and Ottawa's determination to capture the oil revenues of Alberta (according to the NEP formula). It would also synthesize Kierans's answer to the principal weaknesses of Canadian resource policies during the 1970s and Hedlin Menzies's answer to a principal deficiency of the Kierans Report.

Kierans had argued for a stronger assertion of provincial powers to capture the unearned revenues flowing to private companies in the mining sector, primarily by means of crown corporations or the return to the crown of lands held under lease by these companies. During the 1970s, however, while the issue of resource rents was indeed highly politicized, the primary target of new tax and royalty measures introduced by both levels of government, at least with respect to oil and gas, tended to be the revenues flowing to the opposite level of government, not private firms. The same might be said for the proliferation of crown corporations at both levels of government. As resource prices have softened in recent years, these clashes among governments have quieted, and the industry is enjoying the restored atmosphere of intergovernmental calm.

Even where governments made substantial moves in the areas of taxes, royalties, and crown companies, they overlooked one whole area of possible policy responses. There were practically no moves taken in the direction that Kierans had recommended tactically, and Hedlin Menzies and F.J. Anderson endorsed theoretically, as part of a strategy to capture private rents – forcing return of, or obtaining higher revenues from, mineral leases sold to private firms. A central challenge to corporate power in the mineral sector, and an effective and efficient method of extracting rents (and only rents) from the public's resource base, is the introduction of more frequent and competitive bidding for rights to explore and exploit resources on crown lands. The almost total failure of governments to seize upon this instrument of rent capture, even when the potential to do so was at its zenith owing to world price levels, is probably an indication of the sustained political power of the private sector throughout the period under review.[44]

Ironically, this failure also meant that governments missed the opportunity to turn to their greater advantage the one irreversible source of corporate power that Eric Kierans had paid insufficient attention to: their market power. Resource processors and refiners that lack confidence in their ability to earn substantial income from their sales of resource-based products will not buy raw-material production from provincial crown corporations. Likewise, they will not bid high prices for leases on crown land. Firms that do have high expectations of such profitable sales will do both. However, in the case of the competitive sale of leases, when there are no rents to be collected, there is no idle publicly owned capacity, either. The implication of this is that, in the end, Kierans may have made one of the most convincing arguments ever for the urgent importance of the public capture of resource rents, but he also may have missed the most efficient and effective way of accomplishing that end.[45]

Nevertheless, Kierans's report for the Manitoba government has proven very durable indeed, and its reach has been long. It still appears in the list of references for significant articles on resource policy, and in 1986 it was the only work by Kierans held in the Library of Congress in Washington, DC. However, while exposure of the study has been extensive, it is difficult to make the case that it has had a major impact on policy outcomes in Canada, or that it has produced the turn-around in resource policies that Kierans was undoubtedly looking for. When asked about this – in particular, when asked for his own sense of what the report accomplished – Kierans has said, simply, that it drove home the point that, in Canada, resources are the property of its people.

However, things have come full circle, and in a roundabout way Kierans has refuted his own contention. As recently as 1987, in the foreword to a book on resource rents and public policy in western Canada, Kierans was still reminding Canadians of the significance of the fact of their ownership of their resource base, which suggests that they either have lost sight of the idea over the years since he first promoted it in 1973 or never fully grasped it in the first place.[46] Indeed, Kierans referred later in this same foreword to an assessment by an unidentified observer, who had impressed economist John Deutsch at the 1961 Resources for Tomorrow Conference with the comment that "Canada is a country rich in resources, but poor in policy." To this Kierans added, "The description fitted then and it still fits." Perhaps Kierans was unaware that, to the extent that the latter half of his formulation is, in fact, true, it contradicts the idea that he had a lasting, substantial impact on Canadian resource policy. If this is the case, Kierans's report can still serve to remind Canadians how much cause they have to regret the fact, if not resent it.

CHAPTER TEN

Globalism, State, and Community

During the two decades since release of the Manitoba resources report (1973), Eric Kierans has remained an unremitting critic of federal policies on a number of fronts, resource policy among them. He presented the CBC's 1983 Massey Lectures, published as *Globalism and the Nation-State* (1984); was a regular panel member – along with former Ontario NDP leader Stephen Lewis and Progressive Conservative adviser Dalton Camp – on CBC's "Morningside"; and wrote, with Walter Stewart, *The Wrong End of the Rainbow* (1988). He testified in 1987 before the parliamentary committee on the constitution concerning the Meech Lake Accord and in the late 1980s published articles (including one called "A Cruel Joke") on the Canada–United States Free Trade Agreement. Most recently, he headed Nova Scotia's working committee on the constitution, which reported in 1991.

Kierans has been, in short, one of Canada's most prominent public commentators, although he has not held elected office for more than twenty years. While for some of this time he was formally an academic, his "post-retirement" career has more closely resembled that of a public commentator. He is probably best described as an "engaged intellectual," on the European model – a rarity in North American political life.

The present chapter reviews what Kierans has had to say across this wide range of public policy issues. While most of his pronouncements do not represent major departures from the views discussed above, some amount to a consolidation of earlier concerns, produced by the heightened intensity that some major issues, such as national unity, took on during the 1980s. Increasingly, Kierans's political outlook came to be dominated by his opposition to overcentralization of power within Canada and the world domination of the multinational corporation.

Natural resources policy – more and more confined to the specific issues of oil and gas exports and the Mackenzie Valley pipeline – was the first area that Kierans attacked in his new role. If it is true that the Kierans Report made no lasting difference to the way in which Canadians treat their resource endowment, it was not for want of effort on Kierans's part. In fact, the report proved to be only a beginning. Its release almost coincided with the explosion in world energy prices, and directly or indirectly the OPEC price hikes in the fall of 1973 placed several issues of Canadian resource development at the top of a very heavy agenda for national, provincial, and federal-provincial politics. The proposal for a Mackenzie Valley pipeline, which gained impetus from the perceptions of energy scarcity in North America, was one of the favoured developments that Kierans continued to oppose, for the kinds of reasons that he had raised in his letter to Trudeau during the 1972 election campaign. In every forum, from academic journals to public conferences and television panels, he also widely publicized the specific, "energy-industry" version of his attack on the distortive effects of the Canadian tax system and the privileges that it extended to extractive industries.[1]

For example, he wrote this about John Turner's 1974 budget:

A significant aspect of the November budget lies in the determination of federal government to reduce the share of provincial revenues and to restore control of the petroleum industry and the responsibility of assuring future energy supplies to the private sector. Thus, 'We have pulled back from our original proposals. We want resource industries adequately taxed, but we want to see their financial position sufficiently strong to enable them to develop and to deliver the supplies needed in the years ahead. We have done our part. I now appeal to the provinces ... to do their part. I have no doubt that if the provinces respond to the needs of the industries and the nation as I have tonight the problem will be resolved.' Mr. Turner's own estimate of the amount of the pull-back from the May [minority-government] budget valued the increase in savings for the resource companies at $185 million for the year 1975.[2]

Noting that the minister of finance had admitted that Canada's reserves of oil and gas were declining while demand was rising, "it would seem to follow," Kierans wrote, "that a thorough review of existing energy policies is required, not a blatant, thrice-repeated endorsement of the private sector and its performance to date."[3]

The mineral-fuel sector was dominated by very few firms which have exerted enormous political pressure on the government in matters ranging from tax reform to commercial policy. Indeed, in 1971, Statistics Canada reported that "17 firms out of a total population of 835 corporations controlled 55 per cent of the assets, 73 per cent of the product sales and 83 per cent of the profits before taxes in the mineral fuels sector."

Kierans related how the industry had pressed for rapid exploitation of Canada's energy reserves through massive exports of oil and gas, and he quoted William Twaits, chair and chief executive of Imperial Oil Ltd., to the effect that "a barrel of oil in the ground has almost no value today even at a price of $4–$5 a barrel twenty years hence."[4] Kierans responded: "Of course, this is the whole point. The private sector, facing political risks to their ownership or control, must maximize the immediate sales value of an asset. But the public sector must be concerned with the needs of tomorrow, stability, security, and a whole quantum of social, political and economic effects. For a nation the quick buck will be the last consideration. The conservation and orderly exploitation of natural resources simply cannot be entrusted to the private sector as Mr. Turner and Mr. Twaits demand." Thus, Kierans concluded, it is "disheartening, in this day and age, to see the Minister of Finance adjusting his budget so as to make it attractive for a handful of oil giants to include Canadian economic and energy objectives with the pursuit of their own objectives of growth in assets, power and profit."[5]

In this and other ways, the energy crisis of the 1970s provided a perfect focus for Kierans's economic and political beliefs. It involved some of Canada's largest companies, most of them foreign-controlled, extensive corporate tax privileges, natural resources and the public's claim on resource rents, and, especially in the latter respect, federal-provincial relations. All these themes Kierans drew together in a paper, "Federal-Provincial Treatment of the Extractive Industries," presented to the annual conference of the Canadian Tax Foundation in November 1974.[6] The budget of May 1974, while appearing to exhibit belated recognition "that the petroleum and mining industries are mature and have outgrown the need for special and open-handed tax concessions," had more than a suggestion in it that "the federal government did not become interested in resource revenues until it became clear that provincial governments were positioning themselves to increase substantially their income from the sale of their own wealth."

Kierans made two main arguments about this development. One was, simply, that "if the resource sector has paid too little in taxes on the mining of natural wealth, this has principally been the result of federal policies and definitions of taxable income, not provincial legislation." Kierans thus raised his long-standing concern with the tax breaks enjoyed by these firms, "depletion, accelerated write-offs, exploration expenses, exempt mining income, etc." The other argument was that Ottawa was attempting to "ensure that provincial royalties, provincial mining taxes and other arrangements having similar effects do not unreasonably erode the corporate tax base" and was massively centralizing Confederation and invading provincial prerogatives. With prescience, he argued that "unless the federal government realizes that it has to co-operate and co-ordinate its activities with the provinces, we have an explosive situation on our hands."

In his concluding paragraph, Kierans underscored the predictable result of failure to do this: "The federal thrust outlined in the May 6 budget is an attempt to detach the provinces from the revenues implicit in the ownership of their own lands and resources. It can only strengthen the resolve of some provinces, and eventually all, to take over themselves the exploration for and development of their wealth. The Crown cannot then tax the Crown." He predicted that federal intransigence would awaken Canadians to the shortcomings of resource policies and inflame sentiments attached to their ownership of natural resources. Kierans concluded with this passage from Karl Polanyi's *The Great Transformation*: "What we call land is an element of nature inextricably interwoven with man's institutions. To isolate it and form a market out of it was perhaps the weirdest of all undertakings of our ancestors."[7]

More and more, Kierans's consideration of resource policies drew him towards a vision of a decentralized Canada, largely because the provinces were vested with primary responsibility for the kind of public stewardship over natural resources implicit in Polanyi's statement. One sees gradually developing through the resource-policy debates of the 1970s Kierans's deep conviction that a community consists of the relationship between a land and its people. Thus, by 1979, Kierans was attempting to inspire a graduating class in Fredericton, New Brunswick, to recognize "the unity of man and environment."[8] Over time, Kierans argued, a group that has gathered together in a particular place will experience "a gradual harmonization of values, expectations, and viewpoints" and realize a unity that to some degree will be imposed by nature itself, "for the possibilities inherent in the environment and the resource base determine the scope if not the limit of man's activities."

In such a community, Kierans reminded his audience of hopeful youth and proud parents and kin, horizons embrace all modes of human existence – religious, economic, social, scientific, and cultural: "And it is principally at this level, while still members of the community, that men and women have the greatest freedom of choice for all the principal directions of living are open to them." Community can support a government empowered to define and enforce rules of conduct, "so that man may know and be free to choose among the principal directions and modes of existence." Community in this sense is both an expression and a buttress of individual responsibility, while at the same time it is a source and expression of political power. The conclusion? "The problem of Canadian unity, our problem, is to find a way in which the primary importance and fundamental values of community can be maintained in the face of escalation, concentration and regimentation at both the political and economic levels. I do not see how this can be accomplished unless our political leaders start from the beginning with the objective of strengthening our communities and reinforcing our provinces."

If he were a provincial leader, he said, he would find it increasingly difficult to insist that Canada, with its distinct economic regions and cultures, should be a strong, centralized country – a heartland centred on Ottawa, Montreal, and Toronto and with all the rest a periphery. No doubt looking up from his notes, he added, "In effect I would be telling the best young people of my province, the educated and the intelligent to go away. There is no room for you at home."

COMMUNITY VERSUS "COMERGENCE"

Kierans was asked by the CBC to deliver the 1983 Massey Lectures, later published as *Globalism and the Nation-State* (1984). Despite their brevity, these five lectures set out the foundation for just about everything that Kierans has had to say since then about the Canadian constitution and the Free Trade Agreement, matters taken up in this chapter. However, because of the philosophical tenor of these lectures, it seems appropriate to focus on Kierans's spiritual and philosophical outlook.

Kierans opened the second lecture – "Should There Be a Nation-State?" – with lines from "Anecdote of Men by the Thousand" by poet Wallace Stevens:

The soul, he said, is composed of the external world.
There are men of the East, he said,
Who are the East.
There are men of a province

Who are that province.
There are men of a valley
Who are that valley."⁹

Surely all of us would admit, and certainly Kierans would agree, that at present one is more likely to find men and women of Quebec "who are Quebec" than to find men and women of Canada "who are Canada": English Canada seems to be increasingly populated with people who are either "North America" or, if not that, then "Alberta" or "British Columbia" or "Nova Scotia" rather than "Canada."

In other words, Canada as a whole is unlikely to put together as effectively as has Quebec the proper relationship between the economic and the political life of the community that Kierans feels is at the core of a distinctive national existence capable and worthy of survival. Worse, Quebec's success on this score seems to be yet another nail in the coffin of Canada's viability as a united and autonomous community. Kierans is convinced that this need not be so, but that if Canada is to avoid this fate, Canadians will have to acquire (or apply) a deeper appreciation of the proper relationship between the economic and the political dimensions of their life as a nation. Kierans's understanding of this problem contains some distinctive elements, and it is important to develop them carefully.

R.H. Tawney observed in *Religion and the Rise of Capitalism*:

The medieval theorist condemned as a sin precisely that effort to achieve a continuous and unlimited increase in material wealth which modern societies applaud as a quality, and the vices for which he reserved his most merciless denunciations were the more refined and subtle of the economic virtues. 'He who has enough to satisfy his wants,' wrote a Schoolman of the fourteenth century, 'and nevertheless ceaselessly labours to acquire riches ... all such are incited by a damnable avarice, sensuality, or pride.' ... The essence of the argument was that payment may properly be demanded by the craftsmen who make the goods or by the merchants who transport them, for both labour in their vocation and serve the common need. The unpardonable sin is that of the speculator or middleman, who snatches private gain by the exploitation of public necessities. The true descendant of the doctrine of Aquinas is the labour theory of value. The last of the Schoolmen was Karl Marx.[10]

This passage touches on the philosophical principles qualifying the capitalism of Eric Kierans, particularly concerning the relationship between the economy and society. This is not to say that there is a general affinity between Kierans and Marx, or between Kierans's philosophical tenets and the labour theory of value or any of its forerunners. Nothing in Kierans's thinking about economics shows any sign of a direct subscription to socialist thought, despite the fact that, in view of his Manitoba resources report, more than one mining company president has condemned him as a Marxist – a strange charge to lay against a former President of the Montreal Stock Exchange. Rather, the clue to Kierans's thought contained in Tawney's paragraph lies in the phrases having to do with the unacceptability of either "continuous and unlimited increases in material wealth" or "exploitation of public necessities" and the importance, instead, of "serving the common need."

Kierans shares with the Schoolmen and (according to Tawney) Marx a sense of limit – the idea that individual economic pursuits are bounded by constraints derived from common needs and subordinate to principles and priorities established for the promotion of collective purposes beyond that of material well-being. The most distinctive and characteristic notion pervading the public philosophy of Eric Kierans is the idea that the economy is embedded within a set of other relationships among the members of a given society; moreover, and for that reason, the economy is subordinate to the authority established by the members of that society for the achievement of their common aims. The quotation from Tawney resonates throughout a review of Kierans's career because his outlook is rooted in a Christian view of humanity in society and condemns as meaningless, if not pernicious, the boundless pursuit of wealth. These elements bear on the durability of Canadian nationalism in an age and on a continent dominated by American liberalism and corporate capitalism.

The quickest way to get to the heart of this matter is to pose the straightforward, but hardly simple questions of the connections between liberalism and nationalism, and between capitalism and the state. If, as Donald Smiley and George Grant would have it, liberalism is inimical to the survival of most states, if not indeed "the State," then Kierans's nationalism must be partial repudiation of his liberalism, or his liberalism must qualify his nationalism.[11] The economic credo of liberalism gives the state no valid, extensive role in the economic system. If there is no role for government in the economic affairs of people, why should we be concerned about countries, especially in an era in which the greatest economic promise and chance for world peace are thought by many to lie in the direction of international corporate rationalization and global economic interdependence. As one of the targets of Smiley's criticism has put it: "the multinational corporation, *precisely because* it is a threat to the sovereignty and independence of the nation state, may well be a harbinger of further evolution of human society toward a more humane, equitable and non-discriminatory civilization."[12]

Kierans's view could hardly be more opposed. For him, a key development of the twentieth century has been the growing divergence or incompatibility between those two great hallmarks of economic liberalism, "laissez-faire" and market competition. When "leaving business be" means elimination of competition through ever-larger firms devouring smaller ones, only the state can restore competition in the national market and resistance to American oligopoly in the international market. (The invisible hand will probably not spread the oligopolistic treasure produced by global corporate Sumo wrestling.)

Our economic and political well-being are served best by resistance to the centralization of economic and political power, especially when a huge country like the United States has begun to turn its large, transnational corporations into arms of the state. Resistance may embody a liberal principle, challenging economic concentration in favour of market competition; it could also be considered a nationalist principle, in that it opposes foreign political domination. Kierans's "liberal nationalism" – or possibly "nationalist liberalism" – could be defined roughly as liberalism that perceives a major role for the state in its national economy when the free play of economic forces no longer guarantees competition and when the practices of big business are already subordinate to political authority – namely, that of a foreign super-state.

Kierans bases this understanding in a philosophical, even spiritual conviction that there are limits to humanity's material pursuits. George Grant has drawn a useful distinction between a liberalism that holds to "what is true about political liberty for all sane people" and the American liberal ideology of domination and mastery.[13] For Grant, the struggle between nationhood and modern liberalism is a sub-case of the more universal tension between preservation of community and tradition and the technological, homogenizing power of advanced capitalism. S.J.R. Noel summarizes Grant's work on this question:

The overpowering image which emerges from Grant's writing is of a world in which domination is the ever-present reality, its particular instances arising from, and made inevitable by, the ideological dominance of a crude faith in technology ... Even the severest critics are ultimately ineffectual because they too are captivated by the deeper assumptions of technological liberalism. As it is for individuals so it is for nations. Canada, ultimately, is not a quiescent satellite of the United States because of direct American intervention or control, but rather because Canadians, and especially the Canadian ruling classes, share the values of their American masters; they 'see themselves at one with the continent on all essential matters.'[14]

Both Grant and Kierans stress the inability of liberalism to admit of the notion of limit, of constraints on human acquisitiveness. Grant holds that liberalism is a set of beliefs centring on the assumption that the human essence is freedom and that therefore what chiefly concerns human beings is to shape the world as they see fit. Kierans, therefore, is a liberal, not because he subscribes to the tendencies towards technological domination and homogenization inherent in advanced capitalism, but precisely because he would preserve the liberty of all communities against both. In 1983, the centre-piece of his Massey Lectures is a condemnation of "Williamsburg" (the American-hosted summit of the Western economies) for its alleged hidden agenda of economic centralization and political integration of the Western alliance under the hegemony of the United States: in a word, comergence.[15] Once this perspective on the Canadian experience is established, it should not be difficult to understand how a liberal could call for extensive state intervention in the national economy.

Even more, it should be easy to see how a liberal in such circumstances would insist that the government must reverse the general direction of Canadian economic policies over the last forty years. Kierans has consistently had a reputation for economic nationalism, radicalism, and anti-Americanism because of what has been, more often than not, simply his attack on the Canadian tax system. Yet taxation is one of the least intrusive of policy instruments: it can finance provision of public goods and can allocate the social product without imposing direct controls on individual producers or creating direct agents of state power such as crown corporations. A desire to provide for public welfare, while avoiding centralization of political or economic power, is thus a key element in Kierans's political economy.

The purest expression of this desire might consist of the complete substitution of individual moral responsibility for state power, and Kierans does argue for individuals' enhanced social conscience and an expanded sense of citizenship.[16] In fact, Kierans comes close to saying that state action is necessary because corporations, as opposed to individuals, do not have the capacity to love:

When forms of business organization were personal – partnerships or proprietorships – there was no problem about defining business ethics. Business ethics were personal ethics, and the ethics of the person may be described by the one word – 'love.' '[Love] and do whatsoever thou wilt,' was the commandment of St. Augustine, but he was not inviting anarchy. A true love would not infringe the rights of others, and this boundary to one's actions preserves community and freedom.

To command a corporation to love would be madness. Commanding a corporation to love would be asking it to distribute its wealth, to commit suicide. On the other hand, the corporation cannot be concerned simply with itself; it cannot be the object of its existence. It can and must be forced to conduct itself so that its activities correspond with the aims of the community, with the state itself as the seat of power and elected spokesman of the people.[17]

So, the state serves the community and freedom by constraining the inhuman (or a-human) appetites of the corporation for the sake of collective purposes, since individual conscience cannot be relied upon. It is, no doubt, in this spirit that Kierans quotes Baron Thurlow's rhetorical question, "Did you expect a corporation to have a conscience, when it has not soul to be damned, and no body to be kicked?"[18] But imposition of public constraints on corporate conduct is complicated by the sheer scale of the modern corporation, so that decentralization, competitiveness, and openness in the economic system are to be preferred on this ground to corporate expansion and rationalization of industry. Hence, for example, the tax system must promote the entry of new, and the exit of old, firms.[19] Hence, also, control of corporations must be returned to the individual shareholders who own them, because these are capable of acting as moral agents as well as the economic ones that we saw applauded in chapter 2.[20]

Ultimately, Kierans locates the roots of the Canadian quandary in the fundamental nature of the modern business corporation. He perceives that for Canada, and for all societies striving for the proper relationship between economic pursuits and social ends, something crucial was lost as business enterprises gradually arrogated the corporate form to the entrepreneurial function. This achieved for the firm the privilege of institutional immortality that had hitherto been reserved to such incorporated institutions as the church and university in exchange for their service to the common good of their societies.[21] Businesses' achievement of indefinite longevity has categorically transformed the operation of market forces:

From Adam Smith through to John Stuart Mill writing in 1849, economists viewed the firm as a proprietorship or partnership, mortal like the owners or operators, certain to disappear in time, thus providing the openings for new men, new initiatives, new ideas. If entry was not easy, exit at least was certain. It was this constant turnover in a dynamic, evolving economy that theoretically prevented a large number of firms from controlling prices and production. This is not the appropriate manner of looking at the economy of 1983 or the multinational, although the model still survives in economic theory.[22]

What model, then, does describe the descendants of these immortalized agents of capital accumulation – the multinational corporations of today? "Their control of their markets, their absolute size ... and their independence from those who own them means that society has created institutions that can grow without limit through time. As they grow, they burst through national boundaries and demand the right to range across the world – anonymous institutions that acknowledge no citizenship and would be free of all responsibility except the single objective of creating wealth."[23]

Kierans is concerned, at a minimum, that the Canadian tax system cease to feed the growth of the domestic subsidiaries of these foreign giants (and their locally based counterparts); beyond that, he would set policies to ensure that in Canada, at least, their pursuit of profit and growth is carried out within the constraints set by the peculiar requirements of Canada's economic setting and the distinctive aspirations of its people. Echoing Tawney, and like George Grant, he would appeal to us to restore our commitment to a view of humanity that can serve to constrict the limitless horizons visible from atop the "new cathedrals" – the soaring office towers of the modern corporation.[24]

THE CANADA–UNITED STATES
FREE TRADE AGREEMENT

For Eric Kierans, the FTA was, essentially, "a pact" between "the Canadian giant corporations and the American conglomerates."[25] As such, it was absolutely at odds with the philosophical outlook elaborated in *Globalism and the Nation-State*. Citing the example of Sweden's economic strategy, which restricted foreign economic control but kept the national market generally open to international competition, precisely so that consumers could not be exploited by protected domestic firms, he did not oppose, and indeed supported, the removal of obstacles to the free international exchange of goods.

But this, for Kierans, was not at issue in the FTA, which he argued was not about free trade, in any significant way, at all: "The words, FREE TRADE, used in the context of this agreement are not only meaningless, they are misleading and intended to be so. The reduction or elimination of the few tariff and some non-tariff barriers are the least substantial and significant elements of the agreement ... In fact, we are entering into a continental corporate network in which concepts such as free trade have been made as irrelevant as the money exchanges made the system of barter."[26]

Thus, Kierans was one of the few commentators about the FTA to argue that any discussion of free trade is largely beside the point when most trade between the United States and Canada occurs not between firms but within firms. "The market" is not "free" but rather is largely administered by major American and Canadian corporations. He was also one of the few to cite statistics connecting corporate concentration in Canada, as well as the prominence of foreign-controlled firms in Canada's economy, with the issue of international trade. In the same article, he injected information such as the following: "In 1983, 30 percent of all goods and services produced in the Canadian non-financial corporate sector were produced by foreign enterprises. If networking policies direct purchases from captive sources because it is in the interest of the global corporation, then the market is suppressed ... When is a trade not a trade? When one is exchanging with oneself or with someone not at arms length. In 1980, foreign-controlled firms imported some $42.1 billion of goods and services."

After pointing out that in 1983 foreign controlled firms realized 43.6 per cent of profits in the Canadian non-financial sector, Kierans reminded Canadians that they are subject to the joint problems of corporate concentration in general and foreign-dominated concentration in particular: "736 foreign-controlled firms sold $164 billion of goods and services or 25 percent of the $658 billion output of the non-financial corporate sector of 391,212 firms in 1983. The 736 largest foreign firms earned $12 billion or 38 percent of total corporate profits in 1983, while the 1,040 largest Canadian firms earned $7 billion or 22 percent." Canadians are not generally reminded of the fact that one half of one per cent of the companies in the country earn 60 per cent of Canadian corporate profits and that over half the profits earned by that select group accrue to foreign-controlled firms. Had they been so reminded more often, they might have been more inclined to see the FTA less as a potential cause of further economic integration with the United States and more as a culmination of past economic integration.

On the Meech Lake Accord (1987–90), Kierans focused his interventions on federal decentralization. Here, his views owe much to his years in the Quebec government. As described above, during that period he "lived out" one of the main requirements of his political economy – the close relationship among government, economy, and society. But there is a more direct connection to this discussion. Ever since he, as a Quebec minister, suffered intense frustration with Ottawa's overbearing and overcentralizing tendencies, Kierans has been a strong anti-centralist. And yet, as we saw briefly, he was a strident and outspoken foe of René Lévesque's separatism, precisely because it threatened the survival of Canada as a nation. Why this opposition to what could be seen as simply an extreme form of decentralization? Indeed, why was Kierans himself not a Quebec separatist?

In my view it was primarily because of his conviction that all of Canada's communities can be of invaluable support to one another's survival and autonomy, but only so long as their unity is sustained and renewed among themselves, not compelled by an overriding central authority. Kierans is a Canadian nationalist, but he is also very near to being a confederalist. Canada's union can achieve no greater strength than that sustained through voluntary and continuous subscription to it by its component parts. Kierans believes in "sovereignty-association," but as an approach to all provinces', not just Quebec's, self-realization. It is a good term for what he sees as the appropriate relationship among the provinces, not between English Canada and Quebec. This interesting conceptual synthesis perhaps could come only from the English-speaking, Quebec businessman who spent three years facilitating the public entrepreneurial ventures of Quebec's most inspirational nationalist.

It is, however, Kierans's view more of the spirit of Confederation than of its institutional provisions that promises the national revitalization that he would like to see. It is a little-noted fact that Kierans appeared before the Special Joint Committee on the 1987 Constitutional Accord on the morning of the day (27 August 1987) on which Pierre Trudeau made his first submission on the issue. Kierans himself commented:

What I want to say is that you are talking about centralism and you are not going to meet a centralist [later] tonight; you are not going to meet even a super-centralist. You are going to meet a one-man centralist [i.e. Trudeau], and he is not even going to accept your role. He is going to be talking over your heads. It is not just the provincial governments that he considers nobody, it is the federal government also, because he is going to ignore you and your position as a federal committee and go directly over your heads in order to impose an idea that died a long time ago.[27]

Everyone, of course, is entitled to their own impressions of what Trudeau said, but few could mistake its distance from Kierans's contribution. Consider this, for example, from Kierans: "Provinces are just like people; I have found this. They have pride. They feel they are special. They should feel they are special. They have differences – each one of them, not just Quebec – to protect. They are a fact of Canadian life. They are a fact of Canadian constitutional life, and they are a fact of Canadian reality. Sooner or later they are going to revolt against anyone who attempts to impose on them the slow death of a welfare position."[28]

Kierans expressed difficulty in understanding people's preoccupation with the problem of "distinctiveness" in Meech Lake. "It is not just traditions, history, languages and culture that promote distinctiveness"; rather, it is "[t]he nature of the country and its resources: parts of the country have mines, fish, prairie farmers, financial centres such as Toronto. We have everything here that describes a country different in all of its parts. We are clearly a pluralistic society. Anybody who wants to turn us into one of Plato's unities is going to get the same kind of criticism that Aristotle gave to Plato: that is a mindless conformity you are trying to impose on us." Thus, one of the virtues of the document is that "first of all, it was an accord," one that represents a modus vivendi towards which federal-provincial meetings have been moving since 1945–46.

The comment from Kierans, however, that shows most clearly his cabinet experience is more personal: "I may just add that in provincial politics you learn to adapt to people. You do not get away with making the people adapt to you. I think it is a lesson out of Meech Lake. For once we are attempting to create a Constitution that adapts to what people want, instead of creating a constitution that is going to mould and make people adapt to it." The federal government, in contrast, as Kierans was at pains to convey, has traditionally been distant and almost imperious towards the governments and people across the country.

Kierans thus reveals himself to be a liberal in the profoundest sense possible: he believes unequivocally in democracy, in the sovereignty of the individual. His thinking allows only two qualifications of this absolute belief in democracy – and they are not even qualifications of his belief in individual freedom so much as elaborations of his concept of the individual. One is that everyone is born somewhere, and therefore everyone begins life as part of a community whose character is defined by its physical location and the other people there. As he likes to say, "The roots of a community are two – the land and the people who come to it," and every individual is in some sense a product of such a community.[29] The second is that everyone is under a moral obligation to act responsibly, which comes down to acting out of respect for the others in the community and for the common needs of the community: "It should not be forgotten that Adam Smith was a moral philosopher with a strong faith in the natural order and the capacity of the individual. Self-interest and individualism must be integrated now in the search for a true and generous community. We can no longer respond to the system of values embedded in the individualism of the 19th century but must find and proclaim the originating values, the moral and social principles that arise from our role as members of a community, a nation."[30] In short, "We need a new definition of the individual, not as one who stands alone but as one who is a responsible and involved member of one's community."

Kierans's bedrock faith in such individuals is shown in what seems to have become his favourite metaphor for political action, which he has used at the conclusion of his last two books. The image was provided by René Dubos, in *A God Within: A Positive Philosophy for a More Complete Fulfilment of the Human Potential*, who quotes Michelangelo's observations while looking at a block of marble:

> The best of artists has that thought alone,
> Which is contained within the marble shell;
> The sculptor's hand can only break the spell,
> To free the figures slumbering in the stone.

Kierans comments: "It needs only political leadership, and a belief in ourselves, to break the spell" and thereby release the potential for independence and economic vitality dormant in Canadian society.[31] Less poetically, perhaps, but to the same effect, he quotes favourably this sentiment of René Lévesque's (whom he called, in the

same review, "the most influential political figure of his time"):
"Yet power is not an end but a beginning, the beginning of a chance
to move forward, not alone but with others, *and to bring as many
forward with you as you can.*"[32]

The same bedrock faith also explains his conviction that Canada's economic and political survival will be best served by breaking
down, or at least loosening, concentrations of economic and political power. For Kierans, the key to this is the objective of strengthening Canada's communities and reinforcing its provinces. Kierans
here adopts what I take to be a novel perspective – namely, that
effective subordination of centralizing economic forces to local
political control may be enhanced, not diminished, in smaller
rather than more inclusive political units. The reason for this
conclusion is the more direct and intensive public accountability of
authorities in smaller units – a primary justification for Kierans's
support for the Meech Lake Accord:

Meech Lake means that provincial premiers and governments will have
greater responsibility than ever before for the growth and development of
their communities. The greater scope and need for provincial entrepreneurship and creativity [place] a larger burden on the provinces which is where it
should have been all along ... Meech Lake means the greater freedom that
people need from domination by bureaucratic institutions that are beyond
their control, beyond their influence, beyond their touch. Centralization,
whatever the advantages may be, drains communities, checks their development and thwarts the efforts to provide sufficient scope and opportunity
to challenge their youth.[33]

There are few, if any, other observers of Canadian politics who
insist that national unity and independence cannot be achieved in
isolation from one another and reveal the interrelatedness of these
two challenges by recommending decentralization as the most
effective means of resisting and reversing American control.

Kierans's simultaneous support for Meech Lake and opposition
to the FTA were based on presuppositions at odds with those held by
others who happened to take the same political stand, such as John
Turner and most other Liberals and Canadian nationalists. His
support for Meech Lake originated not out of some hope or belief
that it would somehow "bind" Quebec to the rest of Canada but,
instead, from the conviction that it would free Quebec and the other
provinces to take greater control of and responsibility for their own
needs and prospects and the confidence that all the provinces, in

doing so, would continue to act in concert, as they themselves expect this to be helpful.

An account of Kierans's submission to the Parliamentary Committee on the 1987 Constitutional Accord could well have served to round off the story of his public life. However, as with the question of resource rents following the Manitoba resources study, Kierans's single major contribution to Canada's unity debate also carried momentum and led to further public attention and a continuing public role. Just as the Manitoba report was followed by almost a decade of public appearances and media "spots" on Canadian energy policy and the Mackenzie Valley pipeline, so too his interventions on Meech Lake were followed by an appointment to chair the Nova Scotia Working Committee on the Constitution, a series of addresses on national unity, and occasional bouts of public and semi-public service.[34] Moreover, several dimensions of this most recent public role suggest that it may serve as the closing episode, certainly the dénouement, of Kierans's political life.

First, this episode takes place in a "region," the Atlantic provinces. Here, Kierans was able to live out his philosophical predisposition simply to show respect for a people and a place – this time, Nova Scotia. Kierans had told a parliamentary committee that provinces have feelings, including pride, and he stressed that the role of his working committee was simply to listen carefully to what the people of Nova Scotia were feeling about Quebec, about the rest of Canada, and about the proper place of government in their lives. In sum, he saw it as his duty to facilitate his community's expression of its most pressing and deepest concerns.

What he seems to have heard from Nova Scotians is that economic leadership is the country's most pressing need. In the words of a Halifax daily's editorial response to the release of the committee's report, "What [Nova Scotians] want is stronger leadership; what they often feeling [sic] they're getting is a great deal of talk about Canada's role in the global economy but little action to build a strong economy."[35] However, the people of the province were also prepared to deal with the non-economic issues at the heart of Canada's constitutional impasse: "People do see beyond their pocket books, and what they see is the need for reasonable, pragmatic compromises to keep Canada together."

For a part of the country such as Nova Scotia, concern about the economy and concern about national unity were scarcely separable. Among the very worst outcomes, according to many witnesses, was separation of Quebec from Canada, not least because it would draw the Maritimes into economic dependence on the United States and weaken the ties with other provinces that underpin the case for sharing Canada's wealth. Kierans's "Chairman's Introduction" to the committee's report (1991) is preoccupied with the threat of continentalism inherent in the Canada–United States Free Trade Agreement and contains only a single paragraph specifically on Quebec. As Kierans wrote, "Today, the centre of the nation is no longer a core but is itself a periphery in a continental market. Increasingly, the big decisions affecting us, economic and political, are being made outside our borders. Atlantic Canada is becoming the periphery of a periphery. Is anybody listening in Ottawa? Is anybody home in Ottawa?"[36]

Kierans listened to and respected the intervenors so much that he let them change his mind, particularly about the Charter of Rights and Freedoms and native rights: "It soon became clear, after the early meetings and the vigorous internal discussions, that the committee itself was a microcosm of Canada. Close encounters between different ethno-cultural groups, the aboriginals, the disabled and women's organizations forced us to learn about each other and quickly."[37] Moreover, Kierans warned the province's leaders, Nova Scotians will no longer tolerate exclusion of such groups from constitution-making and economic policy formation. "Empowerment flowing from the Charter of Rights and Freedoms adds force to their efforts to make rights meaningful and our political institutions accountable."[38] Accordingly, it seems, Nova Scotia's was one of only two provincial governments (the other being Ontario's) seriously to consider guaranteeing half of its new Senate seats to women.

The most characteristic Kierans touch, though, to this job was his articulation of why national unity and independence matter. This point was clearly part of the message that he tried to communicate from the platform that came with his position. In a press interview shortly after his appointment, he was asked if Canada made economic sense. He replied,

Oh, no – it never did. I mean, that was the problem right from the very beginning. And that's why eventually we had to have what they call the National Policy of 1879, in order to give us breathing time to build up sufficient infrastructure to knit the country together with all of our highways and railway systems, among other things. Of course, if economics were the only thing, then you'd simply just join in with the United States, accept what their values are, accept responsibilities of being world leaders and military powers and all the rest of it. This is what you would do. But we have a lot more than that to give.[39]

As for the difference that Canadian independence can make, Kierans said that it is really a matter of Canada's giving expression to, and providing an example of, the overriding of economic values with non-economic ones: "We're not really bound by that single, sole criterion of nailing everybody to the cross of competitiveness and efficiency and so on. We have other values ... values of the heart and mind and all the rest that will have a leavening influence on this civilization in the North American continent."

Once again, by implication, Kierans was bringing the discussion of national unity back to the FTA, with its emasculation of government's power to shape the economy and promote public ends beyond those of simple economic productivity, or "competitiveness." There is a subtle conjunction of concerns here that is almost a Kierans trademark. Unlike the neo-conservatives, and most of the Progressive Conservative party of the 1980s and 1990s, Kierans believes that good government and well-constructed national policies are vital if Canada is to survive as a recognizable, autonomous country. But unlike many Canadians who share that outlook, he is generally a decentralist and extremely suspicious of over-concentration of political power at the federal level; he believes that government should be located and acted out at the provincial level. Accordingly, he argues, the country could do a lot worse than simply to return to the substance of the British North America Act of 1867, particularly vis-à-vis division of powers.[40]

His decentralism is much closer in practical terms to the priorities and preferences of Quebecers than to those of Nova Scotians. Kierans, almost alone in English Canada, identifies with a new variation on a Quebec nationalist theme: Ottawa as a dead hand on an otherwise vibrant, assertive, and globally competitive Quebec economy. The Allaire Report, which still carries some political force among Quebec nationalists, characterized "Ottawa" as a bloated, beached whale, unable to do anything except roll over and crush something and defile the general atmosphere.[41]

Kierans is sensitive, as so few English-Canadian observers appear to be, to the fact that a major and genuine redistribution of power in Canada may be the only sustainable basis for national unity. As he put it in his piece in *Canadian Forum*, "Separatism began with the unilateral, illegal and unconstitutional takeover of provincial financial resources and responsibilities by a determined Ottawa bureaucracy in 1946," and, as he stresses elsewhere in the same discussion, the bureaucrats have been at it ever since.

So, a sceptical view of Kierans's role on the Nova Scotia working committee might be that, after all, he was not exactly the right man for the job. Nova Scotia's reliance on federal transfers and national social and development policies makes the typical Nova Scotian – and many of them made this very point before the committee – strong centralists. And little of Kierans's decentralizing inclination is recorded in the report, even in his own introduction. A good and faithful listener, Kierans kept his pledge, and passed on to the government a "true copy" of what the people had asked him to report. He decided in the end, though, to vote against the Charlottetown Accord, and he issued a press release to ensure as many people as possible knew about it.[42] His reasons represented a reversion to form. The accord represented the constitutional entrenchment of matters that were better left to legislatures. There were too many disparate proposals to allow for a simple yes or no answer. Politicians were abdicating to the courts their responsibilities for social and political issues. In sum, "Canadians will not be living in a flexible, political democracy but in the straitjacket of constitutional forms and courtroom procedures that are by nature unresponsive to change, inflexible in their approaches, and insensitive to regional differences." The Nova Scotian statist gave way in the end to the Canadian decentralist.

WHITHER OTTAWA?

Meanwhile, Kierans found a way to get in a real dig at "Ottawa." On the regular segment on CBC's "Morningside" involving "Camp, Kierans and Lewis," Kierans called for transfer of the nation's capital to Winnipeg. This interjection generated, apart from incredulity, little more than amused bewilderment in Kierans's fellow guests, host, and listeners. He was quite serious, but only a few people who knew him best could have realized how serious. Some of his reasons seemed a bit beside the point: the city's location at the geographic centre of the country, if not the continent; the almost representative ethnic mosaic of its population; and its genuine, as opposed to forced or transplanted, local culture. Kierans really wanted to emphasize that if this country is to have a national government with which it can live (or survive), it is going to have to start over – from scratch.

As Allan Fotheringham, among a handful of journalists, understood, the origin of Kierans's proposal was the briefly touted transfer of the seat of government for the Soviet Union from Moscow to Minsk.[43] He was as much as saying to Canadians that if they, like the oppressed citizens of the Soviet Union, want to rid themselves of the dead hand of a bloated, privileged, obstructive, and ossified government, they had better copy them and move the government somewhere else, leaving behind thousands on thousands of apparatchiks. "Ottawa," the creature from the deep lagoon of unwarranted, self-perpetuating, self-reinforcing political centralization, cannot be reformed; it cannot be "renewed"; it must be killed.

For Kierans, this is in fact a program intended to reform, not abandon, strong national government and centrally defined economic policies. For Kierans, there is important work for a national government to do in Canada, but it must be work that only a national government can do, or do properly. It is his view that the financial and human resources necessary to do this work, and do it even better than it is being done now, can be marshalled for a fraction of its current cost. The excess cost is either more appropriately and potentially more effectively spent at the provincial level, or it is sheer waste.

Kierans opens himself to a charge of inconsistency, and certainly to misunderstanding, by attempting to balance the need for good, central government and the need for this central government – standing in a fifty-year tradition of excessive concentration of power in Ottawa – to go. This stance shows that detractors of the decentralist option are caught on a slight inconsistency of their own. They seem more content to defend what federal powers should be like, but to say little about what federal government should be like. This seems to perform politically as a sort of permissive condition allowing the present federal government to lay down the tools of government, as it were, with such acts as the FTA and various measures of deregulation and privatization while holding on to enormous budgets (read: deficits), massive bureaucracy, and continuing intrusions into provincial jurisdiction. For over thirty years, Eric Kierans has been inviting Canadians to join in a serious and focused debate over the proper delineation of federal power, especially the spending power, a position that he has shared throughout that period with a great many Quebec nationalists. It would be tragic for Canadians to discover that Quebec nationalists have wanted little more than this all along but ended up with separation instead.

CHAPTER ELEVEN

A Political Economy for All Canadas

Eric Kierans is unique in having served in the cabinets of both Jean Lesage, during Quebec's Quiet Revolution, and Pierre Trudeau, Quebec nationalism's most powerful and articulate antagonist. He is also one of only a few members of either cabinet – apart, of course, from Trudeau himself – who still contributes to Canadian policy debates. He does so as a politician who has witnessed, often at first hand, the most significant turning points in recent Canadian history. The relationship between nationalism and liberalism in Canada is an important part of most of these turning points, a relationship that Kierans has addressed as a conflict between advanced capitalism and the preservation of independent communities. An examination of the political economy and political career of Eric Kierans, therefore, provides a valuable opportunity to explore the relation between nationalism and liberalism as philosophical doctrines as well as the parts played by both doctrines in the recent history of the country.

A measure of the uneasiness in the relation between nationalism and liberalism in Canada over the past thirty years is the fact that a profound anti-nationalist like Pierre Trudeau and a spirited Canadian nationalist like Eric Kierans were part of the same national Liberal government in 1968.[1] Moreover, while both men counted themselves as opponents of the separatist extreme of Quebec nationalism, they have shown very different reactions to the demands of Quebec and other provinces for decentralization of federal power. In short, Trudeau was an anti-nationalist and a centralist; Kierans was a nationalist and a decentralist. As a consequence, in Kierans's eyes, Trudeau's preoccupation with the defeat of French-Canadian nationalism resulted in his government's neglect of Canada's difficulties in fending off the economic intrusions and political influence of the United States. Meanwhile, Kierans's nationalism and anti-centralism were at odds with the Liberal government and the federal civil service – that is to say, with Ottawa – during the late 1960s and the 1970s. In the early 1970s, however, Kierans and his views gained wider public support – though more outside the ranks of the Liberal party than within it – as it became increasingly clear to many Canadian nationalists that Liberal policies were doing little to prevent, and possibly much to promote, US domination of Canada.

An outline of the career of Eric Kierans can be formed by tracing the ways in which nationalism and liberalism intertwine, like a strand of conceptual DNA, through his public clashes with some of the most prominent Liberals of his time. He received much national attention in 1963 by attacking, as president of the Montreal Stock Exchange, the ill-fated budget of Walter Gordon, the Liberal minister of finance whose memory most Canadian nationalists revere to this day. Many critics of Kierans point to this episode as evidence of Kierans's dilettantism, opportunism, or, at best, inconsistency. While it is often difficult to know whether this criticism betrays a desire to discredit his past anti-nationalism or his later nationalism, the charge of inconsistency seems inescapable. Kierans himself, much later, went out of his way to acknowledge this. In his own exploration of the American threat to Canada in the 1983 Massey Lectures, he paid tribute to Gordon, "who foresaw most of this long before the rest of us."[2]

Kierans's relation with René Lévesque and Québécois nationalism are also topsy-turvy. Almost immediately upon becoming Quebec's minister of revenue Kierans helped wrest the finances of the province from the stranglehold of the English-speaking financial establishment and forcefully advocated within cabinet Lévesque's determined interventions in the economy. After the defeat of the Lesage government in 1966, Kierans (as party president) nevertheless manoeuvred a convention of the Quebec Liberal Federation into presenting Lévesque and other Quebec nationalists with an ultimatum to either renounce separatism or quit the party. Thus Kierans was both one of the strongest English-Canadian allies and one of the most consequential early adversaries of Quebec's leading nationalist.

Oddly, perhaps, one of the earliest signs of Kierans's Canadian nationalism occurred while he was still a member of the Quebec Liberal government. On this occasion (in January 1966), he generated a storm of controversy by doing an "end-run" around Prime Minister Lester Pearson and the governor of the Bank of Canada to

protest, as the federal government had not, the US Johnson administration's declaration of guidelines to American multinational firms.
These guidelines had in effect instructed the parent companies of
American-controlled subsidiaries in Canada (and around the world)
to ensure larger returns to the American economy from their foreign
operations. Kierans was stunned by the apparent complacency with
which Ottawa's leading economic decision-makers were prepared to
greet this (to him) blatant US attempt to use foreign operations of its
multinational companies to advance American economic interests
over the national interests of host countries.

Similar but more protracted conflicts between Kierans and the
Liberal economic establishment ensued upon his arrival in Ottawa
in 1968. Concretely, most of these fights involved the government's
failure to adopt, as directly and as comprehensively as Kierans
would have preferred, the recommendations of the Carter Commission on tax reform. More broadly, they were about the kind of tax
and other economic policies that Kierans felt were minimally
necessary to begin to reverse the growth of American control of the
Canadian economy. By 1971, Kierans's frustration over Trudeau's
economic policies in taxation, foreign investment, and energy had
accumulated to the point that he believed that he had to resign from
the government, and for the remainder of the decade he sustained
media attention as one of the strongest and most vocal critics of
Liberal economic and energy policies.

Some final twists and turns occurred more recently. Perhaps the
most striking, Kierans, like Liberal leader John Turner, opposed the
Free Trade Agreement (FTA) while supporting the Meech Lake Accord. To Kierans, the FTA had practically nothing to do with the un-
hindered exchange of goods between countries (which as an economic liberal he has always supported), and almost everything to do
with formalizing the kind of economic continentalism that Liberal
cabinets – one of them including John Turner as finance minister –
had promoted during the 1960s and 1970s. Kierans thus found
Turner's conversion to economic nationalism a little late and
unconvincing.

As for the Meech Lake Accord, Kierans and Pierre Trudeau, each
in his way a nemesis of René Lévesque as a Quebec separatist, were
directly and profoundly at odds with one another over centralization and decentralization. Trudeau came to Canadian nationalism
by way of opposition to separatism and the increased power of
provincial governments; Kierans, despite his unequivocal rejection
of separatism, has always seen enhancement of the power and
responsibility of all provincial governments as crucial.

Over the years, Kierans has repeatedly celebrated of the creative and productive energies set loose within economies based on individual entrepreneurship and sustained competition – in other words, his belief in capitalism. One can also find evidence of his apparently antithetical view that humanity's material pursuits must be bounded by a higher commitment to the common good, which can be realized only within distinct and autonomous political communities. He believed that both capitalism and community are being undermined by the expanding and tightening control of the modern international corporation.

While it may be that this institution and the "managerial capitalism" that it embodies are justified and rationalized by the new "liberal" ideology, this new liberalism shares practically nothing with the capitalism of Adam Smith or, for that matter, the liberalism of John Stuart Mill. In Kierans's view, the institutional form of managerial capitalism and this new brand of liberalism – not capitalism itself – are irreconcilable with nationalism and the autonomy of communities. Indeed, true capitalism may provide a more effective buttress for autonomous communities than the versions of socialism most familiar to this generation of Canadians. The ultimate conclusion of this study is that, during the last three decades, Canadians have seen the dimensions of their public life diminished by the increasing power of American managerial capitalism, and Kierans's actions and thoughts have had the potential to restore a measure of respectability, responsibility, and autonomy to the politics of the Canadian community.

Like George Grant, Kierans has argued against the limitless capitalist accumulation that has threatened to overwhelm Canadian autonomy. Yet, unlike Walter Gordon, he has not tended to see imposition of national barriers against inflows of foreign investment as a sufficient or even necessary condition for an independent and prosperous Canadian economy. Hence, many Canadian nationalists -including, as we have already noted, George Grant himself – have attacked Kierans for his substantial part in forcing reversal of Gordon's budget. The details of this bitter dispute have already been reviewed. However, the essential difference in outlook between Kierans and Gordon partially explains Kierans's political economy.

Kierans has never looked at foreign control in isolation from other economic conditions, such as corporate concentration and excessive dependence on the export of primary resources, or from other political concerns, such as the excessive centralization. In short, Kierans has always regarded the evils associated with foreign control as a sub-case of the evils associated with the concentration of economic and political power more generally. The answer to American corporate control of Canada is the defeat of managerial capitalism in general, and that defeat is in turn a matter of imposing upon the practices of *all* businesses in Canada, regardless of their ownership, limits and conditions according to the political will and best interests of their national or provincial constituents.

George Grant's condemnation of Kierans for attacking Gordon's budget – followed by almost every self-described Canadian nationalist ever since – is thus misdirected. Having identified Kierans with the service to "international capitalism" that he saw as characteristic of most Canadian capitalists, Grant went on to criticize Kierans for supporting within the Quebec government attempts to expand provincial control of economic development: "The division of powers weakens the ability of public authority to control private governments [i.e., large corporations]; the size of the provinces allows them to be controlled by private economic power. The espousing by American or Canadian 'conservatives' of greater authority for the local states has always a phoney ring about it unless it is coupled with an appeal for the break-up of continental corporations."[3] Kierans had long tirelessly called for the break-up of all large corporations – "continental," international, American or, indeed, Canadian. In short, for Kierans, the problem of foreign business is indistinguishable from that of big business, and his solution to the problems associated with big business in Canada generally would take care of those associated with foreign investment.

Kierans has always been concerned less about keeping (or getting) foreign capital out than about the economic policies and conditions that it encounters once it's in. Moreover, he was convinced that the best policies to apply to foreign investment in Canada were those that should apply to capital in general. Kierans's reaction to the Gordon budget cannot be properly understood in isolation from Gordon's (and Liberal governments') general silence on the more fundamental ailments afflicting the post-war Canadian economy. Kierans's views towards foreign control originated in his more general adherence to the dual principles of decentralization of power and subordination of markets to community authority.

In fact, if Kierans deserves to be condemned for his attack on Gordon's budget, it should be less over any alleged defence of "continental capitalists" than over the unintended – though no less culpable – set-back to assertion of Canadian priorities against the interests of American investors (and, unfortunately, Canadian ones, too, which was Kierans's point). His attack on Gordon was not meant to promote continentalism or what was then often referred to as the "Americanization" of Canada. Kierans was opposed to Gordon's approach not because he felt that it was anti-American or would reduce foreign control, but because he saw it as the wrong answer – certainly insufficient and potentially damaging – to the problems stemming from foreign control.

Nevertheless, the severity of Kierans's reaction and the finality of his objections may have carried an unnecessarily high price, even if many of his objections were justified in economic terms. Kierans may have sincerely felt that he was repudiating a set of unworkable and misdirected budget provisions for which economic nationalism was no excuse, but in fact he helped to discredit for some time all forms of economic nationalism in Canada. He certainly contributed, as the regretful tone of Denis Smith's telling of this episode would help us believe, to the political emasculation and demoralization of Walter Gordon himself, at a time when the Liberal party of Canada might still have held some hope of moving effectively towards a more autonomous economic posture.

Thus it must be conceded that Kierans in 1963 placed too much emphasis on an economic climate conducive to capitalism in Canada and too little stress on the political climate necessary to strengthen the Canadian community. The conversion of Eric Kierans to economic nationalism since 1963, then, can be summed up as a shift in the balance between those two concerns towards the importance of community and the political changes needed to solve some of Canada's long-standing problems. But that change, too, had external causes. One was the part that he played in governing Quebec during a time of greatly strengthened nationalism there. The other was a change in the attitude of the US government towards its multinational firms, which were seen no longer simply as private business agents but as arms of the American state.

The question of whether Kierans or Gordon was "right" in 1963, or indeed whether Kierans was more "right" in 1963 or in 1966, hinges critically on whether or not the character of American investment (that is, of American-controlled companies in Canada) changed substantially as a consequence of Washington's 1965 guidelines. As economic agents pursuing their own economic interests, foreign capitalists hold no dangers for a properly constituted community, for such a community will have established policies to ensure that all the capitalists in its midst act in ways conducive to achievement of its collective ends. However, should a foreign government convert its capitalists to political agents pursuing its own national interests, foreign investment may need to be targeted for special attention from the community – not to exclude it, but to ensure that it is subject to domestic rather than foreign laws and economic priorities. Kierans was concerned primarily with "extraterritoriality," and his solution was to be found in more decisive action by host governments.

As president of the Montreal Stock Exchange, as a member of Jean Lesage and Pierre Trudeau's cabinets, as author of a study of resource policy in Manitoba, as an economist, and as a student of Canadian public affairs, Kierans has learned something about the behaviour in Canada of the subsidiaries of American and other foreign companies and about the special challenge that they present to those who wish to act on behalf of the Canadian community. It is a challenge that Pierre Trudeau and the rest of the Liberal cabinet either ignored altogether or, at best, addressed only superficially. It was a challenge that Eric Kierans not only met head on himself but placed before Canadians in a forceful and distinctive manner.

KIERANS'S POLITICAL ECONOMY

Thus one of the most important bridging acts that Eric Kierans performed was linking the politics and economics of Canada's survival as an autonomous and united community. Not only is he simultaneously an economic thinker and a political actor, but his economic thought itself has politics – and the relation between politics and economics – at its very core. In short, Kierans's thought amounts to a particular type of political economy, and parts of it are original. One such part is the way in which his thought implicitly runs along the lines of the growing discipline of public choice. As we saw in the previous section, Kierans is a "radical democrat" and believes in the "sovereignty" – that is, the ultimate political responsibility – of the individual. In other words, the foundation of his political-economic position is an individual very similar to the "rational actor" of the public choice theorists. Another such part is the distinctive point of intersection that he establishes between politics and economics – namely, the creative powers of agency that the political actor and the economic entrepreneur have in common. I elaborate briefly on each of these elements of his political economy, in turn.

Public Choice

How do the ideas and public life of Eric Kierans intersect with theories of public choice? There appear to be two possible applications, both involving Buchanan and Tulloch's fairly elementary observation that all rational actors face a trade-off between two types of unavoidable costs. The first is the possible consequences for each actor of the unpredictable, unregulated conduct of other actors – what economists call "externalities." The second is the cost of joining together with others to establish institutions for prevention of such conduct or its negative consequences through exercise of authority over all actors – what economists call "organizational costs" or "decision-making costs."[4] Two aspects of Kierans's political economy can be highlighted using this basic framework.

The first application is Kierans's belief that providing a good example to others is the cheapest possible way of helping to prevent actions by others that are costly to oneself. It may not be much protection, but any benefit so derived represents a positive return because the investment in it is zero, since it is free of any expenditures on organization. Thus Kierans's conduct as a politician was, at least in part, simply intended to be exemplary. Moreover, something of this logic lies behind his use of St Augustine's injunction, "Love, and do what thou wilt." A sensibly self-regarding actor would never undertake action harmful to others in the community, or to the community itself, given the benefits that the rational actor knows that he or she obtains from the community. To "free ride" on the community is ultimately to undermine its capacity to provide general benefits. Thus, at many points in Kierans's life one can see him seeking, if not acting, to expose those whom he believed to be conducting themselves irresponsibly – either other politicians or public servants whom he thought were "on the make," if not "on the take," or indeed any individual whom he felt to be wasting his or her talents and taking an insufficient share of responsibility for the public good. There is a moralistic streak in Kierans, and it is a form of public morality, in contrast to (say) the intrusive self-righteousness of fundamentalist Christians.

A second application of insight from the public choice perspective has to do with the proper exercise of public authority. A good deal of Kierans's life in government, as we have seen, was devoted to resisting the erosion of public authority by private interests and self-regarding authorities. Kierans's fundamental understanding of government was not that far different from Hegel's conception of the transcendent, absolute state or, at least, some democratically accountable version of it. If governments habitually give way to the particularized demands of special interests, they can do so only by adopting policies that impose heavy external costs on other members of the society or, indeed, on the community as a whole. The acceptance by the state of a particular individual's or group's demands represents a sort of "public policy rent," and such behaviour merely intensifies competition among groups for such rents – a condition described earlier as "hyperpluralism." The record shows that Kierans was concerned that the governments of which he was part serve the comprehensively defined national interest, and he suffered unmistakeable isolation when he resisted decisions that conferred special benefits or gave special concessions to particular interest groups.

A third, and final, application of the public choice perspective is entirely speculative, but it may provide a fundamental link between the political economy of Eric Kierans and that of Harold Innis, a connection explored in greater detail below. The efforts that an individual may be inclined to expend in organizing demands for institutional reform – that is, energy spent on political action – are costly to individuals, and it is difficult, if not impossible, for those individuals to "capture" the benefits that flow from their efforts. Political organizations and individual activists are constantly confronted with this consequence of the problem of "free riders," who can benefit from social change whether they contribute to its realization or not.

Two dimensions of Kierans's life are illuminated by this line of analysis. First, he largely eschewed political organization; he was indeed a "maverick" within the Liberal party – happy to run for office as a Liberal, but spending very little effort on the collective fortunes of the party, as such. This facet of his political career is explored below, but the public choice perspective reveals the rationality of this sort of "under-investment in institutional reform." Second, most of Kierans's efforts concerning social reform were essentially economic: he has shown much more sympathy for small firms than for small groups and for entrepreneurs than for "organizers." Agents of economic change – entrepreneurs – are likely to benefit directly from the innovations that they bring to the marketplace, while political agents of change are not. As the next section shows, the most fundamental tenet in the political economy of both Kierans and Harold Innis is the importance to society of economic agency, and both see individual entrepreneurship as a vital factor in the freedom and welfare of human societies. While neither man justifies entrepreneurship explicitly in such terms, their grounding of the indeterminacy of human affairs in economic, rather than political agency could well reflect instinctive appreciation of the inherent irrationality that confounds political action. For both thinkers, the "creative destruction" that can undermine the economic monopoly which supports the over-centralization of power is likely to be typical more of economic than of political markets.[5]

Political and Economic Agency

The second major dimension of Kierans's political economy, then, has to do with a synthesis of politics and economics through his central concern with human agency, which is a prized characteristic in both the economic and the political realms. For Kierans, the essence of both politics and economics is creativity, newness, and the making of beginnings. His economic agent is not the manager of a global corporation (or worse, of one of its subsidiaries) but instead the individual entrepreneur. His economic concerns all centre on creation of new enterprises, not consolidation or perpetuation of existing ones. As a result, he favours death duties, opposes existing barriers to entry of new firms, and – like the Schoolmen – condemns those who ceaselessly labour to acquire riches so that they may some day live without labour (or pass on riches to their children).

Moreover, as a businessman and cabinet minister, Kierans himself placed emphasis on getting things started: he built a new company out of the ruins of an old one. He lent his experience and energy to the public entrepreneurship of the province of Quebec. He made an essential contribution to the origins of Telesat. All his life he has sought new beginnings. Even "the community" that he brings into his arguments for primacy of politics over economics is new: "a community is made of a land and the people who come to it," as he has said so often. Finally, time and time again he has emphasized a concern for the youth of Canada and Quebec in major addresses.

Kierans's economic and political orientation also holds significance for a specifically Canadian political economy. Most of the Canadian academics and intellectuals who today consider themselves practitioners of political economy share two qualities. First, they see themselves as working in the tradition of Canadian economic history stemming from the work of Harold Innis and his followers – the "staples school" or "staples theorists." Second, they tend to place themselves on the political left – they call themselves variously Marxists, socialists, social democrats, or democratic socialists.

While Innis, like Kierans, was an anti-monopolist and strongly resented all kinds of American influences as alien to Canada's traditions and circumstances, he was in no way a Marxist or a socialist – a characteristic that he also shares with Kierans.[6] J.R. Mallory finds a possible source of the confusion of the Marxian and Innisian perspectives in the minds of those who do not think through the ideas of either carefully enough. At the time when Innis and his immediate followers did their path-breaking work, economic historians "provided the only hard data there was" on which to base explanations of Canadian political development. The result was a possible bias in their work towards "economic determinism."

Economic determinism is not equivalent to political explanations based on class conflict – an identification that Innis certainly would not have made. The economic factor in his historical determination was surely not class conflict, but rather technological innovation and adaptation. Because of Innis's inattention to Marxist stress on class cleavages as a determinant of political evolution, Innis's ideas are closer to Kierans's than to those Canadian political economists who treat him as their mentor. It is possible, then, to explore some central issues by examining both the similarities between Kierans and Innis and their differences with the current mainstream of Canadian political economy.

There are two principles on which the two men agree and on which both disagree with Canadian socialists and political economists. One is avoiding unrealistic degrees of centralization in Canada; the other is recognizing the central significance of the creative individual as an agent of economic change and growth. To begin with the principle of decentralization, Robin Neill succinctly reminds us that "Innis wanted to decentralize planning as much as possible to the provincial level and to construct a strategic balance between government and private enterprise."[7] As we have seen, this fits rather closely Kierans's own views on returning power from Ottawa to the provinces. Equally, Kierans would have agreed with Innis's preoccupation, as Neill puts it, with "the self-accelerating bias of centralization that increasingly used [centrally stimulated] growth to overcome its problems."[8]

Moreover, Neill summarizes Innis's rejection of the Rowell-Sirois Commission's recommendations (1940) in terms that could be taken as an intellectual profile of Eric Kierans on the same subject. Innis, Neill tells us, saw the commission's policy proposals as "a type of Keynesian manipulation of national income that could not be carried out without prejudice to democracy in Canada," and he believed that the commission had constructed "an artificial division of functions at the national level ... while the real need for equilibrium adjustments was ignored in favour of grants to the depressed areas."[9] Innis, in contrast, thought that Canada's most fundamental economic problem was the highly uneven incidence of the country's tariff structure in the face of profound regional differences, and he contemplated a variable tariff to operate in the manner of fiscal policy.[10] While Kierans has never mentioned that approach specifically, he has certainly identified equalization payments and other federally determined grants to the provinces as second-best solutions to problems created by misguided national policies.

On the role of creative individuals, again Kierans and Innis display similarities – and distance from Marxists. For both men, political-economic agency originates with individuals, not classes. Here, also, one can detect the possible source of the Canadian socialists' failure to appreciate their differences with Innis. He, like Kierans, feared for the preservation of individual agency in an era of monopoly: huge corporations smother or displace entrepreneurs as effectively as they oppress workers. However, sharing a common enemy in the forces of economic concentration does not mean that entrepreneurs and "the working class" see the role of individual creativity in the same light. Clearly, a thinker who condemns, as Innis did, British intellectual socialists for promoting "labour imperialism" and dismisses the strategy of their Canadian counterparts as a campaign to "work up sentiment in favour of government intervention and then to accept positions in Ottawa to carry it out" is not looking to political mobilization of the working class to solve economic problems.[11]

Indeed, Innis and Kierans share a bleak vision of what Innis called a "New Dark Age" of bureaucracy sustained by the new social sciences. Moreover, both see the answer to this in the creativity of the individual, which is still a key factor in deciding the direction ultimately taken by societies whose environmental constraints never exclude room for significant moral choices made by the individuals within them.[12] Thus, Neill's understanding of how, for Harold Innis, the price system ("the market") must always be indeterminate runs parallel to the argument put forward here that, for Kierans, economic behaviour is conditioned by the beliefs that define a community. Because human preferences and beliefs are not only diverse, but also themselves derived from more deeply embedded values, the non-economic (or "extra-economic") ends of men and women will channel, contain, and redefine more purely economic activity – or, at any rate, they should. The role of values for Innis thus resembles the role of "limits" for Kierans, and both fit very neatly with the dawning realization within mainstream economics that social norms and conventions – even quite localized and peculiar ones – affect the efficiency of markets.[13]

In fact, it is the deterioration of such limits that places both Innis and Kierans in a comparable position of antagonism to the United States. However, the evil that both men associated with the United States was not the result of a fundamental malaise that had somehow uniquely afflicted Americans; rather, the United States is condemned as the epitome, or culmination, of a malaise in Western civilization. If, for Lenin, imperialism was the highest stage of capitalism, then for Innis and Kierans the highest stage of imperialism was the United States. Kierans has generally been more reticent than Innis had been to attribute "totalitarianism" to the United States,[14] but he would have no difficulty subscribing to Innis's dark view of the direction in which the United States was taking humanity:

The economic development of the United States had put it at the forefront of developments in the technology of mass production. Because it had deliberately turned away from the cultural heritage of Europe, the United States had founded its traditions on the techniques of mechanization. For an unrepentant individualist like Innis, and for someone with his deep appreciation of the difficulties of creativity, this could only forbode the cretinization of the English-speaking world: 'mass production and standardization are the enemies of the West.' Yet the post-war years saw the emergence of the United States as a world power, an object for emulation. And those who would not emulate would be crushed. Art, culture, and creativity were severely threatened by the rise of the mass man.[15]

It is not relevant here to explore how Innis traced this problem to such factors as the "mechanization of public opinion," the aforementioned loss of the Augustinian concept of limits, and the "militarism" of the American constitution. Kierans, in his writing, has not explicitly addressed these same factors, or indeed provided as thoroughgoing and penetrating an analysis of the dimensions of this problem as Harold Innis. Both men, however, saw one of the few sources of hope in this situation in human creativity, particularly in human economic creativity. In the context of meeting the modern challenge of reconciling freedom and order, Innis once declared, "I am more and more convinced that we need to know the background which admits of the entrepreneur's emergence and that we can then see a little more clearly the conditions which will admit of his continuance."[16] Kierans has never so deeply explored this problem, but he gravitated towards the same solution – institutional and economic conditions encouraging to the individual economic agent.

This discussion has come full circle to Kierans at the Montreal Stock Exchange. It has also returned to Kierans as the president of a stock exchange in the province of Quebec, where he experienced so strongly and personally how the economic acquisitiveness of individuals must be directed towards the requirements of a community. Both Kierans and Innis, unlike typical Canadian political economists, take more inspiration from Adam Smith than from Karl Marx or the famous Fabian Socialists. Of course, the Adam Smith that they admire is not, as Neill has put it, the advocate simply of prices and competition but, rather, the philosopher of techniques, habits, customs, tastes, aspirations and resources – of, in a word, community.[17] For both Innis and Kierans, the goal of preserving Canada as an autonomous community – and, indeed, Quebec, too, should it decide to go alone – is justified primarily as an instance of decentralization in opposition to the power of monopoly – in this instance, the centralizing tendencies of American capitalism. It is accurate to say of Kierans and Innis what Donald Theall has said of Innis and McLuhan: "Their major contribution in one way was their unself-conscious discovery of the value of Canada as a marginal culture from which to study the central phenomena of the contemporary world. McLuhan tried later to crystallize this in his concept of the DEW line, Canada as an Early Warning System ..."[18] It seems highly likely that the correspondence between the thought of Innis and that of Kierans (for Kierans has said that he had never read much Innis) is a result of the fact that both were spiritually attuned to the "animal spirits" of genuine, competitive capitalism in a society on the geographic margin of the world's greatest concentration of monopoly power.

It is in this sense, too, that Eric Kierans's political economy makes him "the man" for all the other "Canadas" in the world that are similarly trying to cope with their marginal status within the American, Japanese, or European economic empires. As brought out in the above discussion of both the Gordon budget and the US guidelines, Kierans came to economic nationalism neither directly nor comfortably, and indeed he did so only tactically, in a sense. The strategic goal served by the tactic of small-country nationalism – by preservation of the autonomy of small communities – is freedom: from overweening global or regional power, from economic and political over-centralization, from monopolistic control. Innis, too, came to nationalism only warily, for it shares some of the characteristics of collectivist doctrines in general, but for him, too, greater values were in peril. As he once said,

Whatever hope of continued autonomy Canada may have in the future must depend on her success in withstanding American influence and in assisting in the development of a third bloc designed to withstand the pressure of the United States and Russia. But there is little evidence that she is capable of these herculean efforts and much that she will continue to be regarded as an instrument of the United States ... Neither a nation, nor a commonwealth, nor a civilization can endure in which one half in slavery believes itself free because of a statement in the Bill of Rights and attempts to enslave the other half which is free ...[19]

This is a passage that, with some stylistic amendments, could just as easily have appeared in *Globalism and the Nation-State*.

So, again, while distant from Canadian political economy on the question of Marx versus Smith (or even Mill), Kierans and Innis are nevertheless at a common distance with Canadian political economy from the mainstream, American-dominated economics of this century. One litmus test of this difference is precisely the incapacity of mainstream economics to address the economies of actual countries, as opposed to abstract "markets," a lacuna that is reflected in, among other things, the discipline's misreading of Adam Smith. (At times one senses that the difference between most liberal economists and most political theorists corresponds exactly to the distinction between those who have read one paragraph of *The Wealth of Nations* and those who have read more than one paragraph.)[20] As discussed earlier, Kierans sees in Adam Smith an understanding of both the individual and the "nation," and hence of the relation between the two, different from that which one finds represented in the vast majority of modern economists, who love to seize on the metaphor of the "invisible hand" as a prescription for the elimination of government. At the heart of this issue we can see the question of limits to and constraints upon human acquisitiveness and, indeed, the profound question of the whole point of economic activity. The creative economic initiative extolled by Innis and Kierans contrasts dramatically with the ceaselessly acquisitive, "rational actor" of economic theory.

Hannah Arendt offers a superior formulation of this difference. There are some strong affinities between Innis and Kierans's idea of entrepreneurs and technological innovators and her celebration of the political world as a source of the new. Arendt locates the ontological basis of human beings' capacity for action in their "natality" – the fact of their being born into an existing world with an inherent capacity, in due course, to show it a new "one" that it has never seen before.[21] Kierans's creative entrepreneurs and Harold

Innis's purposeful economic agents partake of this distinctly human quality; a typical corporate manager (as such) does not.

The difference, which R.H. Tawney's Schoolman would not have missed, is that the economic agent of Kierans and Innis is creating (or adapting) new products and practices in order to answer some need or interest in a particular society, while the corporate manager is overseeing production and innovation in his firm in order to sustain and enlarge the process of production for its own sake. For Arendt, where the human capacity for action is diminished or neglected, and where respect for the collective needs of communities is lacking, the very point of doing and producing things for others – the principal justification of market activity – disappears, or, rather, circles in on itself. According to Leah Bradshaw:

for Arendt, he who crafts the objects that constitute an objective world does so only for utility and, sometimes, beauty; his activity must always be directed at some purposeful end that is outside his realm of technical understanding. But in a world that is empty of meaningful political action and community, the craft of *homo faber* loses its purpose. In such a world, 'worldliness' would then become confused with the making of things for their own sake, and human existence would be seen as an endless extension into the future where the production of one object is simply the means to produce another. Eventually, *homo faber* would cease to regard his activity as one of providing a stable, objective home for men in the world, and come to see it as a constant transformation of the world ... .

... Once men start to view the products of their own hands as having no other end but to make more products, it is a short step from there to treating all the world, both natural and man-made, as the means to man's infinite making ... If one permits the standards of *homo faber* to rule the world he will 'eventually help himself to everything'.[22]

Kierans believes that the multinational corporation – the triumphal institutionalization of acquisitive humanity – is "helping itself to everything" and, while it is at it, regarding trees and rocks as nothing but paper and metal and all members of every society as nothing but consumers.

POLICY IMPLICATIONS OF
KIERANS'S CAREER

Having seen why Kierans entered public life and the central values and principles that he brought with him when he did so, it is now time to assess the difference that he made once he got there. In this concluding chapter, the quality of the difference that he has made to Canadian politics and public policy will be more carefully considered than its magnitude. Earlier chapters attempted to measure the impact that Kierans had on various events in Quebec and Canadian politics. Quebec government finances during and after the Quiet Revolution, the relations between French and English in Quebec, the structure and role of Telesat Canada, the viability of Canada's telecommunications system, the growth of Canada's aerospace and electronics industries, the attitude of Canadians towards their resources, and a few other facets of Canadian life today show features that developed not only while Kierans was there, but because he was there.

As a record of public service, these marks of Kierans's influence are far from trivial, but even taken together they are far from monumental. Trudeau, Lévesque, several other former Liberal cabinet ministers, some members of national Conservative governments, several national leaders of the opposition, numerous provincial premiers, and even some public servants can boast of larger contributions to the governance of Canada over the past three decades. However, in the realm of ideas and political principles, Kierans's contribution was and still is worthy of attention. Kierans understood better than any Canadian politician of his era what was needed both to make Canada economically independent and to keep it politically united: unlike so many others, he did not buy a solution to one of these problems at the price of neglecting – or exacerbating – the other.

It is appropriate at this point to review some of his ideas critically. I have encountered one very powerful criticism of Kierans (perhaps "challenge" is a better phrase, since it came from someone who regards him very highly). It suggested that Kierans might be seen almost as a "reactionary" – his ideas amount to a perfect solution to the problems of a world that no longer exists. According to economist Thomas Courchene, it is clear enough how Kierans would have reworked economic and institutional policies historically, but much less clear what he would do now, given that his preferred policies were not followed in the past.[23]

This is particularly true of the multinational corporation. The "cosmocorp," as Kierans often calls huge international companies, is now a fact of economic life, and Courchene wants to know how Kierans's much-praised political decentralization (as in his support of the Meech Lake Accord) squares with heightened economic concentration, especially across international boundaries. With prescient insight, Courchene has speculated about what policies

Kierans would devise to come to terms – in ways consistent with his general outlook – with present global economic realities. He might, Courchene posits, insist that mergers be driven only by market considerations, rather than tax provisions; he might apply the Carter Commission's famous "buck is a buck is a buck" formula to the treatment of retained corporate earnings and dividends; he might force firms above a given size to be publicly held and add to this by putting in a "wealth tax" at death; he might subscribe to facets of the Swedish system; and he might endorse "pension-fund capitalism" and workers' control.

Several of these measures in fact were recommended recently by Kierans, in the policy chapter of *The Wrong End of the Rainbow*.[24] Nevertheless, there is something resembling "entrepreneurial nostalgia," if not outright romanticism, in some of the elements of Kierans's approach, and he has failed to deliver on a promise to address directly the issue of the viability of small states in a corporatist world. As Courchene detected, Kierans is caught on the issue of international economic concentration in the era of multi-national corporations. Not only does he prefer smaller political units to larger ones, but his bedrock liberal values dictate that these small political units also be open societies, with as little direct interference by government as possible in business decisions. Kierans cannot simply assume away the cosmocorps, nor can he just take as given the competitiveness of small, national firms. He also expressly denies that he is "talking about Albania."[25] So, what is he talking about?

Kierans is talking in part more about broad directions and tendencies than specific end-states, and he is dealing with questions of more or less, rather than either or. In other words, he is attempting to reverse current trends towards more centralization and larger firms and is not necessarily seriously committed to the breaking up of most existing firms. (He would, however, distribute their profits as income to their shareholders and subject managers to greater accountability to those shareholders.) "Small is beautiful" is a vision with which he would identify, but more as an inspirational ideal than as a fully practical, concrete objective.[26] Yet there can be no doubt that he genuinely believes that the arguments for the greater efficiency of highly centralized and large-scale economic units are greatly exaggerated. Worse, he would add, there are logical flaws in the identification of size with efficiency. For one thing, rationalization of production, even if it did create gains in efficiency, would do nothing to ensure proper distribution of the gains achieved. For another, it is simply not the case that, as the globalists assume, there is "one, true, efficient allocation of all the world's human and material resources."[27] We have seen, too, that he believes strongly in the greater adaptability and flexibility of small firms in response to changing tastes and market conditions.

One possible application of the Kierans philosophy that he did not develop himself, but seems consistent with what he has said, would be to pursue the potential for greater individual initiative and responsibility within large-scale organizations and at local levels. A recent critical analysis of the political thought of Max Weber helps in understanding what this might entail and also places in an interesting light some of Kierans's most significant battles against the Ottawa establishment. In this light, the difficulties that Kierans encountered in Ottawa are simply a Canadian version of the difficulties inherent in the politics and government of large industrial societies, especially their tendencies towards bureaucratization and manipulation of mass publics through vacuous, almost purely symbolic exercises in political and governmental action and utterance.

In a penetrating investigation of these difficulties, Mark Warren instructs us that there are clues within Weber's works that can help us to close the "continuing divergence between the promise and performance of liberal democracies" and arrive at "a meaningful politics in a secularized world."[28] These clues are to be found in studied appreciation of the strengths and weaknesses of Weber's endorsement of charismatic leadership as a means to counter the power of bureaucracy in mass societies – as an answer, that is, to "the bureaucratic displacement of politics and the domination of technocrats."[29]

The outstanding features of Weber's model, according to Warren, were "first, a strong, even Caesaristic political leadership based on the plebiscite and limited by Parliament." Second, Weber expected that this formula for leadership would produce "an equilibrium of countervailing forces between political leadership and bureaucratic power, an equilibrium that would ensure a relatively open and dynamic society." One weakness of this approach, of course, is that the charismatic leadership capable of overpowering or redirecting technocracy is more likely to amount to domination than leadership, especially when, as the sociologist in Weber also saw distinctly, most mass followings of leaders involve "purely emotional and irrational" factors. Plebiscitary leadership, then, may not promote anything that we might want to accept as a democratic process.

During the course of tax reform, to choose one example, Eric Kierans became increasingly frustrated with this ability of technocrats to divert and trivialize the process to the point where it passed as but a pale shadow of Carter's initial design. There is indeed something genuinely Weberian in Leslie MacDonald's account of the power of the "tax professionals" in the field of tax policy.[30]

Meanwhile, and ironically, the cabinet was under the sway of one of the most charismatic prime ministers that Canada has ever seen. However, a less powerful force was directed, in vain as it turned out, against bureaucratic complacency and manipulation. It was a more modest type of political force that Max Weber had seen as another possible challenge to bureaucratic domination – action by courageous, fully responsible individuals. This is the kind of person that, for example, Eric Kierans sees in Tom Kent, and Kent sees in Kierans. Such political actors and public servants exhibit a quality much admired by Weber.

As Warren quotes Weber: "It is immensely moving when a *mature* man – no matter whether young or old in years – is aware of a responsibility for the consequences of his conduct and really feels such responsibility with his heart and soul. He then acts by following an ethic of responsibility and somewhere reaches a point where he says: 'Here I stand; I can do no other.' That is something genuinely human and moving."[31] Neither Kierans nor Kent, sharing at least a touch of this quality in the eyes of most observers, lasted more than three years in the Trudeau regime.

THE LESSONS OF A LIFE IN ITS TIMES

A life is meaningful, it seems fair to say, to the extent that it provides a specific instance of working out the answer to a significant problem of its time. One substantial challenge that seems to have grown more and more unanswerable over the lifetime of Eric Kierans is that of maintaining the identity and integrity of particular communities in an age of increasing global rationalization and homogenization. Kierans saw several important elements of the answer to that problem and, individually, undertook a course of political action that was consistent with his convictions. It is as if he said to himself, "I must do what I can to contribute to the autonomy and integrity of the Canadian community, because if Canada can accomplish this – next door to the world's largest economy, and itself so internally diverse in so many ways – then any country can. But, first, Canada must." Kierans's answer to the Canadian version of this challenge includes, moreover, some distinctive elements. He combined commitment to decentralization of power with affirmation of individual public responsibility, both of which were reviewed in the first section of this chapter.

In Kierans's view, therefore, nationalism and liberalism are not only compatible, but mutually supportive. They are both derived from the same concern for individual Canadians. For Kierans, neither liberalism nor nationalism is a political cause; each is a philosophical principle that he values because he believes that each will advance his real cause – to preserve the capacity of individual Canadians to maintain an open and autonomous community within which they can prosper according to their own priorities and exercise responsibility for the goals that they share with their fellow citizens. Ultimately, Kierans is both a nationalist and a liberal because of his concern to protect the integrity and autonomy of Canadian public life – that is, of the institutions and processes through which Canadians fulfil their obligations as economic, political, and moral actors.

What Kierans sees "slumbering in the stone" is not his model of a perfect Canada into which a mass of people are expected to configure themselves, but a Canadian citizen. His confidence in the individual citizen is the ground of his commitment to the decentralization of economic and political power that we have seen is the key ingredient of his liberalism and economic nationalism. As Kierans sees it, both prosperity and autonomy can be enhanced to the degree that political and economic power and responsibility are drawn down to the community level, where individuals and genuinely accountable institutions exercise and shape events and developments within them. His vision of Canada (which he has tried to use to "break the spell" on its people) can be summed up as that of ten provinces with the same combination of entrepreneurial spirit and strength of community as Quebec, and a national government promoting those national purposes to which the provinces – as "sovereign associates" – have agreed. Kierans has not brought many forward with him in the direction of this vision. But it could happen yet, if more Canadians have as much confidence in themselves as Kierans has in them.

Unfortunately, the universal significance of his answers to the challenges facing Canada is diminished by the fact that, as yet and for the foreseeable future, they have failed. Of course, as an individual, Kierans deserves credit for providing an example of the kind of responsible citizenship that is a necessary part of the survival of any distinct political community. So, one could say that concerned Canadians and concerned citizens of any country could learn from Kierans's example of "political agency" as well as from his ideas about decentralization and entrepreneurial capitalism.

But an even deeper lesson can be learned from the political failure of the Kierans agenda, and his responsibility for that failure. For all the depth of his concern about community, and for all his recognition of the creative energy of individual commitment and political and economic agency, Kierans was largely blind to the significance of collective action. The practical problems of forging and sustaining an effective political coalition around a specific program of action are not to be found in Kierans's writing, nor did he ever enter or try to lead the kind of political movements that seem to be necessary in the modern age, marked as it is by the dual problems of the size and inertia of mass societies and bureaucratic power.[32]

Kierans loved to take on individual bureaucrats (remember the run-in with Louis Rasminsky), and he frequently condemned the mandarins, but I doubt that it ever crossed his mind to lead a "people's movement" against a government agency, or even a neighbourhood's fight against city hall. It is true that he added a strong voice against the Department of Energy, Mines and Resources and the National Energy Board on the issue of the Mackenzie Valley pipeline, but this was as a man of ideas, not as a political leader and coalition builder. Not every Canadian, obviously, can be elected to a provincial or national legislature (let alone both) or appointed to two cabinets. Kierans probably did as much with such successes as anyone could be expected to do. However, good men and women in the right offices will continue to be almost purely matters of coincidence, and of marginal political consequence, unless vastly greater numbers of Canadians are drawn into other forms of action and show themselves capable of taking on the full responsibilities of citizenship that Kierans talks so much about. It was probably not in his nature, but Kierans needed to add to his political agenda a consistent attempt to promote "substantive forms of democracy now lacking in liberal-democratic societies" if he was to achieve any genuine hope of lasting success.[33]

At its peak, in the early 1970s, the Canadian nationalist movement celebrated two champions operating on two different political principles. One was the Waffle "tendency" within the New Democratic Party, and the other was Eric Kierans. It was frequently possible in those days to witness Kierans, Mel Watkins, and Jim Laxer on the same panel, or platform, espousing almost identical goals. But the difference in their approaches to politics was as distinct as the similarity of their goal: returning the control of the Canadian economy to the people of Canada. The Waffle approach was governed by the principle of political and organizational leadership. It was intended to work through (potentially) mass participation, grass-roots organization, and an aggregation of the efforts of a wide range of existing community organizations. It represented an attempt to mix with "ordinary" Canadians – as NDP leader Ed Broadbent was wont to refer to them in the 1988 election – and move them towards creation of "an independent socialist Canada" by means of a redefinition and reorientation of almost all walks of Canadian life. The Waffle Movement operated on the principle that effective political power emanates from – is almost tantamount to – the collective efforts of people acting to promote the public's acceptance of the ends that they share.

Kierans had what most Canadians probably regarded as the better idea – an independent capitalist (or liberal) Canada. (Public opinion polls have for years repeatedly informed us that only about one-fifth of Canadians regard themselves as socialist.) However, Kierans was inclined to give intellectual, rather than organizational leadership to the Canadian public, and the principle governing his view of political action was much closer to the standard approaches of representative democracy – as we have seen, his ambition was to persuade the Liberal party of Canada to adopt different policies. A political realist above all else, he nevertheless did trust the people of Canada to support the right course, given responsible leadership. In short, he was prepared to accept Canadians as he found them. However, this meant that he failed to develop a new political program or mode of collective action, or even to support actively those who did: "I'm not a joiner," he once said in response to precisely this criticism.[34]

Thus, the superior political movement had an unsaleable idea or – more accurately, perhaps – the right idea in an unsaleable form. Meanwhile, the more saleable form of the idea generated no organized, popular movement. Political mobilization was wedded to the inappropriate, politically unacceptable socialist strategy for Canadian independence; the appropriate and acceptable capitalist version was divorced from a broadly based political movement. The people's capitalist declined to become a man of the people, and the principles never met.

It is often said that Canada is a country with too few heroes. This study will not solve that problem, if it is a problem, partly because it has not attempted to make a hero out of Eric Kierans. Kierans does, however, share one characteristic of many tragic heroes. His "downfall" was forged out of qualities that we would otherwise regard as virtues; in the circumstances that he faced, some of his strengths became weaknesses. His forthrightness and independence left him with few political allies and led him to eschew even a limited degree of political horse-trading and coalition building. His strong, almost moralistic commitment to principles and standards of conduct made him some outright enemies. His outspokenness, while it excited the press, cooled his fortunes among those in positions of power. His intelligence and deep engagement with the ideas and ends that must inform good government led, as we have just seen, to near-indifference to the means of promoting broadly based collective action and possibly innovative modes of politics. But one person can only do so much, and the public record supports the conclusion that Kierans pursued energetically and openly the kind of politics that was true to his nature. In other words, he exemplified the kind of politics in which he believed. If nothing else, his is an example that, were sufficient attention paid to it, might at least move Canadians to expect more of their political representatives than they generally do.

Eric Kierans has been an extraordinary capitalist, and an exceptionally concerned Canadian. It is a rare thing for a character to exist whose life exemplifies its most treasured principles. In Kierans's case, this has meant living two "isms" – Canadian capitalism and Canadian nationalism – that need never have even been separated from one another, much less at odds with one another. In doing this in his thinking, writing, speaking, and acting, he set a notable standard for men and women in public life. It is a high standard of integrity, honesty, and public spiritedness, but one that is far from heroic and by no means beyond the grasp of just about any Canadian with comparable gifts and a similarly genuine concern for the state of the country. Indeed, it is a standard to which all Canadians might aspire, but which lamentably few try to reach.

Kierans to Walter Gordon, June 1963

June 18, 1963

The Honourable Walter L. Gordon, F.C.A.,
Minister of Finance,
Parliament Buildings
OTTAWA, Ontario

Dear Mr. Minister:

The financial capitals of the world have just about had enough from Canada. Last Friday, the initial reaction to the budget was one of bewilderment and dismay. Yesterday, it was anger and scorn. Today, our friends in the Western World fully realize that we don't want them or their money and that Canadians who deal with them in even modest amounts will suffer a 30% expropriation of the assets involved. And their reaction? If that is what Canadians want, let them have it!

May I offer a few general comments!

1) The entire series of measures aimed at discouraging non-resident investment is based on a serious error. In the budget address you stated: "As I indicated earlier, it is the policy of this government to encourage direct foreign investment in new enterprises in this country on the basis of partnership with Canadian residents. While this type of investment is a great value to Canada, it is our view that non-resident 'take-overs' of established Canadian companies rarely confer any benefit on the Canadian economy."

This is complete and utter nonsense. A non-resident take-over confers great benefit on the Canadian economy. We may not like it but that is not the point. The new owners bring the advantages of new technology, new reserach and development, new products and ideas which can immensely benefit the Canadian consumer and which will be denied him otherwise. The former owners receive funds which become available for investment in new Canadian enterprises or in government undertakings which contribute to the expansion of our economy. Even if they invest the funds abroad, we reduce the balance of our international indebtedness and the income in dividends and interest from such investment improves our balance of payments by reducing the net outflow on current account. *All this is elementary.*

2) Underlying this series of measures is a misconception about the part played by shareholders. I quote – "I suggest that a 25 per cent equity interest is in most cases appropriate to ensure that a smaller percentage would probably not be sufficient for this purpose. A Canadian point of view is always available when company policy decisions are arrived at. A larger percentage would be neither necessary nor in many cases practicable."

Presumably, you are counting on the Canadian shareholder demanding a larger raw material content, a certified list of fees and expenses paid to management, detailed statements of the subsidiary's export efforts, prices of inter-company transfers of materials and components, etc. A not very proud role is assigned to the Canadian shareholder. His contribution will be to badger, to harass and to torment management and the 75% controlling interest. How futile and how unrealistic! Today, the shareholder does not care that much. If he does not like a company or its management, he sells his stock and quietly goes his way. A greater Canadian voice in the direction of subsidiaries will not be obtained in this manner. The success(?) of the budget depends on Canadian shareholders imposing their will on the majority interest, which cannot be done.

Canadians have been given the opportunity many times in the past to purchase shares in Canadian subsidiaries but the record has not been a happy one as the attached table, which the Montreal Stock Exchange filed with the Royal Commission on Banking and Finance, shows. If subsidiaries do make 25% available and Canadian shareholders do not respond, are we going to solve the unhappy dilemma *by forced payroll deductions?*

3) The burden of the 30% capital levy falls, naturally enough, on those who have saved, have invested and have so managed their affairs that they possess property and investments of a reasonable size. It falls on listed corporations by virtue of the amendment to the Excise Tax Act and it falls on unlisted, privately-held and family-owned enterprises by virtue of the following paragraph from the budget address: – "It will be noted that this measure applies only to the shares of listed public companies. Measures are under consideration, and may be discussed with the provinces at an appropriate time, which will apply to all Canadian companies including private companies. I trust that no flood of sales of established Canadian concerns to non-residents will develop in an attempt to anticipate the further measures to which I have referred, in light of the declared view of the government that such sales are generally undesirable."

In effect, a family or individual, forced to sell a private enterprise to provide liquidity to meet estate taxes and succession duties, cannot sell in the best market if that market happens to be non-resident. In many instances, there may be no offer from Canadians or an offer far below a non-resident offer. The owner has to compare a non-resident offer minus the 30% confiscation demanded by Ottawa with the best domestic bid. A family, unable to obtain a satisfactory offer from Canadians and reluctant to accept a non-resident offer with the attendant 30% Federal confiscation, may, in the end, lose everything if an untimely death forces the liquidation of their enterprise. There are interesting implications here.

Skipping the semantics, we can see that the Securities Sales Tax is not fundamentally a sales or excise tax, - *it is a tax on wealth, a capital levy*. It is far worse than a 30% capital-gains tax because a capital-gains tax falls on an increase in wealth between two points in time, - *between the value of the asset at time of purchase and the value at time of sale*. This new tax simply expropriates 30% of the asset at the moment of transfer. It is not a sufficient defence to say that the tax applies only in the special circumstances of sales of assets to non-residents. It exists and the levy can be extended in its application at the will of the Federal authority.

Secondly, if the Government is not concerned here with revenue (the unbelievable rate is evidence of this), the purpose of the budget must be to destroy (prevent) certain activities engaged in by its citizens. In other words, the Government is using the power to tax really to prohibit the sale, by Canadians of assets for money to citizens of the United States, United Kingdom, France or other friendly powers. I am not a lawyer but it seems to be that legislation of this nature respecting property and civil rights comes under Provincial jurisdiction and is beyond the competence of the Federal government.

Premier Lesage, René Lévesque, Paul Gerin-Lajoie and other members of the Quebec cabinet have repeatedly referred to the gradual erosion of the autonomy of the provinces. The creation of the new Securities Sales Tax, without prior discussion with the provinces would be difficult to justify at any time; it is unthinkable in the present atmosphere of strain and suspicion. It is a perfect example of the manner in which a new tax 'gimmick' can reduce existing sources of provincial revenue or invade a sphere of provincial authority, namely property and civil rights.

The forcing of increased Canadian ownership of the use of Federal taxing powers creates two distinct sets of problems, – a) the effect on existing subsidiaries and b) the capital levy on future share transactions.

a) By doubling the withholding tax on dividend payments and by refusing certain tax concession to companies with less than 25% Canadian ownership, the government is in effect describing 'good' and 'bad' subsidiaries. This raises certain questions in the applied art of discrimination.

1) Are Dupont and c.i.l. 'bad' Canadian companies? Less than 20% of their stock is in the hands of the public.

2) If they raise public participation to 25%, will they become 'good' Canadian companies and qualify for reduced taxation?

3) If Canadians hold 25% of the shares of these companies one month and then reduce their holdings by 5% to buy bonds, do these companies become 'bad' companies through circumstances beyond their control?

4) Abitibi and many other Canadian corporations, operate wholly-owned subsidiaries abroad. Will foreign retaliatory legislation force these companies to spin off ownership?

5) Does the government intend to offer 25% ownership in the subsidiary of Polymer Corp. to citizens of France? Holland?

6) Does the government expect further direct investment (which it approves, see page 18) to be encouraged to come into Canada by these dipsy-doodling and discriminatory methods of taxing profits and repatriated dividends?

7) Does the government not expect other nations to retaliate?

8) Will these discriminatory measures improve Quebec's chances of attracting capital from Europe?

9) Will we not, in the final analysis, find our capital in the Ottawa printing presses rather than the capital markets of the world?

10) etc., etc.,

b) The 30% capital levy is designed to discourage take-overs but makes no distinction between ordinary portfolio investments in the country and actual take-overs. As a result:

1) The liquidity, depth and breadth of our security markets will decrease sharply and we can look for a decline in the market value of Canadian securities. *The Canadian investor will be the first casualty of the proposed legislation.*

2) Supply and demand forces on Canadian markets become distorted. Foreign buying will be discouraged and Canadian owners of securities will face a 30% confiscation if they offer shares to a value of more than $50,000.00 in one day. This is not a large amount.

3) The tax will create two markets and two prices for Canadian securities - one in Canada where the tax is applicable and liquidity reduced and the other in New York where transactions can take place among non-residents free of tax. Thus the New York and London exchanges will grow at the expense of the Canadian exchanges.

4) Arbitrage houses, which operate between Canada, the United States and Europe and bring great depth to the market, will disappear. They cannot operate on one side of the market only.

5) Hundreds of millions of dollars of Canadian shares held abroad overhang the Canadian market. The Canadian exchanges will now provide

restricted and discriminatory markets for these investors. The liquidation of even a small portion of these holdings would be disastrous to the Canadian equity owner.

6) The budget measures will encourage Canadians to invest in American securities where the markets are free and non-discriminatory. Exchange controls are clearly the next step.

7) Funds, trust companies etc. will hesitate to buy Canadian equities because the markets in which they deal will be reduced and restricted.

8) etc., etc., etc.,

We will not lay the foundations of a greater Canada on a budget such as this. Since the days of the Marshall plan, the nations of the West have been working towards a greater economic and political unity. This budget will turn back the clock as we Canadians shut ourselves up in our own tight little corner.

Foreign ownership is a problem in Canada. You are quite right in this but this investment is not financed by foreign governments or inspired by desires to impair our political sovereignty. It is financed by the savings and investments of friends in other nations and is successful because of the initiative and enterprise that accompanies and manages their capital. The antidote lies in our own private sector as we strive to accumulate the savings to invest on our own account and to find within ourselves a similar energy and imagination. This is a long and hard road but we must remember that we have sought, relied on and lived with foreign capital for generations and cannot now suddenly take an axe to murder the record of trust and confidence that has grown up over the years.

Some day, a political leader will rise up in Canada and say to the Canadian people that the solution to the problem of non-resident ownership does not lie in the vote-getting arena at all; only then will Canadians have found true leadership and only then will our friends abroad breathe more easily and be happy for us.

Sincerely,

Eric W. Kierans,
President

Notes

PREFACE

1 Robert Bolt wrote the play *A Man for All Seasons* (1960) and later
adapted and substantially cut it for the screen; the 1966 film won six
Academy Awards, including one for Bolt (his second in two years) for
his screenplay.

CHAPTER ONE

1 "Should Be Silent for Shame," *Montreal Daily Star*, 2 February 1914,
10.
2 Hopkins, *Canadian Annual Review*, 511–16.
3 On the divergent attitudes towards the First World War held by
Canada's French- and English-speaking communities in Quebec, see
Hugh MacLennan's novel, *Two Solitudes*, Part I.
4 Swift, *Odd Man Out*, 10: "So in the wake of the war when Eric was
five or six, he had to bear the brunt of taunts – 'Hun,' 'Boche,'
'Squarehead.' And, being a scrappy fellow, he would respond in kind,
and fisticuffs often resulted."
5 For details of this setting and of Kierans's early life in it, see ibid.,
chap. 1. In addition to the divisions already mentioned, the Irish-
German mix represented by Kierans's father and mother corresponded
with a Roman Catholic–Protestant one.
6 Ibid., 73.
7 Kierans, "Investment, Savings and Taxes," 9.
8 Kierans, "Economic Implications of Depreciation Policies," 2–3.
9 Kierans, "Financing Future Growth," 9.
10 Canada, Dominion-Provincial Conference (1945), *Dominion and*

Provincial Submission and Plenary Conference Discussions (Ottawa: King's Printer, 1946), 419. Cf. Kierans, "Source," 12–13.

11 Ibid., 530.

12 Charles Taylor, *Hegel*, 435–9.

13 Ibid., 452–3.

14 Kierans, "The Kentian Thrust."

15 In his memoirs, Kent expresses at several places his growing frustration with the same two problems with the Trudeau government that plagued Eric Kierans – the style of leadership and the inadequacy of economic policy. The substance of their complaints, on both counts, is remarkably similar. Kent points to "a chaos of too many decisions too little co-ordinated" as a pole towards which the Trudeau government was inclined. And elsewhere, he points to examples of "the extraordinarily vacillating mix of inappropriate and incoherent policies that marked the Trudeau period." *A Public Purpose*, 247, 14.

16 Kierans, *Report on National Resources Policy in Manitoba* (hereinafter Kierans Report).

17 Apart from such references cited in chapter 9 below, see Miller, "Trends in Mineral Economics Research," 52; Watkins, "The Staple Theory Revisited," 86; and Rugman, "The Foreign Ownership Debate in Canada," 172.

18 Richard and Pratt, *Prairie Capitalism*, 261.

19 Gunton and Richards, "The Political Economy of Resource Policy," 1 and 23.

20 Cairns, "Ricardian Rent and Manitoba's Mining Royalty," 558 and 561. In his own words, "In no sense is Kierans's use of Ricardo's and Mill's ideas to be construed as socialist. His advocacy of Crown corporations does not imply advocacy that the workers gain control of the means of production. His is a nineteenth century liberal position, in no way inconsistent with his having been a Minister in the Canadian and Quebec Liberal Cabinets, or a stock exchange president." See also Cairns's more recent "Reform of Exhaustible Resource Taxation," 650.

21 Anderson, *Natural Resources in Canada*, chap. 5.

22 Cohen and Krashinsky, "Capturing Rents," 412, 415, 418–19.

23 Yudelman, *Canadian Mineral Policy*, 67.

24 Kierans, "Economic Effects of the Guidelines."

25 Nevertheless, Kierans has spent his life in a Canada that is preoccupied with, or possibly in awe of, American power. "Bookends" around this fact can be provided by two visits by American presidents, one the weekend before he was born, the other the "Shamrock Summit" between Ronald Reagan and Brian Mulroney in Quebec City in 1987. In 1914, former American president William Howard

Taft was the guest of honour at the local Canadian Club "and was accorded a welcome spontaneous in character and real in spirit, such has been accorded few speakers in the capital." Among those reported in attendance were the governor-general, the Duke of Connaught; the prime minister, Sir Robert Borden; the leader of the opposition, Sir Wilfrid Laurier; and "most of the cabinet." (See "Wm. Howard Taft Grips Big and Representative Gathering in Ottawa," *Montreal Gazette*, 2 February 1914.) The Shamrock Summit was similar, except for the absence of the governor-general and the leader of the opposition. About Mulroney, Kierans was to say, "He looked like a man who brought his boss home to dinner." Author's personal recollection from a CBC radio broadcast, shortly after the event.

26 Kierans, "Notes for Panel Discussion," comments prepared for a session of a conference "Glasnost and the Global Village," York University, Toronto, 19–22 February 1991. Kierans did not appear at the conference. I nevertheless believe that his draft address is an important documentary source for his views on this matter which he continued to inject into public debate, notably on CBC's "Morningside."

27 Kierans, review of Robert Keohane, *After Hegemony*.

28 Notes for glasnost conference.

CHAPTER TWO

1 Service in both a national and a provincial cabinet – Quebec's or any other – has been relatively rare among Canadian politicians. A recent study has established that only 10.7 per cent of federal cabinet ministers since 1867 had previous experience in provincial cabinets, about half of them as premiers. See Barrie and Gibbons, "Parliamentary Careers," 142.

2 Technically, he was President of the Montreal and Canadian Stock Exchanges (hereinafter president of the MSE).

3 See Levine, *The Reconquest of Montreal*, 40–1. Levine is illustrating the point that "the logic of the Quiet Revolution inexorably led to a movement to dislodge the Anglophone elite and 'reconquer' Montreal as the metropole of French-speaking Quebec."

4 See Swift, *Odd Man Out*, 8–11.

5 Jamie Swift and author's interview with Eric Kierans, 7 August 1986. See also Swift, *Odd Man Out*, 11–14. Kierans once concluded a discussion of his economic philosophy by saying, "I'm a classicist more than anything else." Interview with the author, 12 August 1986.

   Following the Second World War, Kierans repaid some of the debt that he felt he owed to his former Jesuit mentors by introducing them to some of his growing circle of Montreal business contacts in order to raise funding for their recently formed Thomas More Institute for Adult Education (38–9). Kierans also published a moving tribute to the co-founder of this institute – one of his former teachers at Loyola. See his review of Eric O'Conner, SJ, *Curiosity at the Centre of One's Life: Statements and Questions of R. Eric O'Conner*, ed. J. Martin O'Hara (Montreal: Thomas More Institute, 1987), published in *Compass* 7 no. 4 (September 1989) 49–51. Kierans describes with approval the agenda of the More Institute: "it sought to answer the 'why' of living, leaving the 'how' to others."

6 See, for example, David Olive, "Ethicists Display Great Tolerance for Moral Outrages of Business," *Globe and Mail*, 11 July 1989, B5. Olive reviews, sceptically, three recent treatises on "business ethics," which he feels come down to "amorality or even banality." Kierans himself complained recently that a book on "trust" versus "betrayal" in the corporation ignored the corporation's obligations to others such as its customers, employees, shareholders, and country. It was concerned instead "with the loyalty of people to their corporation, not with the loyalty of the corporation to the people with whom it deals." See his review of *Corporate Loyalty: A Trust Betrayed*, by Brian Grosman, in the *Montreal Gazette*, 14 May 1988.

7 It is a rare Canadian business story that does not include at least some governmental involvement. In this instance, Kierans acknowledges that Canadian Adhesives Ltd. benefited greatly from an excellent deal on three buildings purchased in 1953 from the War Assets Disposal Corp. These buildings, which were in "very good shape," allowed Kierans to expand his total plant capacity at very low cost. Telephone interview, 19 August 1992. For a summary of Kierans's early business successes, see Swift, *Odd Man Out*, 22–8. In 1952, Kierans bought another small manufacturing concern, and he sold it eight years later for over ten times what he had paid for it. In the mean time, in order to expand his horizons beyond the practicalities of business, he had been studying graduate economics part-time at McGill University since 1948.

8 An interview that I had with Kierans (19 August 1987) contained a most revealing moment. I wanted to discover whether being in Quebec had influenced his desire to add something, such as a political career, to his commercial accomplishments. I asked whether, all other things being equal, his story would have been substantially the same had he owned a medium-sized manufacturing firm in Toronto, rather than Montreal. For example, would he have accepted an invitation to head the Toronto Stock Exchange and followed that up by seizing a chance to join the government of Ontario? Kierans was

silent for considerably longer than usual upon taking a question. He eventually said, "Oh, I think I see what you are trying to get at. And the answer's no." I asked him how so, and he replied, "Guilt."

9 Swift, *Odd Man Out*, 309–15 and passim. The only review of Swift's book to get directly at this issue appeared in the *Westmount Examiner*. The *Examiner's* reviewer felt that Swift's emphasis on Kierans's inconsistency unduly complicated the picture of the man. Thursday, 4 August 1988, 18.

10 Armstrong, *The Crisis of Quebec*, 35.

11 Ibid., 36.

12 This is translated as "one of us, the best among us." See Levine, *The Reconquest of Montreal*, 46.

13 See Sancton, *Governing the Island of Montreal*, 14.

14 Ibid., 60–1.

15 See McRoberts, *Quebec*, 85; Sancton, *Governing*, 61.

16 Coleman, *The Independence Movement*, 101.

17 Levine, *The Reconquest of Montreal*, 42. One of the empirical measures provided by Levine is the fact that "the percentage of total Canadian stock transactions registered on Montreal's exchanges fell steadily from 86 percent in 1925 to 25 percent in the late 1960s." The last vestiges of the city's "commercial empire of the St. Laurence" – Air Canada, Bell Canada, and Via Rail all headquartered in Montreal – are now also giving way to a wave of deregulation and US-centred market penetration.

18 *McGill Daily*, 26 January 1960.

19 Kierans, "Investment, Savings and Taxes" (14 November 1960). Kierans's four other major speeches in 1960 were "More Saving – Personal or Corporate" (19 May), "Combines – the New Look" (6 June), "Financing Future Growth" (23 June), and "Economic Implications of Depreciation Policies" (12 September).

20 Kierans, "Economic Implications of Depreciation Policies," 11.

21 Kierans, "Financing Future Growth," 4.

22 It may seem as though Kierans is here simply selling the services of the MSE. However, if the alternatives are to say that Kierans was articulating these views because of the job that he held or to say that he held the job that he did because of his viewpoint, the evidence would seem to favour the latter interpretation. As one case in point, much of the economic analysis presented in the five speeches of 1960 can be found in some of the writing that Kierans did while a PhD candidate at McGill. One draft paper concludes as follows: "The problem of freeing and enlarging the area of competition is essentially one of deemphasizing the power of capital in the individual enterprise system and restoring the emphasis on enterprise & initiative, for it is

undeniably true that the enterprising elements in many of our largest corporations died with the founder, and that his heirs, the managers of today who play golf in the summer and go south in the winter, exist solely by virtue of their capital and monopoly position." This paper advocated abolishing the corporate income tax and instead distributing all corporate profits annually as (taxable) income to corporate shareholders. See Taxation Policy and Monopolistic Competition, handwritten manuscript, n.d. (probably 1952 or 1953), copy supplied to author by Eric Kierans from his personal records.

23 Kierans, "Financing Future Growth," 4–7. Kierans provided a list of these dangers as follows. (1) The price of its products will have to be high enough to permit the necessary flow. Such prices and profits are bound to keep within the industry many less efficient firms, which will split the market and rob the large firm of its size and efficiency. These high prices will also attract new competitors. (2) Growth will occur only at the expense of profits. High prices will have to be charged to cover normal direct and indirect costs of production and costs of expanding numbers of plants, products, and areas. (3) Just as high prices may disturb consumers, retained profits and nominal dividends discourage investors. This situation only increases the cost of needed external funds. (4) Where all firms expand from internal funds, there is no effective market test of the application of those funds, and the industry will be prone to waste and to excess capacity.

24 Ibid., 4 and 9–10.

25 Jamie Swift's interview with Charles Denis, 4 June 1986. Denis, fluently bilingual, was a former journalist who had immigrated from France in the early 1950s and had been hired as a public relations officer with the MSE shortly before Kierans took over as president.

26 See Swift, *Odd Man Out*, 53–4.

27 See Courchene, "Market Nationalism." Similar arguments inform his *What Does Ontario Want?*

28 See Swift, *Odd Man Out*, 69–73.

29 *Montreal Star*, 28 February 1963, 10–11 (full text of speech).

30 Manuscript version of Swift, *Odd Man Out*.

31 See Smith, *Gentle Patriot*, 153–63.

32 *Debates*, 13 June 1963, 1006, quoted in ibid., 153. Note that these measures worked to reduce the returns to Canadians selling out their firms to American buyers and, correspondingly, raised the relative attractiveness of selling out to Canadian ones, thus serving on balance to increase the dominance within Canada of large Canadian firms.

33 As quoted in Smith, *Gentle Patriot*, 162–3 and chap. 8, n. 30.

34 See copy of letter, reproduced in Appendix.

35 Smith, *Gentle Patriot*, 163.

36 Letter from Eric W. Kierans, President of the Montreal Stock Exchange, to The Honourable Walter Gordon, F.C.A., Minister of Finance, Montreal, July 24, 1963. This letter written, as Kierans pointed out over twenty years later, "when Canada had begged the U.S. not to do in July that which Canada had proposed to do in June." Letter from Kierans to the author, 22 November 1985.
37 Ibid. Kierans was quoting from the minister's statement as reproduced in a story in the *Montreal Star*.
38 Smith, *Gentle Patriot*, 175.
39 See Wright, "Persuasive Influence," and Molot, "The Role of Institutions."
40 See Smith, *Gentle Patriot*, 176.
41 *Le Devoir*, 21 June 1963, as quoted in Swift, *Odd Man Out*, 84.
42 See Thomson, *Jean Lesage and the Quiet Revolution*, 244.
43 See Fullerton, *Dangerous Delusion*, 58–61.
44 Fournier, *The Quebec Establishment*, 93. See also Jacques Parizeau, "De certaines manoeuvres d'un syndicat financier en vue de conserver son empire au Québec," *Le Devoir*, 2 February 1970. Fournier acknowledges his debt to Parizeau's account and describes him as "the only source of information on the 'financial cartel' in Quebec."
45 Lévesque, *Memoirs*, 185.
46 Jamie Swift's interview with René Lévesque, 6 October 1986.
47 Jamie Swift's interview with Gérard Pelletier, Montreal, 12 September 1986.
48 *Ottawa Journal*, 9 February 1966.
49 Jamie Swift's interview with Michel Bélanger, 3 June 1986.

CHAPTER THREE

1 Jamie Swift's interview with Kierans, 11 March 1986; see also Vancouver *Province*, 16 May 1963.
2 Swift, *Odd Man Out*, 72; *Montreal Star*, 12 April 1963.
3 Jamie Swift's interview with Gérard Pelletier, Montreal, 12 September 1986. Pelletier was speaking partly for himself, having urged Lesage to give serious consideration to Kierans. The premier told him that he was the "umpteenth person to do so." This is corroborated in Thomson, *Jean Lesage and the Quiet Revolution*, 138.
4 McRoberts, *Quebec*, 108. See also Levine, *The Reconquest of Montreal*, 30–2.
5 Levine, *The Reconquest of Montreal*, 30.
6 Sancton, *Governing the Island of Montreal*, 62.
7 Ibid., 18.
8 Coleman, *The Independence Movement*, 13.

9 Sancton, *Governing the Island of Montreal*, 21.
10 Coleman, *The Independence Movement*, 8. See also Levine, *The Reconquest of Montreal*, 152: "Thus, in the face of limited economic opportunities in the upper echelons of Anglophone-controlled businesses, increases in public sector employment in Montreal and across Quebec after 1960 provided jobs for an upwardly mobile new Francophone middle class of technocrats, teachers, social service workers and policy entrepreneurs ... Until private corporations in Montreal significantly *francised*, Quebec's public administration and state corporations would represent a crucial source of managerial jobs for Francophones. Moreover, the public sector would serve as an important training ground for Francophone managers who, as Montreal *francised* in the 1970s and 1980s, could then move into the private sector."
11 Coleman, *The Independence Movement*, 92.
12 Levine, *The Reconquest of Montreal*, 153.
13 See Arnopoulos and Clift, *The English Fact in Quebec*, 110–14.
14 Ibid., 110–11. See also Coleman, *The Independence Movement*, 121–2, outlining the reaction along these lines of the Chamber of Commerce of the Province of Quebec and the Canadian Manufacturers' Association.
15 Arnopolous and Clift, *The English Fact in Quebec*, 114.
16 COEQ was formed in 1960 as some francophone businessmen sought "elaborate, corporatist state planning in Quebec," by means of 'a public-private industrial strategy council along the lines of corporatist entities emerging at the time in Europe." See Levine, *The Reconquest of Montreal*, 152–3, and indexed references to the "Economic Council" in Thomson, *Jean Lesage and the Quiet Revolution*.
17 My discussion of SIDBEC, except where otherwise noted, draws heavily on Thomson, *Jean Lesage and the Quiet Revolution*, 214–25.
18 Fullerton, *Dangerous Delusion*, 77.
19 Gordon Pape, "There Is Strength in Diversity ... Quebec Proves It," Montreal *Gazette*, 5 February 1965.
20 "A New Problem for Quebec: The Choice of Investments," 1 February 1965, as cited in Swift, *Odd Man Out*, chap. 6, 24–5.
21 Pape, "Strength in Diversity." This is just one of Kierans's idiosyncratic, if creative interpretations of ministerial responsibility. Kierans likes to blend together, depending on circumstances, features of collective and individual ministerial responsibility.
22 Letter from Eric W. Kierans, Minister of Revenue, to Hon. Jean Lesage, P.C., Q.C., Prime Minister, Province of Quebec, 11 June 1965, Kierans Papers, National Archives of Canada, Ottawa, MG 32, B10, Vol. VI.

23 Letter from Eric Kierans to Gérard Filion, President of SIDBEC, Montreal, n.d., Kierans Papers, Vol. VI.

24 Letter from Eric Kierans, Minister of Revenue, to Hon. Jean Lesage, P.C., Q.C., 4 August 1965, Kierans Papers, Vol. VI. The original letter makes references to several enclosed stories and editorials in *Le Devoir* and *La Presse*, 2 and 3 August.

25 Kierans, "Quebec 1965: A Transformation in Depth."

26 "THE ATTACHED THREE DATA PAPERS ARE MEANT TO BE GUIDE LINES ONLY FOR THE DISCUSSION ON 'THE STATUT DE SIDBEC.'" Untitled paper, n.d., Kierans Papers, Vol. VII.

27 See Thomson, *Jean Lesage and the Quiet Revolution*, 226–32.

28 Author's interview with Kierans, Halifax, 17 August 1987. See also Kierans, "Federal-Provincial Tax Treatment of the Extractive Industries," p. 8: "In 1963, the value of mineral production in the province amounted to $543 million. Total revenues of all kinds, rents, licenses, profit taxes etc., came to $5.6 million or 1% of value."

29 Thomson, *Jean Lesage and the Quiet Revolution*, 228–9.

CHAPTER FOUR

1 Kent, *A Public Purpose*.

2 Ibid., 267.

3 See Morin, *Quebec versus Ottawa*, and Simeon, *Federal-Provincial Diplomacy*. For Ontario's perspective, see A.K. McDougall, *John P. Robarts*, especially chaps. 8, 10, and 12.

4 See, for example, Kierans, "Economic Implications of the Province of Quebec Pension Plan." Cf. Jamie Swift's interview with Claude Morin, 7 July 1986.

5 See Kierans Papers, especially vols. VII and VIII. See also Kent, *A Public Purpose*, 275. The Tax Structure Committee had been instigated at the suggestion of Tom Kent, Robert Bryce, and Gordon Robertson following a March 1964 federal-provincial conference on pensions and related matters.

6 Swift, *Odd Man Out*, 116. A.K. McDougall records in *John P. Robarts* (167–8) that Ontario's premier "harshly criticized" the federal government for its failure to confer with the provinces before setting out the requirements of its medicare plan. He adds that "it was not clear that Ottawa knew the cost of its proposals or their impact on health services."

7 Kierans did not specify which conference, but in outline his description would seem to square with Tom Kent's account of one in November 1963. See Kent, *A Public Purpose*, 271, for a description of how little was accomplished at this gathering.

8 Author's interview with Kierans, Halifax, 14 August 1986.

9 See Kent, *A Public Purpose*, 366–9.

10 Malcolm G. Taylor, *Health Insurance and Canadian Public Policy*, 375.

11 Quoted in ibid., from the proceedings of a federal-provincial conference, 10 February 1969.

12 Quoted in ibid., 365–6.

13 Author's interview with Kierans, Halifax, 22 August 1988.

14 A.K. McDougall shows several instances of protest from Ontario, which would have to count as a "strong" province. However, he also points out that during this same period Robarts became "the least provincial of the provincial premiers" and, in the final analysis, a strong supporter of "a single national economy and a single national government which has control over that economy" (Robarts's own words). Thus Ontario's position was ultimately centralist. See A.K. McDougall, *John P. Robarts*, 169.

15 See Canada, Parliament, *Minutes of Proceedings*.

16 In response to a comment by an anonymous reviewer, I went over this point with Kierans in a telephone interview, 19 August 1992. As I have tried to suggest, Kierans has always favoured decentralization of power in almost every sphere. In federal-provincial relations, this view was, in his word, "cemented" by the kinds of experience reviewed in this chapter. Kierans may, in fact, have arrived thirty years ago at a realization that apparently motivates a "new brand of sovereigntist" in Quebec – the ones like the authors of the Allaire Report who claim that Canada needs a wholesale redistribution of powers in part because Ottawa does so much damage with the excessive powers that it had – what one might call the "Ottawa as a dead hand" argument. See Québec Liberal Party, *A Québec Free to Choose*, 3–5, 17–20.

17 See Canada, Task Force on Canadian Unity, *A Future Together*; Heuglin, *Federalism and Fragmentation*. There is also a parallel between Kierans's thought along these lines and the political economy of Harold Innis. See Neill, *A New Theory of Value*, 66–76.

18 See, for example, Swift, *Odd Man Out*, chap. 8; Desbarats, *René*; and Lévesque, *Memoirs*, chap. 30.

19 Swift, *Odd Man Out*, 293–4.

20 Jamie Swift's interview with René Lévesque, Montreal, 6 October 1986.

21 Desbarats, *René*, 137–8.

22 *Montreal Star*, 5 October 1967, as quoted in Swift, *Odd Man Out*, 176.

23 Lévesque felt that Pierre Laporte, aided by Lesage's machinations, did the bulk of the "dirty work" within the QLF to ensure his ouster. Jamie Swift's interview with Lévesque, Montreal, 6 October 1986.

24 Desbarats, *René*, 125.

25 Bruce Taylor, "Separatism Would Die at the Polls," *Montreal Star*, 23 September 1963.

26 See untitled speech by Kierans, Reform Club Benefit Dinner, Sherbrooke, 1 October 1967, Kierans Papers, Vol. IV.

27 See, for example, Brian Upton, "Johnson Labels Kierans 'Betrayer,'" *Montreal Star*, 9 February 1967.

28 Irwin Block, "Lévesque Defends 2-nation Economy," *Toronto Daily Star*, 5 October 1967.

29 Desbarats, *René*, 134–5.

30 See the report of the debate made by Mark Starowicz, "Lévesque or Kierans Is the Choice," *Montreal Gazette*, 27 September 1967.

31 *Montreal Gazette*, 28 September 1967.

32 Kierans, "Challenge to René," Kierans Papers, Vol. XIV.

33 Ibid. Translation: "We have been able to establish that the Liberal Party of Québec truly constituted the only worthy political group for the young generation of Québec, thanks to its boldness and custom of taking up challenges. The young people of this province consider their government to be the means to realize their national objectives. Thus, they conceive a political party as a means to advance economic opportunities, cultural progress, and their social status. I am particularly proud of the large number of young people who are active in our ranks."

34 Ibid. Translation: "In June, Mr. Lesage and I compared the results of our respective tours across the province. Independently, our conclusions proved to be the same. The population of Québec has a minimal interest in constitutional problems and separatism, while the burden of municipal and school taxes, increasing unemployment, economic and regional development, housing, consumer protection, etc. are of primary interest."

35 Ibid. Translation: "The Liberal Party's image after this convention must be clearer and more precise than ever. We want for the French Canadian nation a status of full equality and we intend to fight to obtain the constitutional changes necessary to achieve this equality. The road to equality is not found in separatism. If that is the decision of the convention, those who propose this solution must in all honesty towards themselves and their party take the appropriate decisions. As for myself, firmly believing that the separatist option in any form is not in the interest of the population of Québec, I am ready

to resign immediately, if that is your choice. To be sure, the challenge is imposing, but the Québec Liberals, wanting a strong Québec in a vigorous Canada while refusing to engage in an endless war of words, will side definitively and clearly with the only option worthy of the people of Québec."

CHAPTER FIVE

1 Thomson, *Jean Lesage and the Quiet Revolution*, 148–9.
2 Letter from Eric Kierans to Mr Henry Fowler, Secretary of the Treasury, Washington, DC, 4 January 1966, Kierans Papers, Vol. VI.
3 Quoted in Kierans, "Dollars across the Border," 3. Kierans has recently placed this quotation from Dales at the head of his chapter on "The Cosmocorps" in Kierans and Stewart, *The Wrong End of the Rainbow*, 138. Dales made the analogy to Trojan horses in an exchange of correspondence with Mr. Edward Carrigan published in *Saturday Night*, April 1966, 22–5. This exchange was, in turn, stimulated by Dales, "Half-vast Ideas."
4 Swift, *Odd Man Out*, 138–42.
5 C.N. Telegram Premier of Quebec to Hon. Eric Kierans, Min. de la Santé, Montreal, 9 January 1966, Kierans Papers, Vol. XIX. Translation:" "Urgent and important cabinet meeting Tuesday night January 11 at 8 you must cancel all other commitments no excuse will be accepted. Jean Lesage."
6 Letter to Jean Lesage, Prime Minister of Quebec, Quebec, 4 February 1966, Kierans Papers, Vol. XIX.
7 See Kierans, "Economic Effects of the Guidelines."
8 Ibid., 1.
9 Ibid., 1–2. Logically, of course, the closing sentence means that Kierans has no complaint against American policy: Canadian policy need only override it. This objection brings two points about this episode to the forefront. First, there were no such Canadian policies, which was part of Kierans's argument against Ottawa; second, "when push comes to shove" – that is, when host countries do attempt to override American directives – the Americans win. We thus see how American control of Canadian firms violates Kierans's values: most of its evils are a direct consequence more of deficiencies in Canadian economic policy than of anything else, and the central danger of American economic power lies not in any economic inefficiencies that it may produce but in the centralization of political power that it represents.
10 Jamie Swift and author's interview with Kierans, Halifax, 7 August 1986.

11 See Swift, *Odd Man Out*, 135–42. Evidently, Lesage left for Florida some time between this exchange and Kierans's writing of his letters.

12 See, for example, Press Release, Office of the Minister of Finance, Ottawa, 5 December 1965, in which Canada won further exemption from application of the American tax in return for a promise to keep its reserves of US dollars below a certain ceiling. See also Swift, *Odd Man Out*, 138–42.

13 Canada, Task Force on the Structure of Canadian Industry, *Foreign Ownership* (Watkins Report); Levitt, *Silent Surrender*.

14 Kierans, "Economic Effects of the Guidelines," 13–15.

15 Jamie Swift and author's interview with Kierans, Halifax, 6 August 1986.

16 Letter to Kierans from Prime Minister, Province of Quebec, Quebec, P.Q., 7 January 1966, Kierans Papers, Vol. XIX. "I answered him that, when a [prime minister or premier] gave his opinion, he would commit the [cabinet] and that, given the circumstances, the latter not having been consulted, I could not express an opinion."

17 Thomson, *Jean Lesage and the Quiet Revolution*, 149.

18 See Swift, *Odd Man Out*, 147.

19 Letter to Mr. Edward Carrigan, Toronto, 25 May 1966, Kierans Papers, Vol. XIX.

20 See, for example, Dominique Clift, "National Ambitions Reported Sparking Kierans' 'Crusade,'" *Toronto Daily Star*, 15 January 1966.

21 Dominique Clift, "Kierans Steps Forward as Iron Man," *Toronto Daily Star*, 16 October 1967.

22 "Will René Lévesque's Moment of Truth Be Bitter?" *Globe and Mail*, 13 October 1967.

23 See references in Swift, *Odd Man Out*, 177–8, 183.

24 Political theorists refer to this as the "autonomy of the state." See Nordlinger, *On the Autonomy of the Democratic State*, and Krasner, *Defending the National Interest*. This point also connects with Hegel's "universal state" as discussed in chapter 1, above.

25 Lévesque makes this clear in Jamie Swift's interview with him, 6 October 1986.

26 See "Anatomy of Defeat," *Montreal Star*, 22 July 1966; "Why Lesage Lost in Quebec," *Globe Magazine*, 23 July 1966.

27 For a full account, see Thomson, *Jean Lesage and the Quiet Revolution*, 248ff. See also Fullerton, *Dangerous Delusion*, 62–74.

28 Letter to the author, Halifax, 10 February 1988.

29 Quoted in Swift, *Odd Man Out*, 67–8; the "Charles" referred to is in fact Charles Denis.

30 Jamie Swift provides numerous instances of Kierans's growing

enthusiasm about his work in Lesage's cabinet. Twenty years later, Richard Daignault, a journalist who had covered politics closely then and had, in a sense, been part of it all, interviewed Kierans." 'Do you remember, Dick?' beamed Kierans in reminiscence. 'Didn't we have a hell of a time?' " Quoted in ibid., 85.

31 An aide of many years summed this up neatly. André Houle, Kierans's executive assistant in the office of postmaster general, recalled that Kierans "would never let you carry his bags." Several of his Ottawa associates, including Allan Gotlieb, remember how little he enjoyed the Ottawa cocktail-party circuit, noting that he left several of them early and soon stopped attending them altogether. Jamie Swift's interview with André Houle, 4 June 1986; see also Swift, *Odd Man Out*, 254. Author's interview with Allan Gotlieb, Washington, DC, 21 April 1987.

32 Granatstein, *The Ottawa Men*, 273. See also chap. 1.

33 See French, *How Ottawa Decides*, 154–5. See also Richard Van Loon's chapter in this book, 157–90.

34 Evidence for this sweeping judgment is provided in the next three chapters. This evidence is corroborated in far greater detail and more broadly in the first book-length academic history of the Canadian post office, in preparation by Robert Campbell of Trent University. Campbell credits Kierans with much of what I have said here and, if anything, faults him for attempting fundamental changes on too many fronts. The substance of Kierans's attempted reforms, however, is not called into question in Campbell's treatment. I am grateful to Campbell for the extraordinary generosity of providing me with a draft of this chapter.

35 French, *How Ottawa Decides*, 154.

36 Ibid., 155.

37 Ibid., 158.

38 Memorandum to the Cabinet, 18 March 1971 (Cab. Doc. 324–71), 1. Copy provided to the author from Kierans's personal files. Mimeo.

CHAPTER SIX

1 Leslie MacDonald's interview with Eric Kierans, Halifax, 5 December 1983. Except when otherwise noted, all further references to Kierans's views of the politics of the Carter Commission are taken from this source (hereinafter MacDonald interview). Liberal cabinets of this era were coalitions of highly divergent interests, which may be classified for convenience as "Business liberals" and "Welfare liberals." See Canada, Royal Commission on Taxation, Report, mimeo.

2 See, in addition to MacDonald, "Taxing Comprehensive Income,"

Swift, *Odd Man Out*, 247–54. On corporate and provincial-government responses, see Bucovetsky, "The Mining Industry and the Great Tax Reform Debate." The tone of Kierans's account is also consistent with Kent, *A Public Purpose*, 50–1 and 352.

3 MacDonald interview.

4 Ibid. For similar observations see Kierans, "Problems of Tax Reform."

5 The mimeographed documents set out over 38 questions – some of them broken down into subsections – in continuous sequence. These questions, however, form two separate sets of notes. The first, "RBB'S NOTES ON DISCUSSION OF TAX REFORM QUESTIONS OCT. 30/69," runs from pages 1 to 3 and contains points 1 through 15. The second, "JRB'S NOTES ON DISCUSSION OF TAX REFORM QUESTIONS OCT. 31/69," runs from pages 1 to 7 and contains points 16 to 38. Given to the author by Eric Kierans from his personal records.

6 Three strong examples appear in the Policy Paper Series, Institute for the Quantitative Analysis of Social and Economic Policy, University of Toronto: Douglas G. Hartle, "Impact of New Tax Policies on National Unity" (no. 1) and "The Six Studies on the Carter Report Prepared by the Institute of Policy Analysis for the Department of Finance" (no. 2), and Richard M. Bird, "Taxes and Tax Reform in Canada" (no. 5).

7 MacDonald interview.

8 Kierans was not alone concerning the government's handling of tax reform. Tom Kent says: "[Edgar Benson] took until November 1969 to produce a White Paper embracing only a greatly diluted version of the admirable Carter proposals. Worse, it was not until 1971 that the Trudeau government, harassed by the vehement objection of vested interests, legislated minor tax reforms that were a massive retreat from even its own White Paper and meant Carter's work had come to almost nothing." *A Public Purpose*, 352.

9 MacDonald interview. See also Swift, *Odd Man Out*, 251.

10 MacDonald, "Taxing Comprehensive Income," 180.

11 Author's interview with Allan Gotlieb, Washington, DC, 12 April 1987.

12 On these practices and Kierans's dissatisfaction with them see Stewart, *Shrug*, 161–72.

13 MacDonald interview.

14 MacDonald, "Taxing Comprehensive Income," 688–99.

15 Kent, *A Public Purpose*, 247.

16 Ibid., 114.

17 Ibid., 413; cf. 420.

18 Ibid., 428.

19 Ibid., 431.

20 MacDonald, "Taxing Comprehensive Income," 641.

21 *Debates*, 8 October 1968, 928.

22 Clive Baxter, "Kierans Points Post Office towards 'Total Competition,'" *Financial Post*, 3 May 1969, 1–4.

23 Thus Kierans was using "There is no alternative" as the justification for tough, economizing measures a decade before Margaret Thatcher popularized the term by setting out to make the entire British economy "thriving and efficient." In his zeal, sense of purpose, clear sense of direction, and commitment, Kierans acted in a manner comparable to that of Thatcher, but without making unlimited pursuit of wealth the definitive social good.

24 Hyman Solomon, "The Managers Move into the Post Office," *Financial Post*, 10 January 1970, 5.

25 "Kierans Plan for 6-cent Letters Will Abolish Rate for Local Mail," *Globe and Mail*, 14 September 1968, 1.

26 Swift, *Odd Man Out*, 213.

27 *Globe and Mail*, 14 September 1968, 1.

28 "No Voice," ibid., 16 January 1969, 6.

29 *Debates*, 16 October 1968, 1210.

30 *Financial Post*, 13 May 1969, 4.

31 *Debates*, 21 October 1968, 1601.

32 Swift, *Odd Man Out*, 211.

33 *Debates*, 19 November 1968, 2909.

34 See Stewart-Patterson, *Post Mortem*, 142–3.

35 Clive Baxter, "Post Office Shakeup Put in Deep Freeze," *Financial Post*, 17 October 1970, 1.

36 Simpson, *Spoils of Power*, 336.

37 Ibid., 15.

38 See Stewart-Patterson, *Post Mortem*, 139–43.

39 Swift, *Odd Man Out*, 221–4; Stewart-Patterson, *Post Mortem*, 142–5.

40 Baxter, "Post Office Shakeup."

41 Stewart-Patterson, *Post Mortem*, 76–7.

42 Ibid., 76.

43 See Swift, *Odd Man Out*, 216–17.

44 See Commission of Inquiry into Mail Transport in Montreal (H. Carl Goldenberg, Commissioner), Report (hereinafter Goldenberg Report), 25 March 1970, 4. Kierans's memorandum to cabinet on which this action was based is attached as Appendix A (n.d.) to Memorandum, Deputy Postmaster General to the Postmaster General, Ottawa, 5 February 1970, Kierans Papers, Vol. xv.

45 *Debates*, 20 March 1969, 6887.

46 The editorial approach of the *Montreal Star*, sampled below, reflects

this attitude. On the violence involved, Auf der Maur and Chodos (*Quebec: A Chronicle*, 43) cite post office sources to the effect that the violence was anything but incidental: 662 trucks were attacked; 104 post office stations hit; 75 people injured, including one Lapalme man shot by security forces; 102 arrested; 7 dynamite bombings; 1,200 post boxes and 492 relay boxes damaged.

47 Stewart-Patterson, *Post Mortem*, 82.

48 Swift, *Odd Man Out*, 215.

49 *Montreal Star*, 19 March 1970, 10. The editorial pointed out that Kierans had "earned the disrespect of such labor-attuned ministers as Mr. Mackasey and Jean Marchand."

50 *Debates*, 15 April 1970, 5912.

51 Stewart-Patterson, *Post Mortem*, 82. There is a lot to support this view. The CNTU demanded recognition of the existing union within the public service, which promised to give it a foothold there. This also seems to have been the one demand that the cabinet was adamant in not accepting. See Swift, *Odd Man Out*, 225.

52 "The Key Issues in the Mail Dispute," *Montreal Star*, 12 February 1970, 10.

53 Swift, *Odd Man Out*, 223.

54 Goldenberg Report, 6.

55 Ibid., 8–9.

CHAPTER SEVEN

1 Author's interview with Allan Gotlieb, Washington, DC, 21 April 1987. See also Dewitt and Kirton, *Canada as a Principal Power*, 328–31.

2 See R.M. MacIntosh, Memorandum on the Corporate Structure of a Canadian Satellite Communications Corporation, mimeo, hand-dated 31 July 1968, passim and 1–6.

3 Dewitt and Kirton, *Canada as a Principal Power*, 332. The same point emerges in sources cited in notes to their discussion.

4 Because of some of the nationalist claims during the debate, I would point out that RCA Ltd. is a subsidiary of the American multinational RCA Inc. I trust that the reader will not be misled by references below to RCA Ltd. (RCA) as a "Canadian" firm. Those who emphasized numbers of Canadian jobs tended to describe RCA as "Canadian" and Hughes as "American," based on location of production facilities, not locus of ownership. Meanwhile, those who emphasized Canada's capacity to penetrate new world markets with independently generated technology tended to describe RCA as "American" like Hughes, or even as a "global" conglomerate, stressing instead RCA's

corporate ownership and the secondary status of its Canadian operations in the corporate planning of the international company.

5 Dewitt and Kirton, *Canada as a Principal Power*, 332.

6 Author's interview with D.A. Golden, chairman and past president, Telesat Canada, Ottawa, 16 July 1986.

7 See "Procurement of Satellites and Financing of Telesat Canada," Memo, 6 July 1970, containing a review of the cabinet decision of 29 May 1969, Kierans Papers, Vol. VII.

8 See "TELESAT: Film des événements," Kierans Papers, Vol. VII, n.d., 3–11.

9 Ibid.

10 See Dewitt and Kirton, *Canada as a Principal Power*, 333–4.

11 In fact, the chairman of the Science Council stated publicly that it would be "complete madness" to send satellite production out of Canada and disperse the existing Canadian satellite team. This move, he argued, would, among other things, confirm Canada's reputation for approaching scientific brinks, only to back away from them. See "What's the Rush to the Sky?" *Globe and Mail*, 23 July 1970, 6.

12 Dewitt and Kirton, *Canada as a Principal Power*, 334.

13 Author's interview with Kierans, Halifax, 11 August 1986.

14 A recent study of US energy policy refers to the pervasiveness of "hyperpluralism" in that government's policy processes – that is, "the belief that any organized group has some almost divine right to dictate that its policy preferences be reflected in government decision-making." This description may be a little strong for the present case study, but it highlights a tendency illustrated by some aspects of the Telesat story. See Uslaner, *Shale Barrel Politics*, 77.

15 Memorandum, "Procurement of Satellites by Telesat Canada," Minister of Industry, Trade and Commerce to Cabinet, 6 June 1970, Kierans Papers, Vol. VII.

16 Memorandum, Bryce Mackasey to Cabinet, 7 July 1970, Kierans Papers, Vol. VII.

17 See Kierans Papers, Vol. VII. The source of this memorandum is not clearly identified, but the document is addressed to cabinet and dated 9 July 1970.

18 See "Procurement of Satellites and Financing," Memo.

19 See Memorandum, Minister of Communications to Cabinet, n.d. (probably 10–17 July 1970, Kierans Papers, Vol. VII.

20 See Memorandum, A.E. Gotlieb to the Minister, 23 June 1970, Kierans Papers, Vol. VII.

21 An earlier memorandum to cabinet read: "My discussion with the President of RCA. Ltd. and the ruling given by the president of his parent company indicate that the company would demand to be

absolved from risk of loss through failure or delay in the program, unforeseen difficulties in development or from possible abridgment of U.S. patents. ... Unless Telecanada can negotiate a satisfactory arrangement with Hughes for more Canadian content at an acceptable price the government will have declared a change of policy relating to domestic communications satellites, making the manufacture and assembly of satellites in Canadian industry the prime objective of the Telesat program as opposed to the provision of communications facilities on a commercial basis as stated in the Act." See Memorandum, Eric Kierans to Cabinet, 8 July 1970, Kierans Papers, Vol. VII.

22 See Allison, *Essence of Decision*, chap. 7.

23 Jamie Swift's interview with Richard Gwyn, Ottawa, 10 May 1986.

24 Author's interview with David Golden, Ottawa, 16 July 1986.

25 Author's interview with Kierans, Halifax, 14 August 1986.

26 The phrase "flame out" might suggest a failed rocket-launch of the satellite, but this is not what was meant. The satellites themselves have a limited capacity for self-propulsion, allowing for remote control of their final positioning in their space orbit. Such propulsion systems, especially untested ones, could fail. It is entirely possible, however, that Kierans made no effort to clarify this distinction for the benefit of Trudeau or the rest of his colleagues.

27 Memorandum, A.E. Gotlieb to Minister of Communications, 6 July 1970, Kierans Papers, Vol. VII.

28 Memorandum, O.L. Britney to File, notation from A.E. Gotlieb, 15 July 1970, Kierans Papers, Vol. VII.

29 See Yale, "Telesat Canada's Membership in the Trans-Canada Telephone System." See also Doern and Brothers, "Telesat Canada," 240–2.

30 The president of SPAR gives credit to Kierans along these lines; author's interview with Larry Clarke, Toronto, 9 April 1987. Two studies consider the Canadian aerospace sector one of the few success stories in recent industrial strategy. It is not hard to trace this success to the late 1960s and early 1970s, when Kierans was active in the Ministry of Communications. See Dewitt and Kirton, *Canada as a Principal Power*, chap. 9, and Atkinson and Coleman, *The State, Business and Industrial Change*, especially chap. 6. I was particularly pleased to see Atkinson and Coleman's praise (106) for the part played in this success story by Dr John Chapman, Kierans's assistant deputy minister of research. Kierans called Chapman "the real father of Telesat," repeating several times in interviews that I must find a way to acknowledge his contribution. I do so gladly here. The only item in this biography that Kierans "insisted" I include was this one – a tribute to a subordinate for the quality of his public service.

CHAPTER EIGHT

1 See, in particular, Smith, *Bleeding Hearts ... Bleeding Country*, and
Jamieson, "Overkill."

2 Gwyn, *Northern Magus*, 119, quoted in Swift, *Odd Man Out*, 241.

3 See the FLQ Manifesto, reproduced in English in Golden and Haggart,
Rumors of War, 277–81. One passage (280) reads, "We live in a society
of terrorized slaves, terrorized by the large owners like Steinberg,
Clark, Bronfman, Smith, Neapole, Timmins, Geoffrion, J.L. Levesque,
Hershorn, Thompson, Nesbitt, Desmarais, Kierans. Beside them
Remi Popol, the gasket, Drapeau, the dog, Bourassa, the sidekick of
the Simards, and Trudeau, the queer, are peanuts." I did not ask
Kierans how he felt about being included along with economic giants,
although some of them might have regarded him as a "financial
peanut," or at least not in their league. He appeared perhaps because
he was also in government, or because he was a resident of Hampstead
(another category of oppressors vilified in the manifesto), or, most
likely, because of his role in the Lapalme affair. But one doubts that
one is looking at a meticulously drafted document.

4 See Kierans, "Democracy and Social Change in Canada," 2–7; mimeographed copy provided to me by Kierans from his personal files.

5 Ibid., 15 (emphasis added by hand).

6 Jamieson, "Overkill," 29.

7 See Trudeau, *Federalism and the French Canadians*, 168–9.

8 Author's interview with Kierans, Halifax, 14 August 1986.

9 Author's interview with Allan Gotlieb, Washington, DC, 2 April 1987.

10 Perhaps 80 per cent of the parliamentary record reporting Kierans's
answers and speeches in the house involved his role as postmaster
general rather than as minister of communications (which job he
found much more interesting and rewarding). Moreover, at least 60
per cent of those questions had to do with the closing of post offices in
opposition members' constituencies. (Some government MPs occasionally asked such questions, but naturally their tone was not as
critical.) Such questions seemed a constant feature of Kierans's
parliamentary existence. I doubt that there was a single instance of a
rural post office closing that was not raised, and raised specifically, at
some point by an opposition MP from its riding or from the province
concerned. (Kierans frequently had to provide an updated list of post
office closings in particular provinces.)

11 A good example was the "progress report" that he gave the House on
the changes that he had made to the postal service over the previous
two years. A portion of this address reads as follows: "Mr Kierans: It is
a service that is complete and satisfactory as soon as people realize

and become accustomed to a simple little thing called change. During the past 23 months many motions have been moved relating to the Post Office. It is quite evident that the Postmaster General must be guilty of something, and I guess I am guilty of something. And of what am I guilty? I think I am guilty of waking up the sleeping giant that was the Post Office. Not only was it a sleeping giant; it was a giant that was drugged. An hon. Member: Don't be modest. Mr. Kierans: It was drugged by the nonsense of previous governments ranging from John A. to John G. [Diefenbaker]."

Kierans summed up his defence, a little more prosaicly: "I say quite honestly and sincerely that no improvement made in the Post Office will be the work of one man or even a number of men. The only way to improve the Post Office is through the work, the involvement and participation of each and every member of the Post Office. We have to earn the trust and confidence of the people in the Post Office Department who have been left alone for far too long. We have to ask them to help us, and I hope I can ask my colleagues in this House to help us shape the future of the Post Office." See *Debates*, 22 May 1970, 7234–7.

12 Ibid., 9 June 1969, 9871.

13 At any rate, Heath Macquarrie, Kierans's "shadow minister," allowed that "for me it was an education to be called the many names that I was called in the previous session by the minister. I was designated as a Cassandra, as Falstaff and as the Merry Monk of Hillsborough." The record suggests, though, that the exchanges between the two men began to wear thin the patience of both. A few months later, for example, Kierans began to reply to Macquarrie by saying, "Mr. Speaker, this has become an almost weekly event in which I stand sprinkled with the, I suppose, the sweet ambrosia of the irony and satire of the man least likely to be the next Postmaster General of Canada." See *Debates*, 17 November 1969, 922; 25 May 1970, 7318.

14 Ibid., 2 June 1970, 7646–8.

15 Ibid., 22 May 1969, 8971. See as well "What's the Rush to the Sky?" *Globe and Mail*, 23 July 1970.

16 Letter from Eric Kierans, Minister of Communications, to the Prime Minister, Ottawa, 28 April 1971, given in Appendix C to Kierans, *Globalism and the Nation-State*. The prime minister's reply is also reproduced there.

17 Kierans, "Contribution of the Tax System" (address).

18 See, for example, Neill, "The Passing of Canadian Economic History," 80. Neill cites Harold Innis and Kierans's contributions to a proper appreciation of Canada's distinctive political economy, a theme picked up in chapter 11, below.

19 Kierans, "Contribution of the Tax System" (address), 7. Thomas Courchene has shared with me his recollection of observing Kierans delivering this address. He also gave me a xerox of the copy of the paper that he had with him at the time. The passage just quoted is marked "Great" in Courchene's hand. He had also scrawled "Wow" beside Table 2, discussed below.

20 Wolfe, "Economic Growth and Foreign Investments."

21 Ibid., 7.

22 Molot, "The Political Implications of North American Capital Flows," 178.

23 Letter from Eric W. Kierans, P.C. to the Right Honourable Pierre Elliott Trudeau, P.C., M.P., Prime Minister of Canada, Ottawa, 13 October 1972, provided to the author from Kierans's personal records.

24 Kierans, "Contribution of the Tax System" (address), 20.

25 A detailed analysis of this study is presented in the next chapter.

26 See Swift, *Odd Man Out*, 288–9.

27 Letter from Kierans to Trudeau, 13 October 1972.

28 Letter from Eric Kierans to the author, Halifax, 22 April 1988.

29 Quoted in Swift, *Odd Man Out*, 257.

CHAPTER NINE

1 Kierans, *Report on Natural Resources Policy in Manitoba* (hereinafter Kierans Report).

2 Hedlin Menzies & Associates Ltd., *An Analysis of the Kierans Report* (hereinafter Hedlin Menzies Report), Book II, 67, 74–5. See also Manitoba, News Service, "Task Force to Study Kierans Report: Premier," 2 March 1973. While "repudiation" may seem too strong a word for the premier's reaction as reported in this press release, it does describe fairly his government's reaction over the months between his press release and the premier's CBC television interview cited in the Hedlin Menzies Report. (See below.)

3 Kierans Report, 2.

4 See ibid., 27–33. The industry's argument is that excessive tax and royalty rates scare off resource investments which produce, directly or indirectly, thousands of jobs in mining and ancillary industries. Kierans made an aside that to apply the mining industry's famed "multiplier" to investment across the board in Canada would mean elimination of all existing unemployment and the appearance of six million job vacancies in the country.

5 Ibid., 28.

6 Ibid. See also Table 12.

7 Ibid., 33. The same point is made even more effectively earlier in the analysis. In a footnote to Table 9, Kierans explains his use of "an unusual ratio" – total taxes as a percentage of total income. This ratio "gives an interesting insight into the distribution of the wealth created by the transformation of our national resources. On average, 25% of the resources mined were converted into new capital during the 5-year period [1965–69]. This surplus belonged to the operators. Canadians obtained 14.7% of these profits in the form of taxes or 3–4% of the value of the depleted resources. When we boast of our wealth, we are only about *1/25th* as rich as we think we are.

8 Ibid., 37.

9 For a response to Kierans's economic theory and financial data that is reliably representative of the industry as a whole, one need go no further than the Hedlin Menzies Report. Its criticism of Kierans's study was both detailed and exhaustive. It thus provided the economic substance of much of the mining companies' criticism of Kierans's approach in later phases of the debate. Many of the industry's public criticisms of Kierans's treatment of rents, for example, were closely argued and extensively documented in the firm's analysis. Prominent among these criticisms were several complaints. Kierans's data on the growth in the industry's profits between 1965 and 1969 reflected merely a reclassification by Statistics Canada which added nine large firms to the data in the final year. His use of data tended to confuse many distinct groups within the mining industry, such as metals, minerals, smelting and refining, commodity groups, and active and inactive firms. He similarly moved inconsistently between industry data at the national and provincial levels. And he failed to acknowledge that the new Income Tax Act was about to answer several of his central objections to the tax advantages allegedly enjoyed by mining enterprises as compared with the broader corporate community. (See Book I, 2–25, 31–4.)

   However, the crucial differences between the Hedlin Menzies Report and the Kierans Report had less to do with Kierans's data than with the construction that he placed on that data, as Hedlin Menzies expressly pointed out (ibid., 2).

10 According to the Hedlin Menzies Report, "Economic rent *by definition* is simply that portion of revenue or profit which could be taxed away or removed *without affecting prices, output, or the allocation of resources*" (16). According to Kierans, economic rents (or "super profits" or "super returns") represent "a return in profits, wages or rents in excess of what would be required, under normal market conditions, to call forth the required supply of such factors of production. ... When the scarcity is eliminated by competition or

increases in supply, the economic rent, super returns, will disappear
without reducing the supply of the factors of production" (Kierans
Report, 41).

11 John Stuart Mill, *Principles of Political Economy* (Penguin edition),
169, as quoted in Kierans Report, 46–7.

12 Mill, *Principles of Political Economy* (Laughlin edition), 547, as
quoted in Hedlin Menzier Report, Book II, 19 (emphasis added in
report). The report's discussion, moreover, had anticipated this
problem in another quotation (Book II, 18) from Mill's *Principles*
(284): "The extra gains which *any* [report's emphasis] producer or
dealer obtains through superior talents for business, or superior
business arrangements, are very much of a similar kind [to rent]. If all
his competitors had the same advantages, and used them the benefit
would be transferred to their customers through the diminished value
of the article; he only retains it for himself because he is able to bring
his commodity to market at a lower cost, while its value is determined by a higher."

13 See Hedlin Menzies Report, Book II, 19.

14 Ibid., 20, quoting Mill, *Principles* (Laughlin), 282.

15 Kierans Report, 48.

16 See Hedlin Menzies Report, Book II, 13–14: "a private operator
acquires clear ownership of minerals mined provided that all
conditions of the lease (including true royalty liabilities) are fulfilled.
Tax liabilities, as distinct from true royalties are not normally a
condition of the lease. The real issue concerning mining leases signed
with provincial governments is the extent to which a government
can, or should, fairly and justly use its special powers in relation to
the mining rights it has previously granted under *existing* leases. Any
departure from the terms of an original grant obviously requires
careful consideration. As is the case with leases between private
citizens, it is also useful to review current leases in order to provide
guidance for drafting of future leases."

17 Ibid., 20.

18 Author's interview with George Miller, managing director, Mining
Association of Canada, Ottawa, 17 July 1986. Miller did say at the end
of the interview that he "kind of liked the guy as a person" but that
Kierans, through his report and subsequent public appearances on the
resource issue, had failed to contribute what he might have to a
"mutual understanding" between economists and the mining
industry.

19 "Manitoba Miners Question Politics of Takeover Report," *Northern
Miner*, 8 March 1973, 19.

20 "Mr. Kierans's Credibility Comes into Question," ibid., 6.

21 See *CIM Bulletin*, Vol. 66 (January–June 1973), 12; *Canadian Mining Journal*, Vol. 94 (July 1973).

22 "Mining Takeover Proposal Roasted," *Winnipeg Free Press*, 28 February 1973.

23 Ibid., 14.

24 "100 Per Cent Socialism," ibid., 17.

25 See *Horizons Noranda* (Summer 1973), 10, 12 (inset).

26 Mining Association of Canada, full-page advertisements placed in major Canadian newspapers. See, for example, *Toronto Star*, 25 July 1974, A15.

27 Author's interview with John Bonus, Ottawa, 18 July 1986.

28 See the centre's self-description in most of its publications. This represented the mining industry's "carrot" for the academic world in the resource field. The present story reveals that it was also prepared to use a "stick." McGill University came under substantial criticism from at least two sources in the mining industry after the release of Kierans's report, the title page of which had identified him with the university's Department of Economics. Lorne Gales, executive director of the McGill Fund Council at the time, recalls: "[Kierans] made my life a bit difficult. Noranda was pretty damned mad with him and one of my major donors was so mad he threatened not to give any more money to McGill. It wasn't a sore that healed quickly." Jamie Swift's interview with Lorne Gales, Montreal, 5 June 1986.

29 Hedlin Menzies Report, Book II, 74–5.

30 Manitoba, News Service, "Task Force to Study Kierans Report: Premier," 2 March 1973.

31 For good overviews of changes in mineral taxation in such provinces as British Columbia, Saskatchewan, Ontario, and Quebec, see Nicholas, *Canadian Taxation of Mining Income*, chap. 1, and Brown, "The Fight over Resource Profits."

32 Owen and Kops, *The Impact of Policy Change*, 22.

33 Chandler, "State Enterprise and Partisanship in Provincial Politics," 738.

34 See Prince and Doern, *The Origins of Public Enterprise*, 109–112. All provinces except Prince Edward Island are represented on the list. Dates of incorporation were obtained from other sources.

35 See Vining and Botterel, "The Origins, Growth, Size and Functions of Provincial Crown Corporations," Tables XIII and XIV.

36 For an excellent analysis along such lines, see Bucovetsky, "The Mining Industry and the Great Tax Reform Debate." The Kierans Report may be in part a product of Kierans's frustration with the government's inadequate response to the Carter Commission's recommendations in this area of taxation.

37 Deutsch, *The Nerves of Government*, 203.
38 Author's interviews with George Miller, Ottawa, 17 July 1986, and with John Bonus, Ottawa, 18 July 1986.
39 Jamie Swift's interview with Alf Powis, Toronto, 25 September 1986.
40 Jamie Swift's interviews with the following: George Davies, member of Planning Secretariat for Ed Schreyer's government in Manitoba, Winnipeg, 18 June 1986; Mark Eliesen, former head of Planning Secretariat, Winnipeg, 3 September 1986; Wilson Parasiuk, minister of energy and mines, Manitoba, and former head of Planning Secretariat, Winnipeg, 2 September 1986. The following analysis of Manitoba's stance based on these interviews largely follows Swift, *Odd Man Out*, 273–4.
41 In a similar vein, in the largest rent capture in Canadian history, average citizens were as horrified by the unearned income enjoyed by the province of Alberta as by that received by Imperial Oil. The "policy instrument" adopted by Ottawa in the 1970s to capture a share of Alberta's income (with the deafening approval of the rest of Canada) was not a crown corporation (although there was PetroCan) or new taxes and royalties (although there were new taxes) but a "made-in-Canada price" for Alberta's oil. After the world price of oil subsided to levels below the old Canadian ceiling, talk of capturing rents – in any resource field – also subsided across the country.
   Meanwhile, as the softwood lumber case illustrated in the late 1980s, rents on Canada's resources probably still existed, largely uncollected by the people of the provinces who own them, a fact that was ironically protested more loudly by American senators than by Canadian MPs. Canadians seem less determined to appropriate the rents that flow to resource-producing firms than those that might benefit the people of resource-producing provinces.
42 I am alluding to the National Energy Program (NEP) of 1980. See Jenkins, "Reexamining the 'Obsolescing Bargain,'" 139–65.
43 Yudelman, *Canadian Mineral Policy Past and Present*, 78–9.
44 I cannot attest to the total absence of such government redefinition of the terms of leases and the procedures for their sale and renewal. However, such policy changes are absent from Yudelman's outline (ibid., Table 9) of the "goals" and "means" of "Canadian Mineral Policies" from 1945 to the mid-1980s. See also Anderson's excellent discussion of the technical dimensions of this issue in *Natural Resources in Canada*, 158–9 and 175–7.
45 I am intruding on much-disputed territory here – comparative economic analysis of instruments of rent capture. For some useful reviews of contending perspectives, see Gunton and Richards, "Political Economy of Resource Policy," 34–48; Cairns, "Reform of

Exhaustible Resource Taxation"; and Pearse, "Property Rights and the Development of Natural Resource Policies in Canada."

46 Gunton and Richards, eds., *Resource Rents and Public Policy*, xii.

CHAPTER TEN

1 An example of his participation in public conferences was his contribution to "The Atlantic Provinces and Canadian Energy Policy" Halifax, 6–7 April 1974, which included a session for the general public attended by close to one thousand people. See also Kierans, "The Day the Cabinet was Misled."

2 Kierans, "Notes on the Energy Aspects of the 1974 Budget," 427–8. The internal quotation is from John N. Turner, Budget Speech, 18 November 1974, 14. The ellipsis in the quoted passage is Kierans's.

3 Ibid., 429.

4 W.O. Twaits, chairman and chief executive, Imperial Oil Ltd., Remarks to Second Annual Canadian Investors Converence, 16 November 1972, 7, as quoted in ibid., 430.

5 Ibid., 431.

6 The paper was published without its own title in *Reports and Proceedings of the Twenty-Sixth Tax Conference* (Toronto: Canadian Tax Foundation, 1975), 11–19.

7 Karl Polanyi, *The Great Transformation* (New York: Beacon Press, 1944), 178, as quoted in ibid., 19.

8 See Kierans, "Canadian Unity – a Perspective," 2–5.

9 He used the same quotation to start "The Community and the Corporation."

10 Tawney, *Religion and the Rise of Capitalism*, 38–9.

11 Smiley, "Canada and the Quest for a National Policy," 49–52; George Grant, Foreword, 11.

12 Harry Johnson, "The Economic Benefits of the Multinational Enterprise," as quoted in Smiley, "Canada and the Quest," 52.

13 Grant, Foreword, 12.

14 Noel, "Domination and Myth in the Works of George Grant and C.B. Macpherson," 541.

15 Kierans, *Globalism and the Nation-State*, chap. 1. "Comergence" is defined in the first sentence of the fourth lecture (97) as "integration of economic policies, particularly in the monetary, fiscal, and exchange-rate fields."

16 Kierans, *Challenge of Confidence*, chap. 9.

17 Kierans, *Globalism and the Nation-State*, 92–3. The square bracket denotes the substitution of "love" for "have" in the original text, an obvious mistake, given the context.

18 Quoted as the head to part one of Kierans and Stewart, *The Wrong End of the Rainbow*. Kierans and Stewart, along with just about everybody else, misquote Chancellor Baron Thurlow (1731–1806), who wrote: "Corporations have neither bodies to be punished, nor souls to be condemned, they therefore do as they like"; *The Oxford Book of Quotations*, 3rd edition (New York: Oxford University Press, 1979), 550.

19 Two of Canada's most prominent economists have argued recently that economics must be more realistic in conceding that markets no longer function in the manner assumed by classical theory – Thomas Courchene to the effect that Galbraith's "planning sector" must be exposed to the discipline of the market if that market is to do the job that economists claim it does, and Richard Lipsey to the effect that Schumpeter's "creative destruction" must continue to operate if the liberal economic case against government intervention is to have any force. See their contributions to Lermer, ed., *Probing Leviathan*.

   J.K. Galbraith, in *Economics in Perspective*, shows how mainstream American economists have studiously neglected the importance of the corporate "managerial revolution" as argued in 1933 by Berle and Means in *The Modern Corporation and Private Property*. Galbraith sums up the latter's understanding of the modern oligopolistic corporation: "Not Marx's capitalists but the professional managers were now extensively in control. There now existed power without property. The corporate bureaucrat, not the celebrated entrepreneur. Bureaucracy not entrepreneurship" (198).

20 Kierans and Stewart, *The Wrong End of the Rainbow*, 192.

21 Ibid., part II, "The Rise of the Corporation."

22 Kierans, *Globalism and the Nation-State*, 88.

23 Ibid., 89.

24 "The New Cathedrals" is the title of chapter 4 of ibid.

25 Kierans, "A Cruel Joke," 21. From Kierans's perspective, one of the ironies of the controversy that developed in the mid-1980s over a free trade agreement with the United States was the stark horror with which so-called Canadian nationalists opposing the deal reacted to the possibility that it might prompt American-owned firms to leave the country.

26 Ibid., 22.

27 Canada, Parliament, *Minutes of Proceedings*, 52.

28 Ibid., 43. Remaining references are to 43, 48–9, and 54–5.

29 Kierans, *Globalism and the Nation-State*, 39.

30 Kierans, review of *Ethics and Economics*, by Duncan Cameron and Gregory Baum, 75–6.

31 See Kierans, *Globalism and the Nation-State*, 110–11, and Kierans and Stewart, *The Wrong End of the Rainbow*, 224.

32 Review of *Memoirs* by René Lévesque, 2 (italics added by Kierans).

33 Submission to the Special Joint Committee on the 1987 Constitutional Accord, 27 August 1987, 8, provided to the author from Kierans's personal records.

34 A good example of such semi-public service is his position as a lay member of the Nova Scotia Barrister's Society, where he has been recently praised, on the occasion of his reappointment, for his "tremendous time and effort" and "wise counsel and advice." Copy of a letter from the executive director of the society to Eric Kierans, Halifax, 29 June 1992, from his personal files.

35 "Seeing an Honest Broker," *Halifax Mail-Star*, 29 November 1991, c1.

36 See Nova Scotia Working Committee on the Constitution, *Canada: A Country for All*, Report, 28 November 1991, v.

37 Ibid., iii.

38 Ibid., vi.

39 Mark Renouf, "Eric Kierans," *Sunday Daily News*, 16 June 1991, 4.

40 See Kierans, "The Source of All Our Troubles."

41 Québec Liberal Party, *A Québec Free to Choose*.

42 See press release dated 13 October 1992. Copy provided to the author from Kierans's personal files.

43 See Allan Fotheringham, "Move over Minot, Winnipeg Has It," *Maclean's Magazine*, 20 January 1992, 52.

CHAPTER ELEVEN

1 Ever since the NEP of 1980, it has jarred some people to describe Pierre Trudeau as an anti-nationalist. However, in his most widely read writings, the essays collected in *Federalism and the French Canadians*, he not only excoriates French-Canadian nationalism but holds up all of Canada as a possible model of the "multi-national state." The so-called nationalism of the Liberal governments of the 1970s and early 1980s was more anti-provincialist than anti-continentalist. See my "Natural Resources," 169–73. FIRA, in effect, raised 20 per cent of the drawbridge after the enemy forces had entered the castle.

2 Kierans, *Globalism and the Nation-State*, dedication.

3 Grant, *Lament for a Nation*, 77.

4 See Buchanan and Tulloch, *The Calculus of Consent*, especially chaps. 6–8.

5 For an excellent discussion of the possible role of Schumpeterian competition in political markets, see Young, "Tectonic Politics and Public Choice."

6 An impression of this can be gleaned from Daniel Drache's efforts to

find common ground between Innisian and Marxist (class) analysis. See "Rediscovering Canadian Political Economy," 3–18. J.R. Mallory's comment immediately following Drache's essay (18–20) suggests Drache's limited success: "while there are numerous efforts to incorporate the national question into more or less Marxist terms, it does not yet seem that this effort has been successful." It seems unlikely that Mallory would ascribe a similar ambition to Innis and his direct descendants.

A more recent work on Innis and McLuhan has allowed that "Innis was not entirely opposed to Marxism" but also points out that Innis claimed to stand with John Maynard Keynes in rejecting the Benthamite tradition, which rejection – in Keynes's words – "served to protect the whole lot of us from the final reductio ad absurdum of Benthamism known as Marxism." See Graeme Patterson, *History and Communications*, 18–19. Patterson suggests that the part of Marx that Innis did assimilate and try to extend concerned the mode of economic production – most notably, technology – as a determining factor in all societies.

7 Neill, *A New Theory of Value*, 68–76.
8 Ibid., 75.
9 Ibid., 76.
10 Ibid., 66.
11 Ibid., 87–9.
12 On Innis in this respect, see ibid., 26, 81, and 114–24.
13 For a superb overview of the "new institutional economics," see North, *Institutions*.
14 On Innis, see Pal, "Scholarship and Politics," 98–9. See also Carey, "Canadian Communication Theory," 44: "[Innis] believed that the fundamental form of social power is the power to define what reality is. Monopolies of knowledge then in the cultural sense refer to the efforts of groups to determine the entire world view of a people: to produce in other words an official view of reality which can constrain and control human action." This is a good definition of totalitarianism.
15 Pal, "Scholarship and Politics," 96.
16 Letter from Innis to A.H. Cole, 19 March 1945, as quoted in ibid., 101.
17 See Neill, *A New Theory of Value*, 22–3.
18 Theall, "Communication Theory and the Marginal Culture," 20.
19 Innis, quoted (apparently from "A Plea for Time") in Carey, "Canadian Communication Theory," 56.
20 See Galbraith, *Economics in Perspective*, 60–72.
21 Arendt, *The Human Condition*, 177–8, 247.
22 Bradshaw, *Acting and Thinking*, 18. Bradshaw has quoted from Arendt's *The Human Condition*, 158.

23 Written comments on my first draft, June 1988.

24 Kierans and Stewart, *The Wrong End of the Rainbow*, 192–210. Kierans's own list is as follows: "1. Require Corporations to Restore Power to Shareholders 2. Make Corporations Distribute Their Earnings 3. Abolish Non-Voting Shares 4. Establish a Tax on Business Costs 5. Remove the Corporate Tax [and instead tax profits as income to shareholders] 6. Replace the Federal Sales Tax with a Value Added Tax 7. Eliminate the Unequal Treatment of Capital Gains 8. Stop Corporations from Deducting Takeover Costs 9. Canadianize Our Capital Markets [by adopting several Swedish policies on foreign capital] 10. Create a Real [multilateral] Free Trade Regime."

Kierans has frequently remarked that John Stuart Mill stopped short of endorsing an inheritance tax, and he himself feels that preventing intergenerational transfer of wealth is crucial to reducing economic concentration so that the economy can be subjected to effective political control.

25 Kierans, *Globalism and the Nation-State*, 53. See also his strongly critical review of *After Hegemony*.

26 For example, he quotes favourably from E.F. Schumacher's book *Small Is Beautiful* in his review of *Ethics and Economics*.

27 Jamie Swift and author's interview with Kierans, Halifax, 7 August 1986.

28 Warren, "Max Weber's Liberalism," 49.

29 Ibid., 43–5.

30 MacDonald, "Taxing Comprehensive Income," 688–99.

31 Warren, "Max Weber's Liberalism," 41.

32 See ibid., 45–6.

33 Ibid., 49.

34 Jamie Swift and author's interview with Kierans, Halifax, 7 August 1986.

Bibliography

I have relied on three main types of material: the Kierans Papers (National Archives of Canada, Ottawa, MG 506b 32 B10) and other primary records, secondary works (listed below), and interviews with Kierans and people who knew him. My method can best be described as a combination of standard approaches to the history of public policy and contemporary biography.

There is one special circumstance regarding the research for this volume – namely, the relationship between the present work and Jamie Swift's biography of Kierans, *Odd Man Out* (1988). I had done some preliminary work on my project and had applied for a research grant from the Social Sciences and Humanities Research Council of Canada (SSHRC), when Swift approached Kierans about a possible biography. Kierans saw no reason why he should not cooperate with both projects, and the arrangement between Swift and me (of which SSHRC was informed) was that Swift would work for one year as my research assistant under the SSHRC funding which had by then been approved and I would be provided with copies of all interviews and records that he accumulated while so employed.

Thus, as Swift kindly acknowledged, he drew on some of my early work on Kierans for *Odd Man Out*, while this study has benefited from – in particular – my review of the complete transcripts of over one hundred interviews that he conducted during the year in which we worked together. (I also relied heavily on Swift's extensive reading of the newspaper clippings in the Kierans Papers.) I conducted over thirty hours of interviews with Kierans, and several more with six people connected to him. I examined at least once every item of the Kierans Papers (excluding two volumes of clippings). I also received records and communications from Kierans, who has also read and commented on the entire manuscript at one stage or another of its preparation. However, all chapters were composed initially on the basis of the documentary record – including Kierans's speeches and publications, which form a substantial portion of the sources cited.

Allison, Graham T. *Essence of Decision: Explaining the Cuban Missile Crisis.* Boston: Little, Brown, 1971.

Anderson, F.J. *Natural Resources in Canada: Economic Theory and Policy.* Toronto: Methuen, 1985.

Arendt, Hannah. *The Human Condition.* Chicago: University of Chicago Press, 1958.

Armstrong, Elizabeth H. *The Crisis of Quebec 1914–1918.* New York: Columbia University Press, 1937.

Arnopoulos, Sheila M., and Clift, Dominique. *The English Fact in Quebec.* 2nd edition. Montreal: McGill-Queen's University Press, 1984.

Atkinson, M.M., and Coleman, W.D. *The State, Business and Industrial Change in Canada.* Toronto: University of Toronto Press, 1989.

Auf der Maur, Nick, and Chodos, Robert, eds. *Quebec: A Chronicle 1968–1972: A Last Post Special.* Postscript by Yvon Charbonneau, Louis Laberge, and Marcel Pepin. Toronto: James Lewis & Samuel, 1972.

Barry, Doreen, and Gibbins, Roger. "Parliamentary Careers in the Canadian Federal State." *Canadian Journal of Political Science,* 22 no. 1 (March 1989) 137–45.

Berle, A.A., and Means, G.C. *The Modern Corporation and Private Property.* New York: Macmillan, 1933.

Bradshaw, Leah. *Acting and Thinking: The Political Thought of Hannah Arendt.* Toronto: University of Toronto Press, 1989.

Brothers, James A.R. "Telesat Canada – Pegasus or Trojan Horse? A Case Study of Mixed, Corporate and Crown enterprises." MA thesis, School of Public Administration, Carleton University, Ottawa, 1979.

Brown, R.D. "The Fight over Resource Profits." *Canadian Tax Journal,* 22 no. 4 (July–August 1974) 315–37.

Buchanan, James M., and Tullohc, Gordon. *The Calculus of Consent: Logical Foundations of Constitutional Democracy.* Ann Arbor: University of Michigan Press, 1962.

Bucovetsky, M.W. "The Mining Industry and the Great Tax Reform Debate." In A. Paul Pross, ed., *Pressure Group Behaviour in Canadian Politics,* Toronto: McGraw-Hill Ryerson, 1975, 87–114.

Cairns, R.D. "Reform of Exhaustible Resource Taxation." *Canadian Public Policy,* 11 no. 4 (December 1985) 649–58.

– "Ricardian Rent and Manitoba's Mining Royalty." *Canadian Tax Journal,* 25 no. 5 (September–October 1977) 558–67.

Canada. Parliament. *Minutes of Proceedings and Evidence of the Special Joint Committee of the Senate and House of Commons on the 1987 Constitutional Accord.* Thursday, 27 August 1987, 14:3–57.

Canada. Royal Commission on Taxation (Carter Commission). Report. 6 vols. Tabled 24 November 1967. Mimeo.

Canada. Task Force on Canadian Unity. *A Future Together: Observations and Recommendations*. Jean-Luc Pepin and John P. Robarts, Chairmen. Ottawa: Department of Supply and Services Canada, 1979.

Canada. Task Force on the Structure of Canadian Industry. *Foreign Ownership and the Structure of Canadian Industry* (Watkins Report). Ottawa: Queen's Printer, 1968.

Carey, James W. "Canadian Communication Theory: Extensions and Interpretations of Harold Innis." In Gertrude J. Robinson and Donald F. Theall, eds., *Studies in Canadian Communication*, Montreal: McGill Studies in Communication, 1975, 27–59.

– "Culture, Geography, and Communications: The Work of Harold Innis in an American Context." In William H. Melody, Liora Salter, and Paul Heyer, eds., *Culture, Communication and Dependency: The Tradition of H.A. Innis*, Norwood, NJ: Ablex Publishing, 1981, chap. 6.

Chandler, Marsha. "State Enterprise and Partisanship in Provincial Politics." *Canadian Journal of Political Science* 15 no. 4 (December 1982) 711–40.

Chant, J., ed. *Canadian Perspectives in Economics*. Toronto: Collier-Macmillan Canada, 1972.

Clarkson, Stephen. *Canada and the Reagan Challenge: Crisis in the Canadian-American Relationship*. Toronto: James Lorimer, 1982.

Cohen, J., and Krashinksky, M. "Capturing Rents on Resource Land for the Public Landowner: The Case for a Crown Corporation." *Canadian Public Policy* 2 no. 3 (summer 1976) 411–23.

Coleman, William D. *The Independence Movement in Quebec 1945–1980*. Toronto: University of Toronto Press, 1984.

Courchene, Thomas J. "Market Nationalism." *Policy Options* (October 1986) 7–12.

– *What Does Ontario Want?: The Coming of Age of John P. Robarts' "Confederation of Tomorrow" Conference*. Toronto: Robarts Centre for Canadian Studies, 1989.

Courtney, John C. *The Selection of National Party Leaders in Canada*. Toronto: Macmillan, 1973.

Crowley, David. "Harold Innis and the Modern Perspective of Communication." In William H. Melody, Liora Salter, and Paul Heyer, eds., *Culture, Communication and Dependency: The Tradition of H.A. Innis*, Norwood, NJ: Ablex Publishing, 1981, chap. 17.

Dales, J.H. "The Half-Vast Ideas of Loyalists, Joiners and Consulters: An Economist's Oration on Canadian-American Relations." *Saturday Night* 81 no. 2 (February 1966) 22–4.

Desbarats, Peter. *René: A Canadian in Search of a Country*. Toronto: McClelland and Stewart, 1976.

Deutsch, Karl W. *The Nerves of Government: Models of Political Communication and Control.* New York: Free Press, 1966.

Dewitt, David B., and Kirton, John J. *Canada as a Principal Power: A Study in Foreign Policy and International Relations.* Toronto: John Wiley, 1983.

Dinorcia, V. Review of *The Next Frontier* by R.B. Feich. *Journal of Business Ethics* 4 no. 2 (1985) 91.

Doern, G. Bruce, and Brothers, J.A.R. "Telesat Canada." In Allan Tupper and G.B. Doern, eds., *Public Corporations and Public Policy in Canada,* Montreal: Institute for Research on Public Policy, 1981, chap 6.

Drache, Daniel. "Rediscovering Canadian Political Economy." *Journal of Canadian Studies* 11 no. 3 (August 1976) 3–18.

French, Richard D. *How Ottawa Decides: Planning and Industrial Policy Making 1968–1984.* 2nd edition, with a chapter by Richard Van Loon. Toronto: James Lorimer, 1984.

Fournier, Pierre. *The Quebec Establishment: The Ruling Class and the State.* 2nd edition. Montreal: Black Rose, 1976.

Fraser, Matthew. *Quebec Inc.: French-Canadian Entrepreneurs and the New Business Elite.* Toronto: Key Porter, 1987.

Fullerton, Douglas H. *The Dangerous Delusion: Quebec's Independence Obsession.* Toronto: McClelland and Stewart, 1978.

Galbraith, J.K. *Economics in Perspective: A Critical History.* Boston: Houghton Mifflin, 1987.

Golden, Aubrey E., and Haggart, Ron. *Rumors of War.* Toronto: New Press, 1971.

Granatstein, J.L. *The Ottawa Men: The Civil Service Mandarins 1935–1957.* Toronto: Oxford University Press, 1982.

Grant, George. Foreword to James Laxer and Robert Laxer, *The Liberal Idea of Canada: Pierre Trudeau and the Question of Canada's Survival,* Toronto: James Lorimer, 1977.

– *Lament for a Nation: The Defeat of Canadian Nationalism.* First published in 1965. Carleton Library no. 50. Toronto: McClelland and Stewart, 1970.

Gratwick, J., Fahey, W.R., and Schneider, A. "A Role for Transportation in Canada." *Long Range Planning* 9 no. 12 (1976) 38–43.

Gunton, Tom, and Richards, John. "Political Economy of Resource Policy." In Tom Gunton and John Richards, eds., *Resource Rents and Public Policy in Western Canada,* Halifax: Institute for Research on Public Policy, 1987, chap. 7.

– eds. *Resource Rents and Public Policy in Western Canada.* Halifax: Institute for Research on Public Policy, 1987.

Gwyn, Richard. *The Northern Magus: Pierre Trudeau and Canadians.* Toronto: McClelland and Stewart, 1980.

Hedlin Menzies & Associates Ltd. *An Analysis of the Kierans Report on Mining Policy.* Prepared for the Mining Association of Manitoba, 1973.

Heuglin, Thomas O. *Federalism and Fragmentation: A Comparative View of Political Accommodation in Canada.* Discussion Paper no. 19, Institute of Intergovernmental Relations, Queen's University, Kingston, Ontario, 1984.

Heyer, Paul. "Innis and the History of Communication: Antecedents, Parallels and Unsuspected Biases." In William H. Melody, Liora Salter, and Paul Heyer, eds., *Culture, Communication and Dependency: The Tradition of H.A. Innis,* Norwood, NJ: Ablex Publishing, 1981, chap. 18.

Holsti, K.J. Review of *Globalism and the Nation-State,* by Eric W. Kierans. *Canadian Journal of Political Science* 17 no. 4 (1984) 861–5.

Hopkins, J. Castell. *The Canadian Annual Review of Public Affairs, 1914.* Toronto: Annual Review Publishing Co., 1915.

Jamieson, Donald. "Overkill." *Saturday Night* (April 1988) 23–9.

Jenkins, Barbara. "Reexamining the 'Obsolescing Bargain': A Study of Canada's National Energy Program." *International Organization* 40 no. 1 (winter 1986) 139–65.

Keith, R.F., and Fischer, D.W. "Assessing the Development Decision-Making Process: A Case Study of Canadian Frontier Petroleum Development." *American Journal of Economics and Sociology* 36 no. 2 (1977) 147–64.

Kent, Tom. *A Public Purpose: An Experience of Liberal Opposition and Canadian Government.* Montreal: McGill-Queen's University Press, 1988.

Kierans, Eric W. "Canadian Unity – a Perspective." Convocation Address, St. Thomas University, Fredericton, NB, 14 May 1979.

– *Challenge of Confidence: Kierans on Canada.* Toronto: McClelland and Stewart, 1967.

– "Combines – the New Look." Address to Canadian Manufacturers' Association, Montreal, Monday 6 June 1960.

– "The Community and the Corporation." In C.P. Kindleberger and D.B. Audretsch, eds., *The Multinational Corporation in the 1980s,* Cambridge, Mass.: M.I.T. Press, 1983.

– "Contribution of the Tax System to Canada's Unemployment and Ownership Problems." Address to the Canadian Economics Association, Annual Meeting, Memorial University, St John's, Newfoundland, 3–5 June 1971.

– "Contribution of the Tax System to Canada's Unemployment and Ownership Problems." In *Canadian Perspectives in Economics,* Don Mills, Ont.: Collier-Macmillan Canada, 1972, B2, n.p.

– "The Corporate Challenge to Government." In *The Role of Govern-*

ment in Canadian Society, Walter L. Gordon Lecture Series, Vol. 1, 1976–77, Toronto: Canada Studies Foundation, 1977.

- "The Corporate Impact on Political Authority in Regional Systems." *Revue d'intégration européenne* 3 no. 3 (May 1980) 381–92.
- "A Cruel Joke." *Policy Options* 9 no. 1 (January/February 1988) 21–6.
- "The Day the Cabinet Was Misled." *Canadian Forum* (March 1974) 4–8.
- "Democracy and Social Change in Canada." Address to Sault Ste Marie (Ontario) and District Chamber of Commerce, 22 October 1970.
- "Dollars across the Border: Canadian-American Economic Relations." Address to annual convention, American Society of Newspaper Editors, Montreal, 18 May 1966.
- "The Economic Effects of the Guidelines." Address to the Toronto Society of Financial Analysts, Toronto, 1 February 1966.
- "Economic Implications of Depreciation Policies." Address to the annual conference, Canadian Institute of Chartered Accountants, Banff, Alberta, 12 September 1960.
- "Economic Implications of the Province of Quebec Pension Plan." Address to Canadian Manufacturers' Association, Montreal, 25 June 1965.
- "Federal-Provincial Tax Treatment of the Extractive Industries." Paper to the Twenty-sixth Tax Conference, Canadian Tax Foundation, Toronto, 11–13 November 1974.
- "Financing Future Growth." Address to annual meeting, Canadian Gas Association, Montibello, Quebec, 23 June 1960.
- Foreword to Tom Naylor, *The History of Canadian Business, 1867–1914 Vol. One: The Banks and Finance Capital*, Toronto: James Lorimer, 1975.
- *Globalism and the Nation-State*. 1983 Massey Lectures. Toronto: CBC Enterprises, 1984.
- "The High Cost of a Free Quebec." *Guardian* 13 March 1977.
- Introduction to David Lewis, *Louder Voices: The Corporate Welfare Bums*, Toronto: James Lewis and Samuel, 1972.
- "Investment, Savings and Taxes." Address to annual tax conference, Canadian Tax Foundation, Toronto, 14 November 1960.
- "The Kentian Thrust." *Policy Options* 2 no. 5 (June 1988) 34–6.
- "More Saving – Personal or Corporate." Inaugural address, Montreal and Canadian Stock Exchanges, Montreal, 19 May 1960.
- "Notes on the Energy Aspects of the 1974 Budget." *Canadian Public Policy* 1 no. 3 (summer 1975) 425–32.
- "Problems of Tax Reform." *Canadian Taxation* 1 no. 4 (winter 1979) 22–4.
- "Quebec 1965: A Transformation in Depth." Notes for an address to the Canadian Club, Palliser Hotel, Calgary, 7 January 1965.

– *Report on Natural Resources Policy in Manitoba* (Kierans Report). Prepared for the Secretariat for the Planning and Priorities Committee of Cabinet, Government of Manitoba, 1973.
– Review of *After Hegemony: Cooperation and Discord in the World Economy*, by Robert O. Keohane. In *Queen's Quarterly* 93 no. 1 (spring 1986) 214–16.
– Review of *Ethics and Economics*, by Duncan Cameron and Gregory Baum. In *Grail* 1 no. 1 (March 1985) 73–6.
– Review of *Memoirs*, by René Lévesque. In *Montreal Gazette*, 18 October 1986, B1.
– Review of *Storm over the Multinationals – The Real Issues*, by Raymond Vernon. In *Canadian Journal of Economics* 11 no. 4 (1978) 81–3.
– "The Source of All Our Troubles." *Canadian Forum* (May 1992) 10–13.
– "Towards a New National Policy." *Canadian Forum* (January–February 1972) 52–5.
– "Wanted – a New Commercial Policy." *Canadian Chartered Accountant* 80 (1962) 372–7.
– "The White Paper on Tax Report [sic]: What Else is New?" Address to the Empire Club of Canada, Toronto, 19 March 1970.
Kierans, Eric W., and Stewart, Walter. *The Wrong End of the Rainbow: The Collapse of Free Enterprise in Canada*. Toronto: Collins, 1988.
Krasner, Stephen D. *Defending the National Interest: Raw Materials, Investments and U.S. Foreign Policy*. Princeton: Princeton University Press, 1978.
Kroker, Arthur. *Technmology and the Canadian Mind: Innis/McLuhan/Grant*. Montreal: New World Perspectives, 1984.
Lapping, M.B., and Fuller, A.M. "Rural Development Policy in Canada." *Community Development Journal* 20 no. 2 (1985) 114–19.
Laxer, James and Laxer, Robert. *The Liberal Idea of Canada: Pierre Trudeau and the Question of Canada's Survival*. Toronto: James Lorimer, 1977.
LeDuc, Lawrence, Jr. "Party Decision-making: Some Empirical Observations on the Leadership Selection Process." *Canadian Journal of Political Science* 4 no. 1 (March 1971) 97–118.
Lermer, G., ed. *Probing Leviathan: An Investigation of Government in the Economy*. Vancouver: Fraser Institute, 1984.
Lévesque, René. *Memoirs*. Trans. Philip Stratford. Toronto: McClelland and Stewart, 1986.
Levine, Marc V. *The Reconquest of Montreal: Language Policy and Social Change in a Bilingual City*. Philadelphia: Temple University Press, 1990.
Levitt, Kari. *Silent Surrender: The Multinational Corporation in Canada*. Toronto: Macmillan, 1970.

Leyton-Brown, D. Review of *Globalism and the Nation-State*, by Eric Kierans. *International Journal* 39 no. 3 (1984) 672–81.

Lowi, Theodore J. *The End of Liberalism: The Second Republic of the United States*. 2nd edition. New York: W.W. Norton, 1979.

McCall-Newman, Christina. *Grits: An Intimate Portrait of the Liberal Party*. Toronto: Macmillan, 1982.

MacDonald, Leslie T. "Taxing Comprehensive Income: Power and Participation in Canadian Politics 1962–72." PhD thesis, Department of Political Science, Carleton University, Ottawa, 1985.

McDougall, A.K. *John P. Robarts: His Life and Government*. Toronto: University of Toronto Press, 1986.

McDougall, John N. "Natural Resources and National Politics: A Look at Three Canadian Resource Industries." In G. Bruce Doern, Research Co-ordinator, *The Politics of Economic Policy*, study no. 40 commissioned by the Royal Commission on the Economic Union and Development Prospects for Canada (Macdonald Commission), Toronto: University of Toronto Press, 1985, chap. 3.

– "Nationalism, Liberalism and the Political Economy of Eric Kierans," *Journal of Canadian Studies* 25 no. 2 (summer 1990).

MacLennan, Hugh. *Two Solitudes*. Toronto: Macmillan, 1951.

MacMillan, J.A., Tulloch, J.R., O'Brian, D., and Ahmad, M.A. "Determinants of Labour Turnover in Canadian Mining Communities." Centre for Settlement Studies, University of Manitoba, *Research Reports* 19 (1974) 1–133.

McRoberts, Kenneth. *Quebec: Social Change and Political Crisis*, 3rd edition. Toronto: McClelland and Stewart, 1988.

Mallory, J.R. "Confederation: The Ambiguous Bargain." *Journal of Canadian Studies* 12 no. 3 (1977) 18–23.

– "Parliament, the Cabinet and the Bureaucracy in Canada." *Politics* 15 no. 2 (1980) 249–63.

Melody, William H., Salter, Liora, and Heyer, Paul, eds. *Culture, Communication and Dependency: The Tradition of H.A. Innis*. Norwood, NJ: Ablex Publishing, 1981.

Mill, John Stuart. *Principles of Political Economy*. Laughlin edition. New York: Appleton & Company, 1894.

– *Principles of Political Economy*. Books IV and V. A reprint of the Pelican Books 1970 edition. Toronto: Penguin Books Canada, 1985.

Miller, C.G. "Trends in Mineral Economics Research." *CIM Bulletin* 69 no. 776 (1979) 51–7.

Molot, Maureen A. "The Political Implications of North American Capital Flows." In John H. Pammet and Brian W. Tomlin, eds., *The Integration Question: Political Economy and Public Policy in Canada and North America*, Don Mills, Ont.: Addison-Wesley, 1984, chap. 19.

– "The Role of Institutions in Canada–United States Relations: The Case of North American Financial Ties." In Andrew Axline et al., eds., *Continental Community?: Independence and Integration in North America*. Toronto: McClelland and Stewart, 1974, chap. 7.

Morin, Claude. *Quebec versus Ottawa: The Struggle for Self-government 1960–72*. Toronto: University of Toronto Press, 1976.

Neill, Robin F. "Imperialism and the Staple Theory of Canadian Economic Development: The Historical Perspective." In William H. Melody, Liora Salter, and Paul Heyer, eds., *Culture, Communication and Dependency: The Tradition of H.A. Innis*, Norwood, NJ: Ablex Publishing, 1981, chap. 10.

– *A New Theory of Value: The Canadian Economics of H.A. Innis*. Toronto: University of Toronto Press, 1972.

– "The Passing of Canadian Economic History." *Journal of Canadian Studies* 12 no. 5 (1977) 73–82.

Nicholas, H.E. *Canadian Taxation of Mining Income: An Analytic Approach*. Don Mills, Ont.: CCH Canadian, 1978.

Noel, S.J.R. "Domination and Myth in the Works of George Grant and C.B. Macpherson." *Dalhousie Review* 59 no. 3 (autumn 1979) 534–51.

Nordlinger, Eric. *On the Autonomy of the Democratic State*. Cambridge, Mass.: Harvard University Press, 1981.

North, Douglass C. *Institutions, Institutional Change and Economic Performance*. Cambridge: Cambridge University Press, 1990.

Owen, Brian E., and Kops, W.J. *The Impact of Policy Change on Decisions in the Mineral Industry: The Case of Exploration in Manitoba, 1969–77*. Kingston, Ont.: Centre for Resource Studies, Queen's University, 1979.

Pal, Leslie A. "Scholarship and Politics in the Later Writings of Harold Innis." MA thesis, Department of Political Science, Queen's University, 1976.

Patterson, Graeme. *History and Communications: Harold Innis, Marshall McLuhan, the Interpretation of History*. Toronto: University of Toronto Press, 1990.

Pearse, P.H. "Property Rights and the Development of Natural Resource Policies in Canada." *Canadian Public Policy* 14 no. 3 (September 1988) 307–20.

Pepin-Robarts Task Force. *See* Canada. Task Force on Canadian Unity. *A Future Together*.

Prince, M.J., and Doern, G. Bruce. *The Origins of Public Enterprise in the Canadian Mineral Sector: Three Provincial Case Studies*. Working Paper No. 33, Centre for Resource Studies, Queen's University, Kingston, Ont., 1985.

Pross, A. Paul, ed. *Pressure Group Behaviour in Canadian Politics.* Toronto: McGraw-Hill Ryerson, 1975.

Québec Liberal Party. *A Québec Free to Choose.* Report of the Constitutional Committee (Jean Allaire, Chairman), 1991.

Radwanski, George. *Trudeau.* Toronto: Macmillan, 1978.

Reynolds, Stephen Huntley. "The Struggle Continues: An Analysis of Conflict in the Canadian Post Office." MA thesis, McMaster University, 1981.

Richards, John, and Pratt, Larry. *Prairie Capitalism: Power and Influence in the New West.* Toronto: McClelland and Stewart, 1979.

Royal Society of Canada. *Hermes (the Communications Technology Satellite): Its Performance and Applications. Vols. I–III.* Irvine Paghis, ed. Ottawa: Society, 1977.

Rugman, A.M. "The Foreign Ownership Debate in Canada." *Journal of World Trade Law* 10 no. 2 (1976) 171–6.

– "Risk and Return in the Canadian Mineral Resource Industry." *Revista internationale di science economiche e commerciali* 26 no. 5 (1979) 432–4.

Salter, Liora. " 'Public' and Mass Media in Canada: Dialections in Innis' Communications Analysis." In William H. Melody, Liora Salter, and Paul Heyer, eds., *Culture, Communication and Dependency: The Tradition of H.A. Innis*, Norwood, NJ: Ablex Publishing, 1981, chap. 14.

Sancton, Andrew. *Governing the Island of Montreal: Language Differences and Metropolitan Politics.* Berkeley: University of California Press, 1985.

Sayeed, K.B. "Public Policy Analysis in Washington and Ottawa." *Policy Science* 4 no. 1 (1973) 85–101.

Simeon, Richard. *Federal-Provincial Diplomacy: The Making of Recent Policy in Canada.* Toronto: University of Toronto Press, 1972.

Simpson, Jeffrey. *Spoils of Power: The Politics of Patronage.* Toronto: Collins, 1988.

Smiley, D.V. "Canada and the Quest for a National Policy." *Canadian Journal of Political Science* 8 no. 1 (1975) 40–62.

– "The National Party Leadership Convention in Canada: A Preliminary Analysis." *Canadian Journal of Political Science* 1 no. 4 (December 1968) 373–97.

Smith, Denis. *Bleeding Hearts ... Bleeding Country: Canada and the Quebec Crisis.* Edmonton: Hurtig, 1971.

– *Gentle Patriot: A Political Biography of Walter Gordon.* Edmonton: Hurtig, 1973.

Smythe, Dallas W. *Dependency Road: Communications, Capitalism, Consciousness, and Canada.* Norwood, NJ: Ablex Publishing, 1981.

Spry, Irene, M. "Overhead Costs, Rigidities of Productive Capacity, and the Price System." In William H. Melody, Liora Salter, and Paul Heyer, eds., *Culture, Communication and Dependency: The Tradition of H.A. Innis*, Norwood, NJ: Ablex Publishing, 1981, chap. 11.

Stewart, Walter. *Shrug: Trudeau in Power*. Toronto: New Press, 1971.

Stewart-Patterson, David. *Post Mortem: Why Canada's Mail Won't Move*. Toronto: Macmillan, 1987.

Sullivan, Martin. *Mandate '68*. Toronto: Doubleday, 1968.

Swift, Jamie. *Odd Man Out: The Life and Times of Eric Kierans*. Vancouver: Douglas and McIntyre, 1988.

Tawney, R.H. *Religion and the Rise of Capitalism: A Historical Study*. New York: New American Library, 1954.

Taylor, Charles. *Hegel*. London: Cambridge University Press, 1975.

Taylor, Malcolm G. *Health Insurance and Canadian Public Policy: The Seven Decisions That Created the Canadian Health Insurance System*. Montreal: McGill-Queen's University Press, 1978.

Theall, Donald F. "Communication Theory and the Marginal Culture: The Socio-Aesthetic Dimensions of Communication Study." In Gertrude J. Robinson and Donald F. Theall, eds., *Studies in Canadian Communications*, Montreal: McGill Studies in Communications, 1975, 7–26.

– "Explorations in Communications since Innis." In William H. Melody, Liora Salter, and Paul Heyer, eds., *Culture, Communication and Dependency: The Tradition of H.A. Innis*, Norwood, NJ: Ablex Publishing, 1981, chap. 16.

Thomson, Dale C. *Jean Lesage and the Quiet Revolution*. Toronto: Macmillan, 1984.

Trudeau, Pierre E. *Federalism and the French Canadians*. Introduction by John T. Saywell. Laurentian Library No. 48. Toronto: Macmillan, 1968.

Tupper, Allan, and Doern, G. Bruce, eds. *Public Corporations and Public Policy in Canada*. Montreal: Institute for Research on Public Policy, 1981.

Uslaner, Eric M. *Shale Barrel Politics: Energy and Legislative Leadership*. Stanford, Calif.: Stanford University Press, 1989.

Vining, A.R., and Botterel, R. "The Origins, Growth, Size and Functions of Crown Corporations." In J.R.S. Prichard, ed., *Crown Corporations in Canada: The Calculus of Instrument Choice*, Toronto: Butterworths, 1982.

Warren, Mark. "Max Weber's Liberalism for a Nietzschean World." *American Political Science Review* 82 no. 1 (March 1988) 32–50.

Watkins, Mel. "The Staple Theory Revisited." *Journal of Canadian Studies* 12 no. 5 (winter 1977) 83–95.

– Watkins Report. *See* Canada. Task Force on the Structure of Canadian Industry. *Foreign Ownership.*

Wearing, Joseph. *The L-Shaped Party: The Liberal Party of Canada, 1958–1980.* Toronto: McGraw-Hill Ryerson, 1981.

Westell, Anthony. *Paradox: Trudeau as Prime Minister.* Scarborough, Ont.: Prentice-Hall, 1972.

Winham, G. "Bureaucratic Politics and Canadian Trade Negotiation." *International Journal* 34 no. 1 (1979) 61–89.

Wolfe, David. "Economic Growth and Foreign Investment: A Perspective on Canadian Economic Policy, 1945–1957." *Journal of Canadian Studies* 13 no. 1 (spring 1978) 3–20.

Wright, Gerald. "Persuasive Influence: The Case of the Interest Equalization Tax." In Andrew Axline et al., eds., *Continental Community?: Independence and Integration in North America.* Toronto: McClelland and Stewart, 1974, chap. 6.

Yale, Janet. "Telesat Canada's Membership in the Trans-Canada Telephone System: A Critique." Paper presented during third-year LLB program, University of Toronto, 1980.

Young, Robert A. "Tectonic Policies and Public Choice." Papers in Political Economy, no. 12, Political Economy Research Group, University of Western Ontario, London, 1991.

Yudelman, D. *Canadian Mineral Policy Past and Present: The Ambiguous Legacy.* Kingston, Ont.: Centre for Resource Studies, Queen's University, 1985.

Index

House of Commons, 128,
152, 154, 155
housing. *See* social: investment
Howard, Frank, 94
Hughes Aircraft Corp. of
California, 133, 134,
265 n21
Hurtig, Mel, 171, 191
Hydro-Québec, 48, 50, 65,
85
hyperpluralism, 224, 264
n14

Imperial Oil, 197
imperialism, 228
imports, 86; import sub-
stitution, 167
income tax, 22
independent capitalist
Canada, 238-9
independent develop-
ment, 135
independent socialist
Canada, 238-9
individual Canadians, 236
individual initiative, 234
individual ministerial
responsibility, 100
individual participation,
19
individual public respon-
sibility, 236
industrial development,
134, 265 n21
Industrial Development
Bank, 165
industrial strategy, 265
n30
inflation, 115, 159, 161,
166
infrastructure, 212
Innis, Harold, 224-30, 256
n17, 267 n18, 276 n6,
13
institutional reform, 223
instruments of rent cap-
ture. *See* resource
rents
interest groups, 14, 95,
111-12, 114, 124, 133,
148, 222-3, 261 n8

intergenerational trans-
fers, 277 n24
International Brother-
hood of Electrical
Workers (IBEW), 135
international corpora-
tions. *See* multina-
tional corporations
intra-firm transfers, 92,
206, 242
invisible hand. *See* Smith,
Adam
ISIS, 141
Israel, 47

Jacobins, 12
Jamieson, Don, 150-1
Japan, x, 18, 21, 171; empire, 229
Jesuit fathers, 31; Kier-
ans's classical educa-
tion with, 5, 30, 249
n5
Jewitt, Pauline, 172
John XXIII, encyclical of
1961, 35
Johnson, Harry, 173
justice, 4

Kates, Peat, Marwick and
Co., 118
Kent, Tom: Kierans's ad-
miration for, 13-14;
and Pearson's "co-
operative federalism,"
68-73; Tax Structure
Committee, sugges-
tion to create, 255 n5;
and Trudeau's lack of
economic leadership,
115, 248 n15; and
Trudeau's preoccu-
pation with rational
decision-making,
115-16; view of
Kierans, 235. *See also*
Pearson, Lester B.;
Royal Commission on
Taxation (Carter
Commission)
Keynes, J.M., 276 n6;
Keynesians, 226

Kierans Affair (1966),
30, 84-93
Kierans Report (1973, on
Manitoba resource
policies), 24, 156,
171, 173, 177-94,
195, 196, 222;
academic response
to, 15-16; impact of,
187-94; recommen-
dations of, 178,
183-4, 186-7, 193;
on taxation and
royalties, 189

Labrador, 96
laissez-faire, 202
Lapalme affair (1970),
121, 123-31, 133,
150, 151, 263 n51,
266 n3; "les gars de
Lapalme," 127
Lapalme, G., Inc., 130
Lapalme, H., Transport
Ltd., 130
Laporte, Pierre, 149, 257
n23
large corporations, 112,
114, 220, 233
Laurendeau, André, 47
Laval University, 53
Laxer, James, 171, 238
leadership, political,
234; plebiscitary,
234
Learned Societies con-
ferences, 53, 152
left-wing nationalism,
171, 225
Lesage, Jean, 29, 71, 79,
94, 216, 243, 257
n23; and Ames
affair, 47-51, 56; and
Kierans, 41, 51, 53,
82, 253 n3; and
Kierans Affair, 84-5,
88, 91, 93, 258 n5,
259 n16; and Réal
Caouette, 42; and
SIDBEC, 57-61; and
SOQUEM, 64-5. *See
also* Lesage govern-